# Archetypes

~ *unmasking your true self* ~

# Brian Dale

Illustrations by Lily Loy

Revised Edition

Possumwood Publishing
5 Possumwood Place, Mullumbimby
NSW 2482 Australia
possumwoodpublishing@gmail.com

First published in 2012
Revised edition 2015
Copyright © Brian Dale, 2012

All rights reserved. No part of this publication may be reproduced, stored in a retrieval system, or transmitted in any form or by any means, electronic, mechanical, photocopying, recording or otherwise, without the prior written permission of the publisher.

Dale, Brian
Archetypes, unmasking your true self
Archetypes
Personality traits
Psychology
Spirituality

Printed by CreateSpace, An Amazon.com Company
Published by Possumwood Publishing
Typeset by Jan Dale

# Dedication

This book is dedicated to my dear wife, Robyn.

She has been my lifelong partner, my spiritual advisor, my guide. She has recognized qualities and abilities in me that encouraged my personal growth. My knowledge and understanding of archetypes and my ability to assist people and transform their lives are the product of Robyn's faith and insight.

# Table of Contents

Introduction.................................................................. 1
How to use this book...................................................... 3
Section 1 – What are archetypes?..................................... 4
Section 2 – Discovering your archetypes......................... 10
Section 3 – Description of archetypes.............................. 18
Section 4 – Taking action................................................. 337
Conclusion ...................................................................... 344
Index................................................................................ 346

# Introduction

**This book is about you.**

The question is, "Do you want to know about you?"

Maybe you are perfectly content with who you are.
Maybe you are perfectly content with who you think you are.
If not, read on. You may want to discover who you truly are.

The truth is within. It is within you. It is within your archetypes.
It is within these pages.

Why do we need to know who we truly are?

Well, is your life running smoothly?
Would you like more out of life?
Do any challenges trouble you?
Would you change anything about yourself or the life you lead?
Are you happy with your childhood, teenage years and adult life?
Do the people in your life hinder or encourage your growth?

Knowing who you are will initiate change.
How to change is within. It is within you.
It is within the energy of your archetypes. It is within these pages.

**This book is also about your family.**

Do you enjoy being with your family?
Are the members of your family content and accepting of each other?
Is your home a happy place to be?
Is your relationship with your partner all you want it to be?
Are you the person your partner wants you to be?
Are you comfortable and content with your children?
Is your relationship with your children healthy and positive?
Are your in-laws accepting and supporting or a source of anger and frustration?

Knowing who your family is will initiate change.
How to change is within. It is within you.
It is within your archetypal relationships. It is within these pages.

**This book is certainly about your friends.**

Do you enjoy the company of your friends?
Are they fun to be with or are they a challenge?
Do they enhance your life or hold you back?
Do they talk to you or do they talk about themselves?
Do they support you or criticize you?

Knowing who your friends are will initiate change.
How to change is within. It is within you.
It is within the archetypal relationships you have with your friends. It is within these pages.

**This book talks about all the people you know
and are ever likely to know.**

Do you have a professional, comfortable relationship with your boss? Have you an enjoyable working relationship with your peers?
Are your neighbours friendly or do they create discomfort in you?
Do the people with whom you share your leisure activities annoy or frustrate you?
Do you run a business and attract customers from hell?

Knowing who people are and the positions they come from will initiate change.
How to change is within. It is within you.
It is within your recognition of other archetypes. It is within the archetypal relationship you have with these people. It is within these pages.

*Let's Get Started!*

# How to Use This Book

*'Archetypes, unmasking your true self"* is a reference book, to be used at your convenience. There will be times when only some of the information is relevant to you. Happily use it with a specific desire for information, understanding and change.

However, this book is also a personality manual. If you desire a better understanding of yourself and the people you interact with or if you wish to initiate change in your life, then follow the instructions. As with all manuals, if you follow the steps and the instructions, you will achieve the desired results.

These are the steps:

1. Read the introduction.
2. Discover and understand what an archetype is.
3. Answer the 'Let's Get Started' survey.
4. Find your archetypes in Section 3.
5. Devise and begin your action plan.

# ~ Section 1 ~

## What Are Archetypes?

Each and every one of us has a number of archetypes. Archetypes help us understand who we are, why we think the way we do and why we behave in certain ways. In other words, awareness and understanding of our own individual archetypes can answer the pivotal "who am I?" question.

When you identify your personal archetypes, you gain an understanding of your archetypal and personal energy. This energy determines how you and those around you think and behave. Energy is the combination of personal ingredients that allows us to be individual. Each of us has courage, strength, cowardice, humour, charm, deceit, knowledge, perspective and opinion. It is the combination of these ingredients that give you your individual personal energy. When your energy interacts with other energies, the strength and combination of those ingredients change.

As you recognize your personal archetypes you gain an understanding as to who you are and why you think and act the way you do. You will be able to identify why the people in your life think and act the way they do. You begin to understand which relationships are strong and positive and which relationships are harmful and negative. When you understand yourself and others, you are in a position to initiate change.

**We begin with the basics.**

## Archetypes Defined

**Archetypes are personifications of universal energy patterns.**

Patterns do not change. Archetypal patterns display traits and behaviours that are consistent. They follow a consistent structure. We understand that consistency and know what comes next. Therefore, we have the ability to recognize patterns.

For example, when someone says to us "She is a good mother", we have immediate knowledge and understanding of the Good Mother archetypal pattern. We automatically process a picture of a generic mother and recognize an energy pattern that nurtures, cares, protects, teaches and models righteous behaviour for her charges. These personality traits are universal. They are found in all cultures and societies.

**Understand that all archetypes have both positive and negative aspects.**

The Mother archetype also has a negative energy pattern. This pattern displays as the Smother Mother or the neglectful and abusive mother. These are harmful manifestations of the negative side of the Mother archetypal energy.

While archetypal patterns are consistent in their nature, the energy associated with these patterns can and does change. Energy is rarely static. Traits and behaviours associated with the Good Mother - nurturing, caring, protective, and one who teaches and models positive behaviour - will always be present but may vary in intensity. It is the same with the Bad Mother. The smothering will always be there, for it is a behavioural pattern. However, the smothering will occur on different occasions and will vary in intensity. The neglect and abuse of the Bad Mother archetype will persist, but likewise, the frequency and intensity will change.

Energy changes! This means that archetypal energy will allow an individual to move from negative to positive and from positive to negative. This is good news. This means we have the ability to change ourselves and our lives. It allows us to move from the negative archetypal energy pattern to the positive archetypal energy pattern. It also partly explains why an individual can commit heinous deeds and still be a loving and generous partner or friend.

This does not mean change is easy. How many New Year's resolutions have been broken within a month? How many times have we determined to lose weight, to exercise, to eat healthy food, to give up an addiction, to be more generous with time and money, to be more tolerant with family, to be more caring towards friends and to be a more active member of society? Energy changes and it is easy to fall back into a familiar negative energy pattern. However, once we understand our archetypes and the archetypal energy patterns we are better equipped to see what we wish to change in our lives, to understand that change and to deal with the consequences, both positive and negative.

Major or dominant archetypes are easy to detect and observe in adults. We all know someone who consistently operates in the negative Victim archetype. This is the "poor me" syndrome. Nothing ever seems to go right and these people will often complain about their circumstances and how fortunate others are. These individuals always see life as a glass that is half empty or in some cases, totally empty. Their glass is never half full.

Which of our friends are Damsels? They are continually in and out of relationships and waiting to be rescued by their Knights in shining armour. Who in our life is the Bully, the Rescuer, the Servant or the Martyr? We recognize and understand these archetypes with their positive and negative energies all too clearly. Maybe, up until this point, you haven't been able to put a name to these energies but you certainly know them and react accordingly.

**They are archetypes.**

## Personal Archetypes

There are many archetypes. On a personal level, each of us can claim a relationship with a number of archetypes. We constantly use the archetypal energies associated with those specific archetypes. Some people have a good understanding of who they are. They know their strengths and weaknesses. They are aware of their patterns of behaviour. Others have a much vaguer understanding of self. However, if we have the desire, we all recognize our major characteristics and patterns of behaviour. Within these patterns of behaviour lie our archetypes. Knowing and understanding our archetypes gives us greater insight into who we are and why we behave the way we do. With the help of this guide, you will recognize several of your personal archetypes.

**What you do with this knowledge is up to you.**

Remember, at any given time, there is both negative and positive energy associated with each archetype and we can operate on both sides of the pattern. There are occasions when one singular archetype will dominate your life. For example, the negative Addict archetype may be so overpowering, an individual will suppress all other aspects of life in order to feed the addiction. Damsels may become so involved with intimate relationships, that they neglect all other aspects of their lives. Individuals with the Artist archetype may be blocked and frustrated then feed on their own negative archetypal energies and fall deep into the mire of depression and degradation.

On the positive side, a talented and devoted Teacher will have the ability to inspire their students, impart knowledge and allow each student to express his or her own personality. We all recognize a trusty Servant of excellence, who will ensure the proceedings of an event flow with thoroughness, discretion and artistic flair. The positive archetypal energy of the Knight exudes courage, chivalry and determination, and the Knight will battle all obstacles to maintain the pursuit of justice and righteousness.

## Interaction of Archetypal Energies

Adults and children, consistently use archetypes in the various aspects of their life. They interact together using their own archetypal energies. Hands up if you have the Princess archetype! How many fathers do you know who call their daughters 'princess'? They will undoubtedly have a King archetype, but most of these fathers will have absolutely no knowledge of archetypes and archetypal energy patterns. Conversely, how many daughters, from a very young age, respond to that energy without really understanding it? The archetypal bond between these fathers and daughters is forever filled with love and understanding. This is a typical representation of positive archetypal energies that interact perfectly to form lifelong relationships.

Of course, life is never perfect. Imperfection results when negative archetypal energy is expressed and used to manipulate, defend and succeed at another person's expense. Although this may be base interaction at an individual level, it may also be indicative of a negative archetypal interaction. For example, the negative Bully energy is imposing enough for most archetypal energies but imagine how threatening it is for the negative Martyr, Victim or Slave archetype. The balance is completely out of whack and only negative interaction can ensue. Similarly, the negative energy of the Vampire and the Rescuer will form a similar co-dependent archetypal relationship.

As you examine various archetypal energies you begin to understand how individual growth is enhanced by understanding the negative energetic patterns of an archetype and adjusting your behaviour to the positive energetic patterns of that archetype. You also understand relationships that flourish and stand the test of time are built upon the positive archetypal energy of two complementary archetypes. The King and the Princess is the most natural example. The King is drawn to the vulnerability, beauty and cleverness of the Princess. She is drawn to him for his protection, compliments and indulgence. The Warrior and the Adventurer also make an excellent combination. Their physical prowess and love of exploring, and of nature, make them ideal companions. While some archetypal combinations work well together, others fuel a personality clash.

The first step in utilizing your archetypal combinations for personal growth is awareness.

Be aware of how you interact with others, and how your positive and negative archetypes work with the people around you.

## Balance

Those seeking awareness and personal growth are able to determine their archetypes quite easily. They can then make the voluntary move from any negative energy patterns to the positive energy patterns which reside in each personal archetype. As an example, let us use the Queen archetype and examine her positive energy pattern and personal traits. The Queen exudes excellence in leadership. She achieves this by using the positive energetic patterns of her archetype. She strives to achieve success for all individuals in her realm, not just the chosen few. She recognizes her territory and does not encroach upon that of another. When her responsibilities are many and varied, she learns to trust and delegate. She is aware of her finances and when the fun of a spending spree occurs, it is prudent and relevant. She rules with authority and compassion and with the greatest possible balance for the benefit of all her subjects. When the individual with the Queen archetype displays these characteristics and behaviours, she has engaged the positive archetypal energy. This creates balance in that person's life.

When you harness the positive energy of all your personal archetypes, you are on the road to perfect balance. To achieve that balance, you begin to identify which archetypes are dominant in certain areas of your life. For example, I have been a teacher all my working life. I have a strong Teacher archetype that goes into action at any opportunity, but I use my Father archetype in my teaching role. I understand I am not a typical teacher. I have always seen my students as an extended family, encouraging them to do their best, to be themselves, take responsibility for their own actions, and, when time inevitably dictates, allow them to make their own way in the world. By recognizing the fact I use my Father archetype in my teaching role, I am able to then focus on the positive energy and personal traits of the Father archetype. This gives me a greater energetic balance and understanding of my role and performance as a teacher.

Balance is achieved by awareness and use of all personal archetypes. We do not have one-dimensional personalities. If we led our lives using only a single archetypal energy, we would be one-dimensional, but we do not. We have a number of personal archetypes and, to achieve balance in our lives, it is important to use the energy of all of those archetypes. There are occasions when the energy from one or two archetypes dominates our experience. This is fine for a short period, especially in a time of crisis. However, to maintain balance, it is essential to use all of our archetypal energy.

A good example of imbalance is when an addiction dominates an individual. Nothing else is important; not family, friends, work, finances or home. The individual exists solely on the negative energy of the Addict. All other archetypal energy is obstructed by the quest to fulfil the addiction. By having an awareness of your personal archetypes, you are able to recognize situations when you are dominated by one archetypal force. Look at your other archetypes and muster the positive energy they offer. This brings balance back into your life.

# ~ Section 2 ~

## Discovering Your Archetypes

**This is all about you.**

You are about to undertake a process of discovery. We all come from a different starting base. That is fine. What we are about to consider are our personal archetypes. You have used their pattern and energy all of your life, so consider your past:

* What were you like as a child?
* What sort of a teenager were you?
* What type of journey are you currently on as an adult?
* How important is home and family?
* What jobs have you had?
* What are your hobbies and interests?
* Where does your creativity lie?
* What questions fill your head?
* How do you relate to other people?
* Is technology important to you?

Sit down with a pen and paper and work your way through the questionnaire.

As you answer each question, consider all of your attitudes, your emotions and your life experiences. You have begun the process of discovering your archetypes and fully understanding who you are.

How many archetypes are you likely to discover?

**You should be able to recognize between twelve and twenty personal archetypes.**

Some archetypes will resonate powerfully with your energy, while others will emit a mild sensation of familiarity. Within each of these archetypes is a part of your psyche. Keep them all and read about each archetype. They are a part of who you are.

## We are now ready to begin.

The following key questions will give you definitive insight into your individual archetypes.

Consider all the questions. The answer you are looking for is a clear and definite yes. If this is the case, you will have at least one or more of the archetypes listed after each question. Keep note of those archetypes, and when you are ready, flip to section 3 to understand how each archetype works for you.

If you answer no to any question, move on to the next question. Do not worry about the size of your list. The archetypes you write on your list are all you need for right now.

*****

# The "Let's Get Started" Guide to Discovering your Archetypes

*1. Do you play sports or exercise regularly?*
   *Are you into team sports or extreme adventures?*

**Athlete * Adventurer * Disciple * Nature Child * Warrior**

*2. Are you creative?*

**Artist * Craftsperson * Storyteller * Creator * Magician * Pioneer * Actor**

*3. Do you care for or look after people?*

**Carer * Healer * Rescuer * Servant**

*4. Is family really important to you?*

**Mother * Father * Companion**

*5. Do you enjoy being in charge and taking responsibility?*

**King * Queen * Indulged Child * Politician * Statesman * Judge**

*6. Do you work in the service industry?*

**Servant * Martyr * Teacher * Salesperson * Networker * Carer * Diplomat**

*7. Are you into wine and fancy restaurants?*

**Hedonist * Dilettante * Lover * Narcissist * Entrepreneur * Diva**

*8. Are personal beauty, grooming and dress important to you?*

**Damsel * Princess * Knight * Prince * Lover * Goddess * God * Narcissist * Diva**

*9. Are you into computers and computer technology?*

**Computer Nerd * Networker * Engineer**

*10. Is religion important to you?*

**Disciple * Nun * Priest * Monk * Pilgrim**

*11. Do you join groups on a regular basis?*

**Disciple * Networker**

*12. Do you question authority and social structure?*

**Rebel * Philosopher**

*13. Is your head full of questions? Do you constantly take notes?*

**Philosopher * Seeker**

*14. Are you interested in how people think?*

**Detective * Networker * Philosopher * Vampire * Diplomat * Seeker * Judge**

*15. Are rules and justice important to you?*

**Judge * Avenger * Destroyer**

*16. Do you crave solitude?*

**Hermit * Hero * Computer Nerd**

*17. Are you a spiritual person or on a spiritual quest?*

**Seeker * Guide * Visionary * Angel * Priestess * Divine Child * Shaman * Goddess * God * Mystic**

*18. Are you shy and constantly faced with challenges?*

**Coward * Hermit * Hero * Heroine**

*19. Do others come to you for advice?*

**Wise Woman * Shaman * Healer * Witch * Wizard**

20. Is money vitally important to you?

**Banker * Entrepreneur * Thief * Salesman * Prince * Princess**

21. Do you crave adventure and an outdoor lifestyle?

**Adventurer * Nature Child * Explorer * Athlete * Warrior * Peter Pan Child * Knight * Fairy * Shape-Shifter**

22. Do you need protection and indulgence? Do you love shopping?

**Princess * Prince**

23. Do you feel trapped, worthless or undervalued?

**Slave * Servant * Martyr * Victim * Prostitute * Beggar**

24. Are animals important to you?

**Shaman * Rescuer * Carer * Environmentalist**

25. Do you have an addiction?

**Addict * Martyr * Thief * Vampire * Lover * Entrepreneur * Gambler * Bully * Destroyer**

26. Do you need healing?

**Wounded Child * Victim * Slave * Martyr**

27. Are you methodical?

**Servant * Engineer * Scientist**

28. Do you stand up for the rights of others?

**Advocate * Peacemaker * Diplomat * Statesman * Rescuer * Warrior * Disciple * Rebel * Carer**

29. Can you dramatically change a poor situation into a winning one?

**Alchemist * Wizard * Witch * Pioneer**

30. Do you see things from other dimensions?

**Visionary * Angel * Fairy * Goddess * Divine Child * Magician**

*31. Do you treasure your car, tools or possessions and are they well kept?*

**Knight \* Warrior \* Engineer \* Damsel \* Servant**

*32. Are you into research?*

**Pioneer \* Scientist \* Seeker**

*33. Are you knowledgeable, well read and enjoy learning and study?*

**Scholar \* Wise Woman \* Scientist \* Pioneer \* Scribe**

*34. Do you lack direction and change jobs frequently?*

**Wanderer**

*35. Are you loyal and devoted?*

**Companion \* Disciple \* Servant**

*36. Do you throw tantrums or seek attention?*

**Damsel \* Indulged Child \* Princess \* Prince \* Court Jester \* Knight \* Artist \* Clown \* Narcissist \* Diva**

*37. Are you a conduit for learning and education?*

**Teacher \* Mentor \* Facilitator \* Guide \* Shaman \* Witch \* Priestess \* Wise Woman \* Prophet**

*38. Do you make mischief? Do you make fun of yourself or others? Do you seek a stage to entertain others?*

**Puck \* Trickster \* Court Jester \* Joker \* Fool \* Magician \* Thief \* Rebel \* Clown \* Indulged Child**

*39. Have you an aversion to sex?*

**Celibate \* Wounded Child \* Nun**

*40. Do you take risks? Are you reckless?*

**Destroyer \* Gambler \* Adventurer \* Fool \* Entrepreneur \* Rebel \* Saboteur \* Explorer \* Thief**

## Where to Now?

How did it go? By now you should have a list of archetypes you identify with. Choose the ones you feel strongly about. Look them up in section 3 and come to understand their aspects and energy. Remember this is all about who you are.

If you desire personal change, begin with the archetype that feels to be the essential you - the one you most identify with and feel strongly about. Check the description and its negative aspects. Can you identify what negative energy is holding you back? Look at the negative words and phrases. Which negative words and phrases describe your behaviour? Once you have identified these behaviours, character traits and patterns, begin to eliminate them from your life. Look at the positive words and phrases. Is this where you want to be? Is this where you should be? Are these the behaviours, the character traits, the actions and the patterns you desire to incorporate into your life? This is how you move the archetypal energy. Eliminate the negative traits and adopt the positive traits. These actions are the generators of change. With conscious action, the use of positive archetypal energy brings about change.

A warning! Be prepared to fall back into negative energy patterns. They are familiar to you and often the path of least resistance. The important aspect is awareness. If you are aware that you are back using the negative archetypal energy, you now have the knowledge and ability to push aside those traits and adopt your new positive energy traits and patterns. Remember, energy is rarely static. It requires a conscious effort and a program of reinforcement to keep the flow positive. Bad habits are hard to break, but so are good habits. Once you begin to use the positive energy of your archetypes, the effect compounds and each step becomes easier.

As your archetypal patterns of behaviour change, other aspects of your life change as well. When you change, the world around you changes. Your friends are generally the first to notice. You do not react the same way as you always have. You may wish to spend your time doing different activities. You develop other interests. You have changed, while your friends have remained basically the same. Be aware, when you change, the energy within your relationships changes. This may create tension. Invariably, this leads to new friendships.

Perhaps you have the ambition or desire to change and improve your skills. Will this lead to new work opportunities? As you develop consistency and strength with your positive archetypal energy, your personal attributes will come to the fore and you develop skills and abilities you can use to further your career and your relationships. For example, I have a strong Teacher archetype. My archetypal Teacher energy pattern has always been a part of me. The pattern is consistent. Hence, I have always been a teacher. However, the archetypal energy has changed. I consider myself a much better teacher now than when I embarked on my first teaching position. On my journey as a primary school teacher, I discovered I was a storyteller, a writer and, more significantly, a drama teacher. I am now an Archetype Consultant and facilitate workshops with adults, teenagers and families. Many people have entered my life. Many interactions have been short, while a few have been lifelong relationships. This is the nature of energy.

A French proverb, first used by Alphonse Karr, goes "The more things change, the more they stay the same." That is an excellent description of the archetypal energy pattern. The "essential" you is the archetypal pattern. The "energetic" you is what changes. It is your decision as to where and how you want that change to take place.

After you have examined your strongest archetype, choose a second archetype and follow the same procedure. Generally, we are suited to work on two to three archetypes at any one time without overloading our emotional self. Be cautious in your approach. Deal with these archetypes in their entirety and then move on to another. There is no set or recommended time frame. The time you spend on any one archetype is up to you.

With some archetypes, you will instantly recognize your use of the negative energy and negative personality traits and set a plan to change to the positive. This change may come easy. However, other negative patterns and traits may be more obscure. It may take a special set of circumstances to arise before those negative patterns become apparent to you. Some negative patterns are easier to break than others. As you change your behavioural energy patterns from negative to positive, or even strengthen your already positive energy, you will find other archetypes need attention.

As you change your priorities and circumstances, other energies come into play. You may wish to revisit and re-examine some archetypal energies as your life changes. Negative patterns and cycles are stubborn and require constant attention on your behalf. Do not be disheartened. Even if your life doesn't instantly and dramatically change, you do. Be persistent. Remember, you are not static. You are energy, constantly flowing and constantly changing. Your desire is to change from negative personality traits and negative archetypal energy and adopt positive personality traits and positive archetypal energy. Your aim and your desires are not to go backwards or in circles. Your aim is to change your archetypal energy and adopt positive personality traits that are found within that positive energy. Your archetypal energy is your friend. Look after it. Treat it well and you shall be rewarded with change.

**Remember, you change first; your circumstances change second!**

# ~ Section 3 ~
# Description of Archetypes

## Actor

The Actor is an amazing archetype. Actors are entertainers. They have long histories and traditions of reflecting the drama and humour of everyday life. They reflect and question the customs and traditions of society. They bring stories to people to inspire imagination and stir emotions. Actors feel comfortable in many and varied situations. It is just like playing a part. They feel comfortable playing different roles. Often this is used to hide their true identities or conceal a lack of understanding about who they truly are.

Undoubtedly, many Actors end up in films, on television or on the stage. However, it is not essential for professional actors to possess an Actor archetype. Many in the entertainment industry rely on their King, Knight, Damsel or other strong archetypes to succeed. Sean Connery has a strong King archetype and uses this energy effectively in his film roles. Kevin Costner has a strong Prince archetype. He is totally convincing in the role of Robin Hood. Carey Grant always played Carey Grant. He was the Knight. Charming, chivalrous and drawn into adventures where he rescued the maiden and foiled the villain. Marilyn Monroe, in life and in film, was the perfect Damsel.

The negative archetypal energy of both the Actor and the Damsel archetypes often leads to an obsession with body image, the need to be noticed, short-lived romantic adventures and various other misadventures and misdemeanours. An observation of some of the young starlets of more recent years will reveal the same behaviour patterns. Lindsay Lohan and Miley Cyrus are two young performers who come to mind. The strength of both the Actor and the Damsel archetypes needs to be respected. It is a common occurrence for an individual with these archetypes to fall from positive behaviours into negative behaviours.

Individuals with the Actor archetype have the talent and adaptability to be many characters. They have naturalness that lulls viewers into their worlds, no matter what type of characters they play. Daniel Day Lewis and Meryl Streep are two of my favourite performers. Both possess the Actor archetype that allows them to play diverse characters. Johnny Depp and Renee Zellweger are two more modern examples of performers with the Actor archetype. All four of these performers have a variety of characterizations that are extensive and they possess presence that demands attention.

Not all people who possess the Actor archetype end up in the entertainment industry. However, they will find stages and audiences for their performances. We see children perform for family or friends all the time, and, as adults, they are no different. There are bound to be performances for family, friends and workmates. The content is different, but the intent is the same. Give Actors an audience and you are bound to have a show. It fulfils their desire to be noticed. It may also hide the fact that Actors are often more comfortable playing other characters. Often, for the Actor, it is more exciting to be a character than to be oneself.

**Negative Aspects:**

Self-centred ~ Exaggeration ~ Liar ~ Inauthentic ~ Self-deception ~ Drama queen Confused ~ Unable to define who they are ~ Self-absorbed ~ Self-importance Emotional ~ Internal struggle ~ False ~ Pompous

**Positive Aspects:**

Entertaining ~ Creative ~ Adaptable ~ Passing on the message ~ Self-exploration Brings out the best ~ Holds up a mirror to life ~ Keeper of culture ~ Confident ~ Can play many parts

**Archetypal Energy:**

Actors are persons of many parts. It is like they are on a roller coaster ride with many ups and downs, sudden twists and turns and even a few loop-de-loops. There is contentment in their lives as long as there is a stage or an audience. If they are serious about their acting and choose this pathway as a career, there is likely to be frustration. The entertainment industry is about image and money making. Success may not be easy to come by, as even the most talented Actor may not fit into the industry's bottom-line approach. It is not an industry that rewards honour and being true to oneself.

On a social level, Actors are always comfortable as they are just playing another part. They are often fun to be with and can turn on the charm, the wit and the stories, at the drop of a hat. The most critical aspect of the Actor's archetypal energy is balance. An Actor can easily become energetically unbalanced, which may lead to physical and mental instability. Success can inflate the ego. Success, however, can be fleeting. Hence, the roller coaster rides. Some Actors may also suffer an identity crisis. In playing so many parts, some Actors have trouble distinguishing who they really are. It is important they identify their true selves and give those parts of their characters time and energy. Actors also have to remember they have other archetypes. To be consumed with the Actor role and neglect the other energies within them is likely to leave them as unbalanced personalities.

**Archetypal Combinations:**
The archetypal energy of the Actor combines well with the energy of:
Court Jester * Detective * Victim * Clown * Judge * Magician * Queen * King Puck * Rebel * Storyteller * Prostitute * Shaman * Wizard * Teacher

**Effective Use of Actor Energy:**

- Discover your true self and identity.
- Balance your life by using the energy of your other archetypes.
- Remember you are capable of playing many roles and fitting into myriad social situations.
- Consistently monitor your self-esteem. Your self-esteem is controlled by your Victim archetype, so be vigilant.
- Be wary of the ego. It is powerful and has to be controlled.

# Addict

Be prepared! The energy of the Addict archetype is powerful and all-consuming. Those of you who have the Addict archetype know exactly what this means. You may even have partners, family or friends with this archetype and have a good insight into this energy.

The main challenge that goes with this archetype is that negative patterns can easily take control over the individual. So much of the Addict's time, thoughts and actions are focused with the fulfilment of the addiction. This often causes difficulties, especially with neglect of other aspects of the Addict's life. The key to the individual with the Addict archetype is to recognize the energy of addiction. That single-mindedness drives the Addict at the expense of an individual's other archetypes. Other areas of social interaction and responsibility are neglected in the pursuit of a single issue. Addicts have to be challenged about their behaviour.

Admission is the first step. Once the Addict admits an addiction, then, at least, the battle can begin. Action is the second step. Many organizations assist addictions and they are well versed in their programs. From an archetypal point of view, it is imperative not just to focus on defeating an addiction. It is equally necessary to channel the energy into a positive pursuit. Vigilance and persistence are the third step. It is important to monitor the strong energy of the Addict archetype. When there is a constant flow of positive adventures, challenges and responsibilities, it gives the individual with the Addict archetype a well-rounded and balanced existence.

If you know you are an addict, it will come as no surprise that you may have difficulty focusing on the positive side of the Addict. The good news is that it can be done. The best example I have come across was a gentleman who had a typically strong Addict archetype. He could have been a gambler, an alcoholic or a drug addict. No! He avoided the negative energy. Instead, he channelled his Addict energy into the positive, with his love of rescuing boats. Fortunately, he lived near a beach and he used the powerful, positive energy of his Rescuer archetype to assist his positive Addict energy. What a great way to channel the

Addict energy into the positive. By controlling his Addict archetype, he was able to focus on other important areas of his life, his business and his family.

There are two lessons from this gentleman's experience. Firstly, he was able to channel the positive energy into a positive activity. He found a hobby. Hobbies are excellent ways to engage the Addict energy. Sport is another area to channel that energy. Although, just to reinforce how strong the Addict archetypal energy is, notice how many elite athletes succumb to the negative energy of winning at all costs with performance-enhancing drugs and anti-social behaviours. This shows us that addiction is a constant battle. Secondly, this gentleman was able to incorporate other interests into his life. If there is variety in one's life, there is always balance. We have more than one archetype. We have many personality traits. We are multi skilled. We are adaptable. Take advantage of all your capabilities. The Addict needs to be like the young scout: "Be prepared!' Remember, it is a constant battle for the individual with the Addict archetype. It takes focus and resolve to stay in a positive and productive routine.

**Negative Aspects:**

Weak ~ Out of control ~ Consumed ~ Manipulated ~ Selfish ~ Greedy ~ Over-consumer ~ Glutton ~ Manipulative ~ Workaholic ~ Unbalanced ~ Over-zealous ~ Compromised ~ Easily tempted ~ Tunnel vision

**Positive Aspects:**

Strong ~ In control ~ Sharing ~ Strong-willed ~ Organized ~ Focused ~ Balanced ~ Perseverance ~ Flexible ~ Adaptive

**Archetypal Energy:**

The powerful Addict energy, especially on the negative side, requires a strong and continual commitment to stay on track and focus on positive activities. The good news is the strength of this energy allows the Addict to achieve great things. Many inventors, entrepreneurs, discoverers and explorers were driven to success, in part, by the strength of their Addict archetype. Use it to your advantage. Be clear and concise about the path you follow and the goals you strive to achieve. If you are indecisive and unclear in your intentions, the energy of the negative Addict will swiftly confuse and consume you. From there it is only a small step to be condemned to the depths of despair and depravity.

Remember to stay focused and stay positive. Use the positive energy constructively.

The other lesson for Addicts is to be aware of the company they keep. Like minds gravitate to like minds. Negative energy gravitates to negative energy. Consider the example of city slums and areas of high criminal activity. Observe how the negative energy of various archetypes living together feed upon each other. There is the Addict (sex, drugs), the Avenger (the enforcer), the Bully (head of the crime gang or enforcer), the Damsel (using sex to seek love and attention), the Gambler (addicted to money and easy gains), the Prostitute (professing physical and emotional unworthiness), the Thief (looking for easy targets and gain), the Trickster (preying on gullibility and weakness), the Vampire (sucking the negative energy) and the Victim (wallowing with low self-esteem).

It is important for Addicts to surround themselves with positive people. When accompanied by others with archetypes that complement the positive energy of the Addict, then together, they all progress with support and direction.

**Archetypal Combinations:**

The archetypal energy of the Addict combines well with the energy of:

Rescuer * Servant * Entrepreneur * Alchemist * Coward * Explorer * Adventurer * Pioneer * Healer * Companion * Monk * Nun * Pilgrim * Historian * Scribe * Networker * Student * Seeker * Warrior * Engineer

**Effective Use of Addict Energy:**
- The Addict energy is powerful, so use it wisely.
- Always be vigilant for this energy remains strong for your lifetime.
- Choose friends and acquaintances that complement and encourage your positive Addict energy.
- Involve yourself in a sport, hobby, entrepreneurial venture or worthwhile activity that will focus your energy.
- Exercise your mind with meditation, yoga or martial arts so you remain mentally strong.
- Do not be taken in with promises of indulgences that weaken your will power.

# Adventurer

Adventurers are free spirits. These people live for excitement and exploration. They may travel a great deal, although for some, an interesting walk in a different setting may suffice. Adventurers love the great outdoors. They are nature lovers who enjoy the beaches, the oceans, the mountains and the forests. Here, they experience freedom from the other more restricting aspects of their daily lives.

Do you love extreme sports? Bungee jumping, white-water rafting, hang-gliding, snowboarding, canyoning, skydiving, surfing, mountain biking and motocross are not just entertainment for the Adventurer but a form of devotion. Speed, height, challenge and danger are all part of the intrigue. Take a normal sport, make a slight variation to increase the amount of difficulty and danger and the Adventurer will be there.

Given the nature of Adventurers, they won't apply themselves totally to just one activity. There is always a greater challenge and bigger thrill in the next activity. Generally, Adventurers find it difficult to devote their energy to one place, one job and one activity for any great length of time. It is in their nature to move on, look for another opportunity and experience life to the fullest.

**Negative Aspects:**

Lack of commitment ~ No goals ~ Recklessness ~ Purposeless ~ Escape reality ~ Insecure ~ Frivolous ~ Irresponsible ~ Lost soul ~ Financial irresponsibility ~ Changeable ~ Self-absorbed

**Positive Aspects:**

Free spirit ~ New experiences ~ Nature lover ~ Healthy lifestyle ~ Fun-loving ~ Seeker ~ Adaptable ~ Lives life to the fullest ~ Recognizes new opportunities ~ Fitness fanatic ~ Thrill-seeker ~ Enjoys a challenge ~ Tests mental and physical toughness

**Archetypal Energy:**

The Adventurer is a fun person to be with. If you like excitement, love to be outdoors, enjoy travel and rise to a challenge then you, are the type of person people like to be around. Do not expect Adventurers to be housebound or locked into steady routines. You cannot deny them their freedom. Employment is important and, if you are an Adventurer, you may find yourself working in positions that are dangerous, remote or exotic. Monetary rewards for working these situations is important, as it allows for enough cash flow to finance the next adventure. Adventurers are good savers but only for short periods of time as there is always another adventure to be had. A difficult challenge for Adventurers is to come to terms with personal safety. This is not a problem when they only have to answer to themselves, but when there is family involved, Adventurers have to be considerate of their responsibilities and the needs of other family members.

**Archetypal Combinations:**

The archetypal energy of the Adventurer combines well with the energy of:

Athlete * Warrior * Explorer * Pioneer * Knight * Seeker * Hero * Companion * Addict * Artist * Rebel * Nature Child * Peter Pan Child * Lover * Historian * Pilgrim * Storyteller * Wanderer

**Effective Use of Adventurer Energy:**

- Be mindful of your health, fitness, and energy levels.
- Eat healthy food, and drink lots of pure water.
- Enjoy your adventuring spirit, but maintain your responsibilities in the other areas of your life.
- Be considerate of your family, especially if they do not share your enthusiasm for your next adventure.

# Advocate

The Advocate speaks on behalf of others and is usually the central person between two disputing groups. A good example is the person who speaks on behalf of refugees. In all of these cases, a government has the power to decide the fate of the refugees. Refugees have many barriers blocking their paths to freedom in a new land. These barriers can include the law, lack of money, language, hostile media, fear, and prejudice. This places refugees at a tremendous disadvantage in stating their cases. The government has total control. In such cases, the power differential between these two parties is enormous. It is with these types of situations the Advocate has an incredibly important role to play. The Advocate has to have clear knowledge and a good understanding of both parties. Communication is the key for any successful Advocate.

Aside from refugees, there are people with disabilities, at-risk children, the unemployed, the poor, the homeless, the elderly, indigenous people and ethnic minorities who are disadvantaged by a variety of circumstances. As well as disadvantaged people, there are also animals and the environment. In fact, each and every one of us is open to exploitation in dire circumstances. Even in a humane society, equality and justice become the victims of negative energy. On certain issues and on many occasions, those altruistic aspects of our society, that we dearly love to embrace, often go missing.

The Advocate is the conscience of our society and challenges us to define who we are. Of course, we will not agree with what is espoused by many Advocates. Often there are Advocates with diametrically opposing points of view. Nevertheless, this energy exposes us to ideas we either agree or disagree with. In other words, Advocates of all persuasions, while expressing a point of view, force us to define our opinions. We've all had a moment in time when we've used the Advocate archetype, when we had to stand up and be counted. If you have an Advocate archetype, you will have a passion and the endurance to represent causes close to your heart. This representation may be over a short period of time or over a long period, maybe even a lifetime.

**Negative Aspects:**

Power hungry ~ Manipulative ~ Self-important ~ Bossy ~ Dogmatic ~ False or negative causes ~ Seeking personal gain ~ Hypocritical ~ Biased ~ Prejudice ~ Denier of justice ~ Self-glorification

**Positive Aspects:**

Stands up for the rights of others ~ Empathetic ~ Compassionate ~ Caring ~ Networking ~ Good listening skills ~ Good communication skills ~ Egalitarian ~ Defender ~ Social conscience ~ Seeker of social justice

**Archetypal Energy:**

Empathy, compassion, listening and communication are the trademark attitudes and skills of the Advocate archetypal energy. Advocates possess knowledge, skill and endurance. It is important for them to be supported by a strong structure. This may be in the form of an individual who encourages and supports them at a personal level, or an organization that provides facilities, networks and finance. Both support structures are ideal in assisting the Advocate, although an organization is usually capable of supplying greater support.

Advocates possess a huge amount of patience and endurance. If you need some inspiration or understanding of what the Advocate archetype is all about, watch a film titled "Amazing Grace". It tells the life story of William Wilberforce, who fought valiantly and successfully for the abolition of slavery throughout the British Empire. The film successfully shows all of the positive energies that make up the Advocate archetype. Along with compassion, empathy, courage, patience and endurance, he had a conviction that nothing was impossible. Read the story of William Wilberforce, and you will also gain an understanding that the Advocate is not devoted to just one cause but is prepared to tackle all issues that fall within the sphere of injustice.

There are only a small number of Advocates walking among the population, but on an energetic level, their influence is clear and undeniable. If you are an Advocate, you will support causes dear to your heart. If you are supporting an Advocate on a personal level as a friend or partner, be prepared for a long and arduous journey. The archetypal energies of the Servant, Companion, Slave and Martyr provide an excellent personal support structure. At a broader level, we really can make a contribution. Tune in to your own archetypal energies, and you will soon know and understand the depth of commitment to your causes. Be prepared to contribute. Contribution to a worthy cause enhances your self-esteem and taps into positive archetypal energy.

**Archetypal Combinations:**

The archetypal energy of the Advocate combines well with the energy of:

Healer * Carer * Scientist * Teacher * Wise Woman * Queen * King * Artist * Addict * Storyteller * Knight * Judge * Princess * Peacemaker * Prince * Rescuer * Networker * Priest

**Effective Use of Advocate Energy:**

- Do what you can and to the best of your ability, but be aware of your limitations.
- Be conscious of your physical energy and mental strength.
- Choose your battleground wisely.
- Always be conscious of your motives, and be wary of your ego.
- Use your networking skills to gather a trusty and hardworking support group.

# Alchemist

The Alchemist is not as recognizable as once was the case. These days the true Alchemist speaks more of the law of attraction. Traditionally, the Alchemist is a person who can turn lead into gold. This ability is metaphorical, not literal; although, it is an excellent allegory of what the modern Alchemist can achieve. If you have an understanding and the ability to reinvent, to change a bad situation into a success, or to weave a divine substance, then you are using the energy of the Alchemist.

We are all aware of the master chef, and we probably have friends who can randomly throw ingredients together and create a palatable masterpiece. Similarly, there is the individual who can blend essential oils and other natural substances to concoct sublime soaps, face creams and body lotions. You may consider these trivial abilities, but they are perfect examples of the Alchemist's archetypal energy.

Try not to confuse the Alchemist with the Magician. The Alchemist does not do magic tricks. The Alchemist is also not to be confused with the modern day chemist. Today's chemistry is more about research and following a process to produce a desired mass-market compound. The Alchemist has the insight and ability to recognize potential, take what is succinctly good and pure, and visualize and create a final result without a process. Alchemists use their intuition. They have an innate psychic ability or what I call a "knowing". They tune in. They have no need for thinking. Thinking is the opposite of intuition. Thinking is a process that leads to planning and consideration. Intuition, the energy of the Alchemist, is about the knowing and the doing.

**Negative Aspects:**

Mundane ~ Get rich quick schemes ~ Delusions of grandeur ~ Seduction ~ Trickery ~ Misuse of power and knowledge ~ Unethical ~ Fraud ~ Pretence ~ False ~ Deceit

**Positive Aspects:**

Transforming lead into gold ~ Extraordinary ~ Entrepreneur ~ Mystical ~ Spiritual transformation ~ Enhanced expression ~ Transmutation ~ Optimistic ~ Can-do attitude ~ Intuitive

**Archetypal Energy:**

The archetypal energy of Alchemists is a gift. They have the ability to channel the Divine. When used wisely, it can enhance not only their lives, but also their wider communities. The key is to seek the good in every person and every situation. You cannot create a pure and perfect result without trust in your goal, and confidence in your abilities. The success of Alchemists is built on confidence. They are so in tune with using their intuition that it becomes second nature. Many Alchemists see their abilities as no big deal because it is so natural to them. Alchemists have a strong intuitive knowledge of the relationship between the spiritual and the physical. If you are an Alchemist and you find yourself becoming aloof or magical, seek the people in your sphere of influence to bring you back down to earth. Ground yourself back in the physical, where your divine gifts have an impact.

**Archetypal Combinations:**

The archetypal energy of the Alchemist combines well with the energy of:

King * Queen * Entrepreneur * Angel * Healer * Fairy * Wizard * Wise Woman * Artist * Shaman * Rescuer * Pioneer * Networker * Servant * Witch * Goddess * Teacher

**Effective Use of Alchemist Energy:**

- Remember to work with the good in every person and every situation.
- Be wary of the lure of quick and easy monetary gain.
- Remember to stay true to your principles.
- Stay grounded.

# Angel

There are so many books, songs, poems, stories and cards about angels, yet they are a pale reflection of the truly positive Angel energy. The Angel archetype radiates love and goodness in its simplest and purest form. There are no complications with this energy. It looks for the good in all things. It is the total acceptance of who we are.

The Angel archetype has a direct connection with the Divine. This may cause a state of confusion when an Angel is confronted with the negative archetypal energies that prevail in this physical plane. Imagine moving from a state of pure love and joy to a state of seemingly unrelated chaos.

Another source of confusion for individuals with the Angel archetype is the way they have to deal with earthly inventions. Things like money, time, machinery, computers, and motor cars are all too mystifying for the Angel to fully grasp and appreciate. For example, the Angel enjoys shopping, especially for beautiful things, and the best way to pay for these goods is an expectation that the money will be provided. This is the "pennies from heaven" attitude. Why use earthly communications when you have a direct line to the divine? What is there to understand about transport when you can flow freely between the various dimensions? Why is earth time important when you come from a dimension where time does not exist? From the perspective of the Angel life on earth is different, amazing and extraordinary?

**Negative Aspects:**

False claims ~ Angelic guidance for control ~ Ego enhancement ~ Pedantic fall from grace ~ Temptress ~ Frivolous ~ Confused

**Positive Aspects:**

A channel for angel presence ~ Loving all things ~ Carry the light of the Divine ~ Nurturing ~ Giving help without expectation ~ Pennies from heaven ~ Bearers of good tidings ~ Spiritual connection ~ Grace

**Archetypal Energy:**

Angels are wonderful beings to be associated with. They are loving, caring, empathic, and unique spiritual guides. Their energy radiates a presence that is pure joy. If you have an Angel archetype, you have abundant spiritual knowledge. There is very little I can tell you that you do not already know. Tune in to yourself, and you will find the answers to any spiritual matters that seek your attention. If you are in the company of those with an Angel archetype, be they family or friends, enjoy the experience. Learn from their qualities, and listen to their spiritual message.

If those with an Angel archetype are at odds with, or confused by, some of our worldly treasures or practices, it is all part of their journey. Angels are here to learn about this physical world, which is vastly different to the spiritual world. The physical world is dominated by our senses, our learning experiences, our survival, and the slow processes of manifestation. None of these things matter in the world of spirit, so they are important issues for angelic individual to experience. Remember, we are all here for the experience. After experiencing a physical life, Angels have a greater understanding of humanity, the difference between the physical and the spiritual, and their role of Angel guardianship.

You do not have to belong to a religious order or identify with a particular religion or spiritual belief system to have an Angel archetype. Angel archetypes are people of all walks of life. If you observe those who have a pure and loving heart, unconditional compassion, and a spiritual pathway, you shall find the Angel archetypal energy.

**Archetypal Combinations:**

The archetypal energy of the Angel combines well with the energy of:

Mother * Wise Woman * Healer * Carer * Rescuer * Shaman * Advocate * Pilgrim * Mystic * Scholar * Servant * Divine Child * Teacher * Visionary * Nun

**Effective Use of Angel Energy:**

- Remain pure of heart, and seek goodness in every person and in all things.
- Maintain composure amid the frustration of worldly inventions.
- Learn to use money wisely.
- Beware of the temptation of the ego, and be conscious of the temptation that could lead to a fall from grace.
- Assist those in need of spiritual guidance, for they are bound come to you.

# Artist

The Artist archetype covers all those associated with creative arts and many of the performing arts. This list includes painting, stone masonry, photography, woodwork, graphic arts, metalwork, paper crafts, drawing, computer arts, music, dance, poetry and literature.

Art and craft are often associated, but there is a distinct difference between the Artist and the Craftsperson. The archetypes have a different energy. The Artist relies on flair, creativity and originality, while the Craftsperson follows a pattern and a process. The craftsperson participates in knitting, needlework, doll making, lead lighting, scrapbooking and picture framing to name but a few.

Art reflects society. The Artists' work represents not only their creative selves but also their personal views of society. One of art's golden periods, the Renaissance, is full of paintings reflecting religious themes, most of which were commissioned by the church or their patrons. The best known example is that of the Sistine Chapel.

The Artist's work may also be visionary in nature. This archetypal energy can tap into an internal or external source and find structure in artistic expression. This is bound to happen if the Artist also has a Visionary archetype. The two linked to the one personality presents a powerful energetic connection.

**Negative Aspects:**

Blocked ~ Temperamental ~ Suffering/starving artist ~ Depression ~ Eccentricity ~ Self-possessed ~ Self-indulgent ~ Depraved ~ Perfectionist ~ Haughty ~ Lacking confidence ~ Plagiarist ~ Imitating

**Positive Aspects:**

Creative ~ Self-expression ~ Channel ~ Expand the boundaries ~ Inspiring ~ Flow of consciousness ~ Challenging ~ Passion ~ Art holds a mirror to life ~ Uplifting ~ Beauty ~ Visionary ~ Perfectionist

**Archetypal Energy:**

The Artist archetype is found in many people who hold vastly different positions in society. The Artist may be a grand pianist, a Prima Donna, or a well-acclaimed painter or sculptor. The Artist may also be the mother next door; the vague, daydreaming child in your classroom or your workmate at the local hardware store. When you receive a Christmas card, handmade on recycled paper, beautifully decorated with pressed flowers and other natural ornaments, and written in calligraphy with coloured ink, then you know that person has an Artist archetype. As a teacher aide, I assisted and cared for a down-syndrome boy. His functioning level of mathematics and English was well below his chronological age. However, he spent a great deal of time and focus on his illustrations with all his story-writing projects. As a young adult, he is now making his way into the artistic world of gallery showings and exhibitions. His art work is now printed on gift cards which express his unique blend of style and colour.

The most important aspect when dealing with the energy of the Artist archetype is to constantly be working on a project. When Artists are discontent and feel their lives are stuck in ruts, it is usually because the Artist energy is blocked, frustrated, or ignored. There may be circumstances beyond their control, but it is important for Artists to take a little time to satisfy their creative energy. Projects do not need to be monumental. They may be small in nature and design. They may only need a creative change into a different art form, a room to redecorate or an addition to the work place, home, or garden to restore energetic balance.

On different occasions, an Artist, on a personal level, may be artistically blocked. At times, development does plateau out and the Artist hits a flat spot. It is most frustrating when the writer, halfway through a novel, hits a metaphorical brick wall. Patience may be the only answer. From an archetypal point of view, the individual is able to examine the negative energy of the Artist archetype. Is this energy creating negative behaviours on a personal level? Are you consumed by any of these negative patterns? Are you being a perfectionist? Are you being temperamental about your artistic endeavours because of stress and pressure caused by family, friends, or work? Do you consider yourself unworthy of success?

When you recognize the negative energy, work at changing your mindset to work on the patterns of positive energy. Work on your worthiness and self-esteem. Deal with your outside issues, and begin to meditate or take up yoga to release stress. Remember, too, that art is in the eye of the beholder. Perfection is an opinion. Remember to seek excellence rather than perfection. There are some very good exercises and techniques that offer great assistance to the Artist. Julia Cameron has written two excellent books; *The Artist's Way* and *Vein of Gold*. They offer worthwhile information and techniques to harness the Artist's positive creative energy and creative flair.

**Archetypal Combinations:**

The archetypal energy of the Artist combines well with the energy of:

Seeker * Princess * Prince * Queen * King * Monk * Hedonist * Gypsy * Lover * Nun * Rebel * Scribe * Adventurer * Court Jester * Diva

**Effective Use of Artist Energy:**

- Keep your artist archetype content by the regular planning and maintenance of an artistic endeavour.
- Involve yourself in activities and procedures that enhance your creativity.
- Be aware of the pitfalls of perfection.
- Surround yourself with supportive associates as they may be the source of your success and inspiration.
- Do not place limits on your versatility or ability.

# Athlete

The Athlete archetype represents ultimate physical prowess and mental toughness. There is no doubt that elite sportspeople have the Athlete archetype. Those who reach the top in their chosen sports must have both the physical ability and the mental focus to succeed at that level. Those who participate at a junior level of sport have the same archetypal energy.

It is not just sport that attracts Athlete archetypes. They come from all walks of life and may include the soldier, the regular jogger, the skateboarder, or the suburban yoga devotee. Imagine the Athlete archetype in a tribal society. When tribes depended on hunting for their food, Athletes played an important part in the whole tribe's survival. Speed, stamina, endurance, and mental agility were paramount. As we've settled into a more permanent rural structure of towns, villages, and then cities, the role of Athletes changed. They were then valued as soldiers. But since the conclusion of World War II, in many countries, sport has become the dominant arena for Athletes.

Development of the Athlete's body is important, but development of the Athlete's mind is even more critical. There are many sports or physical activities where strength, power, and agility are paramount, but it can be argued that focus and mental toughness are more important. Golf is the perfect example, and it should lead all Athletes to realize that control of the mind is an absolute necessity. The mind plays a much more significant role in harnessing the positive energy of the Athlete archetype.

**Negative Aspects:**

Abuse of body ~ Anorexia ~ Bulimia ~ Obsession ~ Winning is everything ~ Narcissism ~ Worship the body ~ Self-loathing ~ Win at all costs ~ Fear of failure ~ Hero worship ~ Poor loser ~ Verbal abuse ~ Bragging ~ Cheating

**Positive Aspects:**

Physical strength ~ Mental strength ~ Body is a temple ~ Honour ~ Willpower ~ Discipline ~ Being a good loser ~ Being a gracious winner ~ Belief in oneself ~ Energy ~ Vitality ~ Good self-esteem ~ Being part of the team ~ Endurance ~ Resilience ~ Determination

**Archetypal Energy:**

The archetypal energy of the Athlete demands that time and effort is put into regular development of the physical. When this doesn't happen, the energies of an individual's other archetypes are affected. Lethargy creeps in, despondency fills the vacuum, and both physical and mental powers begin to wane. Regular exercise is a must for the Athlete archetype.

The other demand of the Athlete is rigorous mental development. If you are an Athlete, do not be remiss in developing your mental strength and flexibility. This is not a short-term demand, nor is it a simple exercise in the visualization of victory. There is nothing wrong with visualization, but the archetypal energy of the Athlete demands a much stronger and continual commitment. Sure, visualization is good, setting goals is fine, and yoga and meditation are even better. Gentle martial arts like Tai Chi, are excellent for physical and mental control. These are some considerations that satisfy the archetypal energy.

Individuals with the Athlete archetype have to be cautious when dealing with their Athlete archetypal energy. It is so easy to slip from positive to negative. There are many examples of the Athlete exhibiting behaviours of a bad loser, bragging, boasting, being an "in your face" winner, pushing the boundaries of fair play, using performance enhancing drugs, and abusing the body. The true test of the Athlete's ability to use the positive archetypal energy is more to do with attitude than anything else. Athletes have to monitor their attitudes and behaviours. Not necessarily when times are easy but more likely when times are tough. This is when mental toughness is important. However, the real test of their behaviour is when Athletes are successful and in the euphoria of their moments of triumph. Is their behaviour that of gracious winners or of braggarts? It is important to be proud of your achievements, but always be prouder of your behaviour.

**Archetypal Combinations:**

The archetypal energy of the Athlete combines well with the energy of:

Adventurer * Warrior * Knight * Explorer * Hero * King * Queen * Pioneer * Rebel * Seeker * Servant * Shaman * Slave

**Effective Use of Athlete Energy:**

- Develop both physical and mental abilities.
- Physical and mental development is a lifetime program.
- Activity needs to be regular and consistent.
- Be aware of your limitations and the consequences of extreme regimes and behaviours.
- Examine and monitor your attitude and behaviour when you experience the highs and the lows of your endeavours.

# Avenger

As the name suggests, the Avenger seeks justice in the form of revenge or retribution. The energy of the Avenger is a strong energy and suggests action. Generally, for an Avenger, a simple apology is not sufficient. Satisfying the strength of the Avenger's energy requires physical punishment, monetary recompense, or both. The Avenger would agree with Gordon Hewart that "Not only must Justice be done; it must also be seen to be done."

The Avenger archetype is common in young males. Unfortunately, many of these individuals utilize the negative aspect of this energy. This energy is supported by physical strength and the bond and camaraderie of the peer group. Avenging acts usually occur between groups of young men out on the town, street gangs claiming their territory, motorcycle gangs wanting control, and underground criminal gangs conducting profitable but illegal activities. For Avengers, any excuse will do in these circumstances. It is the honour of the tribe that is at stake. The Avenger energy can be strongly associated to a collective tribal energy.

Tribal energy is powerful. It determines such rules as how you look, what to wear, what to like and dislike, how to behave, who to associate with, what position you hold, what needs to be done to move up the pecking order, and what opinions you profess. Individuals give away many of their rights and freedoms when they become members of a tribal structure. What they receive in return is companionship, conformation, security, and support. As mentioned before, tribal energy is strongest in gangs. However, there are other bodies, such as the armed forces, a cult or sect, organized religions, companies, sporting clubs, service clubs, and so on that rely on the tribal energy. History has shown us there will be occasions when the Avenger archetypal energy becomes prevalent in all of these organizations.

As tribal energy lessens in intensity, so does the Avenger energy. In other words, your underground criminal gang has an intense tribal energy and, therefore, an intense Avenger energy. The local cricket club has a softer tribal energy and, so too, a softer Avenger energy. This follows that a criminal gang will potentially have many members with an Avenger archetype, while a cricket club may have only a few.

Not all young men have the Avenger archetype. It is interesting to note that those with the Avenger archetype can also be found in older individuals and the physically weak. Generally, physically weaker Avengers will use means other than physical strength to extract vengeful justice. They may use money to employ another to carry out their desired justice. They may use emotional blackmail to even the score. The negative Avenger has the desire to turn anything into a weapon in order to extract revenge.

The Avenger's motives may, in fact, be pure. There is justification in seeking justice, representing worthwhile causes, and defending others, especially those in positions of weakness. The Robin Hood philosophy of robbing the rich and giving to the poor would be deemed in many people's minds as acceptable Avenger energy. The choice the Avenger has to make is one of balance. If you have difficulty in justifying someone's actions and feel revenge is necessary; how do you act? Do you be brutal? If you decide to go in that direction, then your Avenger energy is on a par as the person you are condemning. The "eye for an eye" philosophy has equal Avenger energy for both sides of a dispute. One party must lower its defences, change the intensity, and shift the balance. Only then does change occur.

**Negative Aspects:**

Seeks revenge ~ Manipulative ~ Unprincipled ~ Eye for an eye ~ Violent ~ Terrorist ~ Lack of empathy ~ Unable to see another's point of view ~ Robin Hood ~ Ned Kelly ~ Bringer of justice ~ Reactionary ~ Lynch mob ~ Taking the law into their own hands

**Positive Aspects:**

Advocate ~ Tribal protectors ~ Seeks justice ~ Defender ~ Independence ~ Represents causes ~ Robin Hood ~ Ned Kelly ~ Bringer of justice ~ Considerate ~ Empathetic ~ Strength ~ Conviction

**Archetypal Energy:**

The Avenger has to consider motives, purpose, and consequences. Will a response to a perceived injustice be for the greater good, or is it for personal satisfaction? Is it justified? What purpose will be achieved? What are the consequences of a vengeful response?

Often the Avenger will act instinctively and instantly. The consequences of the Avenger's reaction to a perceived unjust action are likely to worsen the situation, not improve it. Sport gives us examples of this on a weekly basis. How often do football players who retaliate find themselves in more trouble with the referees than the players who provoked an initial infringement? Consider the student who reacts to the taunts or provocations of another student. It is the reaction, sometimes the over-reaction, which often draws the teacher's attention and discipline.

An important lesson for the Avenger is to take a moment's respite and consider the situation. The passing of time takes emotion out of a response. It also allows the Avenger to consider various options, many of which improve the situation and not worsen it. If you are an Avenger, the challenge is to transcend beyond the negative patterns of the Avenger and move to the positive energetic patterns of the Advocate. Be a voice for the injustice you see around you, not necessarily a reactionary.

**Archetypal Combinations:**

The archetypal energy of the Avenger combines well with the energy of:

Advocate * Rescuer * Knight * Warrior * Carer * Judge * Athlete * Diplomat * Wizard * Witch * Shaman

**Effective Use of Avenger Energy:**

- Ensure your motives are pure.
- Use your energy to liberate or assist those in need.
- Understand the law may not be perfect but it is important for you to still follow due process.
- Be wary of situations that take away your personal freedom and decision making.
- Choose your friends and associates wisely.
- Be constantly on your guard, as negative Avenger energy can arise swiftly and powerfully. Be aware of the trigger points.
  Use time as your friend to assess the overall situation.

# Banker

The Banker is concerned primarily with the organization of money; how to make it and the most effective way to lend it.

In folklore, the ultimate Banker is King Midas, who collects and saves all his wealth. He spends most of his time counting his money and neglecting his responsibilities. One day, a magical fairy appears and grants Midas his favourite wish; that is, everything he touches turns to gold. He runs excitedly through his palace turning everything in his path into gold. His loving daughter, anxious to share her father's excitement, runs to hug him and, at his touch, instantly turns to a statue of gold. King Midas finally realizes there is something more important than money. Most versions of this fairy tale have a happy ending. The fairy reappears and grants Midas another wish. The King touches his daughter, and she returns to her human self.

Isn't it amazing how folklore still resonates with modern history? Human nature rarely changes. It is not to be suggested that all Bankers are like King Midas, but the ultimate negative energy of the Banker is represented by King Midas. Greed, avarice, single-mindedness, and irresponsibility are all part of this energy. We see this negative energy on display through the rogue banker and the cyclical financial crises as displayed by the global financial crisis in 2007 and 2008.

As with all areas of human activity, the majority go about their business ethically and with common purpose. The same standard applies to the majority in the financial industry. Working with the positive energetic patterns of Bankers, these people assist their clients with financial management, financial gain, and even financial independence. Economies are built around the energy of the Banker. The economic strength of a community or a country often reflects the positive energy of the Banker. Bankers are generally conservative, and this is a positive attribute. It provides safety and security for the economic investment of that society and for the individuals within that society. When the economy fails, it is a reflection of those negative attributes that were mentioned in the King Midas story.

Many people with the Banker archetype work in the financial industry. They concern themselves with the making and distribution of money within that industry. However, others with a Banker archetype have employment in other areas. Those with the Banker archetype who do not work in finance may be the people who carefully manage the family budgets; the tradespeople who contract their labour or service; the individuals with small businesses; or the home investors with portfolios in cash, gold, shares, or property. People from all walks of life possess the Banker archetype. These people have money invested or stored safely. They may be frugal or, at the very least, careful with their finances. Wealth does not always dictate a Banker archetype. It is more about the power of saving and living within your means.

**Negative Aspects:**

Greed ~ Manipulation ~ Personal gain at the expense of others ~ Avarice Get rich quick schemes ~ Corruption ~ Over-indulgence ~ Risky ~ Recklessness ~ Mismanagement ~ Money is the root of all evil ~ Overspending ~ Greed is good

**Positive Aspects:**

Financial independence ~ Financial management ~ Live within your means ~ Assistance to business ~ Personal financial assistance ~ Frugal ~ Peace of mind ~ Budget-wise ~ Entrepreneurial ~ Secure ~ Safety first ~ Nest egg ~ Sincere ~ Customer friendly ~ Teamwork

**Archetypal Energy:**

In the modern world of capitalism and consumerism, the Banker archetype is a most advantageous energy. If you have this archetype, you are likely to be financially stable. There is an inbuilt sense of saving for a rainy day. You always have sufficient money to live on and, invariably, have sufficient funds for an emergency. Most individuals with the Banker archetype are excellent people to be with, as they are steady, are reliable, and possess an excellent work ethic. They're cautious when it comes to investment but, at the same time; understand the possible gains when a measured risk is taken.

The Banker has to consider and be careful of the King Midas energy. Money for money's sake does not sit well as an energetic balance. Excessive greed eventually leads to corruption, immorality, and implosion. The Banker also has to be aware of the ego. There are numerous examples of financial rogues who let their inflated egos dominate their self-control and financial good sense. The other area of concern for the Banker archetype is the gambling industry. There's a fine line between a calculated risk and a gamble. If you are a Banker, you need to remember that. Access to money does not equate to easy money.

**Archetypal Combinations:**

The archetypal energy of the Banker combines well with the energy of:

Mother * Father * King * Queen * Pioneer * Alchemist * Networker * Scientist * Advocate * Judge * Servant

**Effective Use of Banker Energy:**

- Be true to your energetic nature with spending and saving.
- Always act as a reliable and worthy financial example to others.
- If you are in the financial industry, remember that you are also in the service industry.
- Both the customer and personal gain are important.
- Control your ego, and be aware of the pitfalls.

# Beggar

Our understanding of the typical archetypal beggar is the person sitting, standing, or kneeling on the sidewalk silently or earnestly asking for money. Some might even follow you around. This is an all-too-familiar scene in cities around the world. If this situation is a permanent state or a state an individual falls in and out of with monotonous regularity, then he or she has the Beggar archetype.

Some wealthy countries have generous social benefit schemes, and those with the Beggar archetype are well disguised. There is little difference in the energy between people who beg on the streets to those who collect dole cheques every fortnight without raising the effort to improve their situations. One is overtly a Beggar, while the other is covertly a Beggar. Let us stress, this does not apply to those who have fallen on hard times or, through no fault of their own, are unable to earn a living. For example, individuals with disabilities usually struggle financially. However, it does apply to those who deliberately choose to be on welfare or who rely on family or friends for their incomes. Those people have the Beggar archetype.

Begging is usually done for money, but money may not be the only commodity Beggars are asking for. It may be shelter, food, clothing, goods, medical treatment, drugs, recognition, or even sympathy. Like all of us, Beggars would like their basic needs met, but there may be emotional needs that can only be met by family and friends. It is the continuity of need that determines the Beggar archetype.

**Negative Aspects:**

Poverty conscious ~ Lack of self-esteem ~ Needy ~ Craves affection ~ Starving ~ Chronic attention seeker ~ Dependent ~ Lack of belief ~ Unworthy ~ Lazy ~ Powerless ~ Owed a living

**Positive Aspects:**

Self-empowered ~ Self-sufficient ~ Independent ~ Confident ~ Generous Compassionate ~ Financially secure ~ Careful with resources ~ Resourceful ~ Adaptive

**Archetypal Energy:**

The negative archetypal energy of the Beggar is a powerful energy of poverty, neediness and low self-esteem. The negative energy pattern is one of continuity and repetition.

Circumstances will dictate the need for assistance to people in dire situations. Natural disasters such as earthquakes, droughts, floods, tsunamis and the like leave survivors in need of assistance. Man-made tragedies such as wars and forced displacement also leave many in dire circumstances. These people may not necessarily possess the Beggar archetype. Most survivors of tragic events make new beginnings with courage, endurance and optimism. They fight their way back to independence and self-sufficiency.

There is a resignation to the poverty consciousness with the Beggar. So to move from the negative Beggar patterns to the positive Beggar patterns requires a deep desire for change and a strong commitment to the process of change. It is only when the desire for change is strong enough that change takes place. By taking action, the individual activates the positive energy of both the Victim and Prostitute archetypes. The Victim archetype determines self-esteem (a strong attitude together with how good I feel about myself), and the Prostitute archetype is about worthiness (how much am I worth?).

If you possess a Beggar archetype and want to change your physical circumstances, there is a requirement for a huge shift in attitude and the realignment of thought processes. When mental processes and attitudes change, the Beggar patterns move from negative to positive and circumstances improve. Confidence, self-belief, personal worth and action create opportunities. Once a positive pattern is established, an individual gains momentum. This move to positive energy and behaviours creates positive outcomes.

**Archetypal Combinations:**

The archetypal energy of the Beggar combines well with the energy of:

Victim * Prostitute * Servant * Athlete * King * Queen * Banker * Warrior * Rescuer * Healer * Pioneer * Alchemist * Advocate * Carer

**Effective Use of Beggar Energy:**

- Anyone can be the subject of challenging circumstances.
- Follow a plan for independence and self-sufficiency.
- Increase your positive energy by attitude change and mindset.
- Understand your destiny is not totally controlled by outside forces.
- Your attitude and thought patterns have the power to change your circumstances.

# Bully

Are you a Bully? To answer this question, you have to be perfectly frank and honest with yourself. Bullies often come in disguise and with a thousand excuses for their behaviours. Adult Bullies are often harder to detect than child Bullies, as children do not have the understanding, façade, or privacy privileges that adults have.

Most children are more open. "I hit him because he took my ball." "He hit me first." "He called me a name, so I pushed him." "He can't play because he's hopeless." "He spoils our game." "I don't like her." "She always wants to be the boss."

Do you notice how most of the physical bullying is still done by boys, while the verbal and emotional bullying is done by girls? It is also interesting to note, from my perspective as a teacher, that as the schools adopt a "no hands on" method of discipline, many boys are now resorting to verbal bullying and name calling.

With the development of modern technology, cyber bullying has emerged. This takes many forms. Communications technology has made bullying more accessible and a lot easier to hide the identity of the bully. The development of the drone may be the next challenge to protect our personal freedom from the vindictiveness of the bully.

It is important to identify the Bully archetype in children and give them the methodology to change their behaviours. Without this, children carry those patterns into adulthood. The person who possesses the Bully archetype has to have an alternative plan to change their actions. This plan has to differ from the bullying behaviour that draws upon negative energy.

For children, the "no hands on" approach adopted by schools is good policy. However, it is important for children to find a circuit breaker. Many children become angry and reactionary, and often it is the decision made in that explosive moment that activates the Bully energy. As adults we can give options. Walk away, get a drink of water, count to twenty, take a moment of solitude, go find a good friend, or talk to a caring and responsible authority, are all options that may diffuse that make-or-break moment. These are options that can help the Bully who is open and explosive in nature. The Bully who is sneaky and deceptive is more difficult to detect and assist. In many cases, this deception is a learned behaviour.

Children continually watch adults and then adopt certain behaviours as their own. This is never an easy situation to deal with, as you must consider multiple factors. Confronting the truth and the reality of the situation is the best method of attacking the problem, but this does not guarantee any change in Bully behaviour.

The adult Bully is a master of manipulation. This may be accomplished by power (real or threatened); emotional blackmail; abuse of an unequal power structure (for example, the boss and the employee, the parent and child); bribery; or the use of a reward system using money, goods, or status and psychological persuasion. Bullies have an overwhelming need to control all that surrounds them. They seldom take responsibility for their own actions but develop a pattern of blaming everyone else. They often use projection to justify their behaviour. Projection is excusing oneself on the basis that everyone else is doing the same thing, or "They did this to me, so it's alright to do the same things back" but with a little bit more payback.

It is difficult to make Bullies understand they are being Bullies. Because they control situations from a position of power, Bullies will be reluctant to give away that power or be blind to it. Power feeds the ego. It sustains the self-esteem with negative Victim and Bully archetypal energy. Bullies may come from positions of low self-esteem, whereby they pick on others to make themselves feel better. Alternatively, they may come from positions of out-of-control self-esteem.

Look at the history of various world leaders, and notice how full of themselves they can be. This is the negative Bully and Victim archetypal energy at work. Likewise, observe the tantrums of the pop star. The Victim and the Bully archetypes work together to enhance the ego; to control situations and people in their way. Notice when this type of person falls from grace and loses popularity, it is the result of the larger community rejecting the behaviour and personality of the Bully. Once-popular leaders lose elections or lose power altogether. The pop diva's fans desert her and focus their attention on a bright, new star. Elite athletes have been known to suffer a similar fate when a scandal escapes their control. Numbers of people, in unison, take away a Bully's power. To challenge the Bully, adhere to the "united we stand; divided we fall" philosophy.

**Negative Aspects:**

Fearful ~ Violent ~ Controlling ~ Needs attention of peers ~ Abusive ~ Power hungry ~ Manipulative ~ Egomaniac ~ Angry ~ Deceptive ~ Gossips ~ Lack of empathy ~ Name calling ~ Vindictive ~ Tantrums

**Positive Aspects:**

Fearless ~ In control of feelings ~ Self-assured ~ Confident ~ Satisfied ~ Relaxed ~ Peaceful ~ Inclusive ~ Team player ~ Encourages

**Archetypal Energy:**

The archetypal energy of the Bully is based on the desire to control. For Bullies to move from negative patterns to positive patterns, they must realize they cannot control every situation. There are factors we have little or no control over. These occurrences affect our lives, and at times, we just go with the flow. Isn't it interesting how the human race has an obsession with controlling Mother Nature, yet the elements always give us another drought, hurricane, or earthquake to remind us of our fragility and over-sized egos? At an individual level, Bullies ultimately meet their match.

The Bully has to understand that positive relationships are built on mutual trust and a spirit of cooperation. People deserve respect. They are not here as ego fodder for the Bully. If you are brave enough to admit you are a Bully, then examine the way you treat others. "Do unto others as you would have them do unto you" is a key aspect of so many philosophies.

The personal history of the Bully makes consistent reading. The Bully, when confronted with reality, should ask the following questions. What was I like as a child? Was I in control of my temper, or did I react with anger and revenge? What devious behaviours did I learn and put into practice? Was I truthful? Did I take responsibility for my actions, or did I blame others? No matter the answers, from this point onwards, the power is in the hands of one person only—the Bully.

When individuals with the Bully archetype recognize and understand that aspect of their personalities, they are able to change their behaviours. When they come to the realization that there are situations that can be resolved with a win-win outcome, they are on the path to utilizing positive Bully archetypal energy. Negative Bully archetypal energy is strong. Positive Bully archetypal energy is powerful. The positive energy is used by individuals who are in control of their emotions. It is used by individuals who are confident in their own abilities. It is used by individuals who gain and benefit through a policy of inclusion rather than exclusion. Negative energy may have short-term gain. Positive energy has lifelong consequences.

**Archetypal Combinations:**

The archetypal energy of the Bully combines well with the energy of:

Peacemaker * Carer * Advocate * Philosopher * Healer * Companion

**Effective Use of Bully Energy:**

- Examine your self-esteem. Are you content with being who you are, or do you put others down to build yourself up?
- Co-operatively working together is an effective path to achievement.
- Control your emotions.
- Delegation of responsibilities and relinquishing control places your trust in others and your individual journey.
- How important is truth to you?

# Carer

Carers offer physical, emotional, and psychological support. They are compassionate and empathetic. The energy of the Carer differs slightly from both the Healer and the Rescuer. Rescuers will generally attract people, objects, or causes that need rescuing. They may also deliberately involve themselves in rescuing operations. Carers stand back a little. Their energy is gentler and subtler. They go into action when asked to do so; whereas, Rescuers are likely to jump in regardless. Carers assist and then allow their clients to go their way, but Rescuers are often dependent on their clients and the outcome of the rescues. Carers do not wish to change their clients but help them improve their circumstances. Rescuers often have the desire to change their clients for the better.

Similarly, the energy of the Carer differs from the energy of the Healer. Again, the Carer has the gentler approach. The best example is to observe and understand the duties and behaviours of a nurse and a doctor. In general terms, the nurse has a Carer archetype, while the doctor has a Healer archetype. The Healer is more hands-on, more interested in manufacturing change in the client's physical condition. The Carer is there to look after and to care for the client emotionally and to make him or her feel comfortable.

Carers are not always trained professionals, such as nurses. Those who carry the Carer archetype may be parents who raise children with disabilities and care for them into adulthood. They may be children who care for their parents suffering dementia or other debilitating conditions. They may be friends who assist others through tragedies. They may be childcare workers who look after and cater for the needs of their young charges.

**Negative Aspects:**

Neglectful ~ Intolerant ~ Pessimistic ~ Complaining ~ Impatient ~ Uninvolved ~ Acrimonious ~ Dereliction of duty ~ Irresponsible

**Positive Aspects:**

Dutiful ~ Empathetic ~ Compassionate ~ Considerate ~ Caring ~ Cheerful Optimistic ~ Obligated ~ Patient ~ Above and beyond the call of duty ~ Helpful Responsible ~ Endurance ~ Stability ~ Multi-skilled

**Archetypal Energy:**

The Carer has a very gentle energy. Often it is hardly noticeable. Carers are willing to respond to the needs of others, and they do so with minimum fuss. Carers are generally undervalued, as there is limited financial reward in dealing with the sick, the elderly, the disabled, the very young, or the victims of tragedy. Carer energy, however, is not particularly bound or concerned with financial reward. Recognition for the job they do and the people they help is much more important.

If you are a Carer, you are multi-skilled, mentally tough, and emotionally stable. Certainly, Carers go through some difficult times. However, Carers are survivors. Their endurance is remarkable. They have the energy and ability to overcome difficulties and continue with the challenges of life.

The positive energy of the Carer archetype shows the character traits of endurance, patience, compassion, and a deep sense of duty. This presents the individual with the Carer archetype a succession of responsibilities. Responsibilities with family, friends, work, and social commitment are at the forefront of a Carer's life. Each challenge requires all the qualities of the Carer to come to the fore. As an example of the continual service that the individual with the Carer archetype is challenged with, I make mention of a former teaching colleague with remarkable Carer energy. She has been a nurse, a policewoman, a senior primary school teacher, and now a principal. She may have changed jobs and careers, but deep down she still uses the same energy—the energy of the Carer.

**Archetypal Combinations:**

The archetypal energy of the Carer combines well with the energy of:

Mother * Father * Servant * Teacher * Warrior * King * Queen * Knight * Healer * Rescuer * Hero * Heroine * Angel * Advocate * Peacemaker * Martyr * Priest * Priestess * Wise Woman

**Effective Use of Carer Energy:**

- The Carer usually has a client or situation to be involved with. This is a lifelong energetic pattern of responsibility.
- Accept the Carer's duty with willingness and grace.
- Carers have remarkable patience and endurance.
- The Carer's motto is often "humility is the foundation of all virtues".
- Use your Carer archetypal energy for success and achievement in other areas of your life.

# Celibate

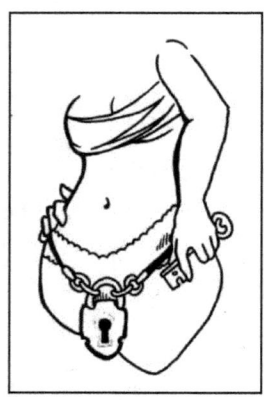

The Celibate generally refrains from sexual experiences and relationships. This may be displayed by total abstinence or, in the very least, a disposition to limited participation in the physical experience. The Celibate channels sexual energy into other forms of expression. Often, these forms are spiritual in nature. Monks, priests, nuns, and so on, represent this type of Celibate archetype. Abstinence is often a prerequisite for certain spiritual pathways. This can lead to confusion with some people, as they may possess spiritual archetypes but not necessarily a Celibate archetype.

The devotion to a spiritual path does not guarantee a sudden influx of Celibate energy. If a person has a Celibate archetype and wishes to follow a spiritual pathway, celibacy is suitable. This allows an individual to focus on religious or spiritual matters rather than physical or sexual desires. Without a Celibate archetype, a person in a strict religious order will face a lifelong battle with the demand of celibacy. The choice of a spiritual pathway deserves nothing but careful consideration. "Know thyself" is the first and essential lesson for both young and old. Knowledge and understanding activates solid decisions, actions, pathways, and directions.

Not all Celibates follow a spiritual pathway. The Celibate may also be found in the healing and caring industries. This is not to say that everyone in these industries is celibate. Far from it! However, these vocations are suitable for moving one form of physical energy into another form of physical energy. Another pathway for the Celibate is in the form of artistic endeavours. This is a great area for the Celibate archetype to drive individual expression, creativity, and physicality.

It is important for Celibates to examine the reasons behind their celibacy. If it is a conscious and well-considered decision, then Celibates are true to their archetypal natures and energies. When they do that, they create balance in their lives and are able to act with precision and clarity.

However, if there is an aversion to sexual expression due to fear, there is a case for serious examination of the cause. Fear is very real. It may have been created by physical intervention, psychological threats, emotional trauma, or a combination of these things.

Those with the Wounded Child archetype are often the product of misused sexual energy. These children are damaged physically, psychologically, and emotionally. As a teenager or adult, it may be extremely difficult to deal with the wounds of abuse and still experience the enjoyment of sexual intimacy. The energy of the Celibate is forced upon these people not of their choosing. Repression, anxiety, poor self-esteem, and a lack of confidence may be the by-products of this energetic imbalance.

Psychological, emotional, and energetic healing is an effective way to deal with these circumstances. The most difficult decision for victims of sexual abuse is to tell of their experiences. Often the truth is told much later in life; nevertheless, it is the beginning of the healing process and better than never telling at all. The choice of celibacy must be of their making, not imposed by other circumstances.

**Negative Aspects:**

Superficial ~ Self-obsessed ~ Self-punishment ~ Holier than thou ~ Repressed ~ Puritanical ~ Withholding ~ Perverse ~ Concealed frustration ~ Anger ~ Wounded ~ Aversion to touch ~ Suspicious

**Positive Aspects:**

Creative expression ~ Commitment ~ Dedication ~ Self-control ~ Prophetic ~ Self-assured ~ Spiritual devotion

**Archetypal Energy:**

The archetypal energy of the Celibate demands personal strength and commitment. Sexual energy is basic to human nature and requires a great deal of self-control to maintain the purity of Celibate energy. Many personality aspects are called into question by the Celibate energy, and the Celibate can be challenged under social pressure. Sex is pervasive in modern society. The pressure to comply with the norm, especially for young adults, is enormous. The strength to say no is an asset that requires the full concentration of positive Celibate archetypal energy.

Motivation is the key. If you have the Celibate archetype and use the energy in a positive fashion, then your direction is clear. Psychologically, you are equipped to deal with any situation and, if required, can enunciate clearly the reasons for your decisions. Remember to be wary of the negative energy of the Celibate, as this is likely to erode your spiritual credibility, your spiritual development, and the grace of your spiritual self. The "holier than thou" attitude represents hypocrisy of the most blatant kind.

The individual with the Celibate archetype has also to recognize that other energies can masquerade as Celibate energy. Understand if you have a Wounded Child archetype, past experiences will likely restrict and inhibit your sexual energy, and therefore, greater self-clarification may define whether you carry the Celibate archetype. Recognize and understand your Wounded Child to clarify the reasons behind your behaviour and overcome your fears. This is the self-examination that is important to all who use the Celibate archetypal energy.

**Archetypal Combinations:**

The archetypal energy of the Celibate combines well with the energy of:

Monk * Priest * Nun * Mystic * Angel * Addict * Martyr * Hermit

**Effective Use of Celibate Energy:**

- Celibate energy provides you with strength of character.
- Use your spiritual energy and your Celibate archetype to lead you down the path of spiritual service.
- Be realistic and practical with the demands of your Celibate energy.
- Make the distinction between Celibate and Wounded Child.

# Child

We all have a Child archetype. There are five different types of the Child archetype.

**Divine or Magical Child:**

These children are creative and intuitive. They seem to have a direct connection with the Divine and often have difficulty adhering to the structure and limitations of the physical.

**Peter Pan or Eternal Child:**

These children are represented by Peter Pan, the little boy who never grew up. These children live for adventure, believe in making the fantastic happen, and generally have an enthusiastic and sometimes irresponsible nature.

**Nature Child:**

These are the outdoor children. They love mountains, forests and beaches and are companions to all plants and animals, especially rare and unusual kinds. These are the children of Mother Earth.

**The Indulged Child:**

I often refer to the Indulged Children as the spoilt brats. Indulged Children are precious. They are loved and adored by their adult families and are granted many favours. The Indulged Children have many talents, as they are exposed to an array of social experiences at young ages and often make excellent leaders.

**The Orphan or Wounded Child:**

These children have been neglected, abandoned or abused. They suffer physically, psychologically, emotionally and socially. Some of these children battle through such hardship with strength and endurance and use that energy to find a way to great success. Ray Charles is a good example. Most, however, grow into adulthood bearing the scars that cause suffering for the rest of their lives.

We never lose our Child archetype. Listen to that inner child voice. You may find as you get older, the voice of the Child becomes your intuitive self. That advice is worth following because, as children, we were far more attuned to our intuition. As we become older, more responsibilities and clutter invade our daily lives.

This external bombardment leaves us at the whim of other energies. Our own internal voices are drowned out by the noise of all that surrounds us. Our inner child also reminds us about our childhood dreams and fancies. Many of these were simple pleasures denied to us. If we, as adults, take the time to engage in some of these simple childlike activities, we become more balanced as individuals and more emotionally content. As adults, look after and listen to the energy of your Child archetype. This archetype is a great friend.

# Child – Divine or Magical

The Divine or Magical Child is the child of trust, innocence, creativity, and fantasy. This Child is often in another world rather than present in the physical. The Divine Child has a direct connection with the Divine and the ability to mentally move between dimensions. The Divine Child is fascinated with many aspects of the physical world yet, at the same time, confused by its complications.

It is important to understand that the Divine Child is either a new soul or a very old soul. If the Divine Child is a new soul, then the child is fascinated by the physical world. Imagine a whole variety of new and different things to experience. Many of the dangers and complications that other children quickly learn about will be a source of fascination for Divine Children. This is the case for the rest of their lives. Therefore, there is an air of innocence and naivety that may surround them. How many of your friends have that trusting innocence about them? How many times have we labelled them as naïve? They often make silly statements and enjoy simple experiences. They have a lovely energy of simplicity and acceptance that makes them totally endearing.

If Divine Children are old souls, then many of the worldly wonders will be simply passé to them. They will be the creative children who love fantasy. These children will excel at art, reading, and creative writing. They live in the world of magical creatures. They are also the intuitive children. There are many things they already know, and many find it difficult to fit in with peers who will be into more physical experiences.

Divine Children may also find difficulty in pleasing the adults in their lives. As students these children are often daydreamers. This is a frustration to many teachers. As natural intuitives, Divine Children automatically know what is best for them. As a child, try getting your parents to understand that notion. However, as an adult, Divine Children have the freedom to follow their creative and psychic passions. There is greater acceptance of their talents and abilities. They become the spiritual workers, alternative healers, visionaries, and expressive artists.

**Negative Aspects:**

Innocent ~ Naïve ~ Impractical ~ Day-dreamer ~ Unaware of time ~ Irresponsible ~ Fragile ~ Difficulty with living in the real world

**Positive Aspects:**

Creative ~ Intuitive ~ Makes things happen ~ Spiritual ~ Creator ~ Has a direct connection to the Divine ~ Inter-dimensional ~ Artistic ~ Visionary ~ Expressive ~ Fanciful ~ Power of imagination

**Archetypal Energy:**

The energy of the Divine or Magical Child is a sublime energy. There are no limits to this energy, and all of this world and other worlds are energetically available to the Divine Child. That is why, on many occasions, the Divine Child may be overwhelmed, impractical, and seem out of touch with reality.

As adults, it is important Divine Children use their abilities with caution and consideration. Adult psychics have enormous potential to guide and heal, but the lesson is to stay within the boundaries of their capabilities. Dark and negative entities are always ready to invade when the naïve psychic opens the doorway for them.

Also, it is important to be truthful with your ability. There is no place for exaggeration or deception. The physical world is full of charlatans. The spiritual world is an existence of grace and purity. The abilities given to the Divine or Magical Child are precious and should be held in the highest regard.

If you are a Divine or Magical Child, you may have suffered difficulties as a child. Dealing with the real world, finding the means to express your creativity, justifying your belief in the fantastic, concealing your intuitive powers from the disbelievers, and possessing knowledge and abilities far beyond your years makes for some interesting times as a Divine Child. As an adult with the Divine Child archetype, you can be confident in your ability and declare who you are. This is not bragging or allowing your ego to take over. This is the quiet expression of your inner nature and your special talents as a spiritual and creative teacher and guide. Do not hide your incredible abilities just because you were disbelieved or discouraged from using those abilities as a child. Do not carry this lack of confidence into adulthood. As adults, we have the ability and understanding to express our true self. We have the opportunity to use out abilities with courage and self-assurance.

**Archetypal Combinations:**

The archetypal energy of the Divine or Magical Child combines well with the energy of:

Angel * Visionary * Fairy * Artist * Shaman * Wizard * Saboteur * Wise Woman * Witch * Healer * Priestess * Mystic * Alchemist * God * Guide * Prophet * Pilgrim

**Effective Use of Divine or Magical Child Energy:**

- As an adult with a Divine or Magical Child archetype, be conscious of your ability and be willing to declare your true self.
- Stay within the realms of your tasks and your abilities.
- Continually seek a suitable and effective outlet to express your creativity.
- Remain balanced; be gentle with yourself and with others dealing with the physical nature of this world.
- Beware of exaggeration and false claims.

# Child – Peter Pan or Eternal

The Peter Pan or Eternal Child is the child of fun-loving adventure, real or imagined. If Peter Pan or Eternal Children are restricted by their environments, they are able to find plenty of scope for imaginative games and escapades. This child is always making and creating. There are indoor games, outdoor games, treasures to find, cubby houses to build, stories, books and weapons to make, like bows and arrows, swords, and shields. Any article that will enhance an adventure will be made with care and enthusiasm.

Peter Pan or Eternal Children are not ones for much social interaction. They are quite content to be alone, as this gives them opportunities to play or to make up their own adventures. When they make social connections, they become the leaders, usually of a rag-tag group of misfits. This is reflected with pinpoint accuracy by J. M. Barrie. Peter Pan is the boy of adventure, never wanting to grow up but leading the Lost Boys with courage and authority. Peter Pan or Eternal Children make great leaders. Like Peter Pan, they are not discriminating when it comes to their followers. They are accepting of all other children and often attract children with special needs, loners, and those with limited social skills. The thrill of acceptance and adventure is special for this type of child.

Responsibility is the one lesson that is paramount for Peter Pan or Eternal Children to learn. Often they get lost in adventure. Time means nothing, and other duties take second place. As they move into adulthood, they take everything in their stride but still maintain that sense of fun-loving adventure. They still have moments of total irresponsibility. Michael Jackson was the perfect example of the Eternal Child. He was creative, talented, alternative, a leader, and a trendsetter. He managed his adult responsibilities but preferred to be a child. Adults with the Peter Pan or Eternal Child archetype make great company. They are accepting, humble, and fun-loving.

**Negative Aspects:**

Irresponsible ~ Lost in fantasy ~ Unrealistic ~ Frustrating ~Lost in time ~ Childish ~ Simplistic

**Positive Aspects:**

Fun-loving ~ Leader ~ Accepting ~ Creative ~ Brave ~ Optimistic ~ Enthusiastic ~ Happy-go-lucky ~ Joyful ~ Courageous ~ Everything is possible ~ Adventuresome

**Archetypal Energy:**

The archetypal energy of the Peter Pan or Eternal Child personifies the simplicity of fun and adventure. This is the energy that encourages us to explore a rock pool, climb a mountain, hang upside down, play a game of tag, bounce on a trampoline, make funny faces, tell a story, have a sword fight, or squirt people with a water pistol. Any activity that is fun, adventuresome, or slightly mischievous will be tackled with joy and enthusiasm by the Peter Pan or Eternal Child. The age of Peter Pan Children will not be an issue, be they children, teenagers, young adults, or in the prime of life. The Eternal Child and Peter Pan have no age barrier.

Eternal Children make great storytellers and authors. They do not tell of great tragedies or deep and dark psychological thoughts and actions. They tell stories of heroism, bravery, skin-of-the-teeth rescues, and slap-stick humour. This energy is a fantastic attribute for a children's author.

Peter Pan or Eternal Children also surround themselves with animals, especially dogs. Peter Pan or Eternal Children have an energetic attraction to unconditional love that makes them so accepting of others, especially animals and children. There is a missing piece in the jigsaw of heart emotion. That piece is the missing love and affection of parents. This parental love and affection is a need of the Peter Pan Child. It is also a need that the Peter Pan Child has for others.

Acceptance and leadership are other components of the energy of the Peter Pan or Eternal Child. These individuals have a canny ability to attract the type of people who can assist them with their projects. They are adaptable yet extremely determined to achieve what they set out to do. They are optimistic and rarely see faults in people. This makes them gullible and sometimes open to exploitation. The other frustrating trait this energy attracts is irresponsibility. Peter Pan or

Eternal Children are often lost in the world of adventure and fantasy. They take pleasure in what is happening now and deal with other issues when absolutely necessary. This can be a constant source of frustration for those who live with these individuals. However, the sense of adventure, creativity, inclusiveness, and fun is a wonderful energy to be around. You have to love Peter Pan.

**Archetypal Combinations:**

The archetypal energy of the Peter Pan or Eternal Child combines well with the energy of:

Adventurer * Explorer * Storyteller * Artist * Wanderer * Athlete * Court Jester * Disciple * Knight * Coward * Companion * Clown * Magician * Seeker * Warrior

**Effective Use of Peter Pan or Eternal Child Energy:**

- Be responsible for those duties that are essential for your well-being, your family, and your friends.
- Use your imagination and creative energy in an artistic and productive capacity.
- Draw to you the people who will not only satisfy your adventuresome nature but who are grounded sufficiently to utilize your talents.
- Beware of adventures, schemes and personalities that prey upon your gullibility.

# Child – Indulged

Indulged Children are treasured, especially by family. They are given opportunities to follow their interests and develop skills and expertise in their chosen fields. Parenting is the key to developing a confident and well-rounded Indulged Child. The Indulged Child loves freedom of opportunity. This is achieved when the parents go to any length to give the Indulged Child the best on offer. They provide educational opportunities, social skills, and the best of technology, stimulating toys, and parental support and encouragement.

By showing encouragement, love, affection, trust, and constant involvement in their child's interests, these parents give an enormous boost to the child's self-esteem. This provides the child with incredible confidence and optimism, and nothing becomes too great a challenge for the Indulged Child. They are ready and willing to take on the world. Another benefit of this confidence is the development of leadership qualities. Indulged Children make great leaders. They have had the parental modelling and encouragement that allows them to take on responsibilities and become leaders in their chosen fields.

Many Indulged Children have a significantly strong personality. These children demand attention from their parents and expect all their needs to be met. When the energy of the Indulged Child is stronger than the energy of the parents, an imbalance occurs. This results in Indulged Children becoming spoilt brats. Indulged Children are happy to use the negative energy of the archetype to get what they want. When the energetic balance between children and parents is maintained, Indulged Children use the positive energy of the archetype to great effect. Balance is so important when raising an Indulged Child.

Imbalance also occurs when you have a "smother mother" approach to parenting. When Indulged Children are wrapped up in cotton wool, their development is stifled. They achieve, but their achievements are limited to the confines of parental expectations. These parents also have a major say in the directional path these children follow. This type of parenting often leaves Indulged Children with potential rather than achievement.

**Negative Aspects:**

Spoilt brat ~ Tantrum thrower ~ Indulged ~ Compensated ~In denial ~ Inappropriate behaviour ~ Emotional blackmail ~ Nagging ~ Workaholic

**Positive Aspects:**

Confident ~ Make excellent leaders ~ Capable ~ High self-esteem Ambitious ~ Treasured ~ Well rounded ~ Optimistic ~ Stimulated ~ Prepared to take on the world

**Archetypal Energy:**

The archetypal energy of the Indulged Child is strong in confidence and self-esteem. Indulged Children feel they can achieve anything and get away with everything. As children, it is important they have good parental modelling of behaviour and guidance. This teaches respect and responsibility. Parents who have high expectations of their children have to have high expectations of their own behaviours. Children see through hypocrisy. When Indulged Children are raised in well-balanced environments, then the positive traits are encouraged and, over time, flourish.

As adults, Indulged Children have to consider their progress. Personal achievement in education, career, material possessions, and relationships is important. However, questions relevant to those achievements have to be examined. What has been the cost of those achievements? Has there been an emotional, physical, or psychological cost? Have the achievements been accomplished ethically? These are important questions. Has your progress been at the expense of others? Have your achievements been purely personal, or have you assisted others with their success? How much negative energy has been used in your rise to the top?

Indulged Children can thrive on negative energy. They can become bullies, manipulators, social climbers, emotional blackmailers, the "win at all costs" personalities, drama queens, and put-down champions. Examine the type of energy that has been used. Negative energy is destructive. Positive energy is inclusive and harmonizing.

Consider the level of your achievements. As an adult with an Indulged Child archetype, have you made the best of your opportunities? Have you underachieved? What potential has been left untapped? Have you wasted opportunities through laziness or self-indulgence? Have you lived up to your expectations? Has the negative energy of the Indulged Child stifled your growth? The good news is that it is never too late to make changes. Set up a program of change. Keep your eye on the big picture, but monitor your step-by-step progress. The Indulged Child can change the put-downs into compliments; send thoughts of love instead of jealousy; channel the energy of tantrums into physical fitness; and turn denial into awareness with measured thoughts, language, and actions. Everything is possible when the positive energy of the Indulged Child is engaged and placed in motion.

**ARCHETYPAL COMBINATIONS:**

The archetypal energy of the Indulged Child combines well with the energy of:

Heroine * Hero * King * Queen * Entrepreneur * Prince * Princess * Mother * Father * Peacemaker * Victim * Diva * Politician * Statesman * Prostitute * Scholar * Diplomat * Artist * Craftsperson

**Effective Use of Indulged Child Energy:**

- Have your achievements been accomplished using negative or positive energy?
- Check your attitude to the people in your life. Do you treat them with love and respect, or are they stepping stones for your ego?
- If underachievement is a pattern of behaviour, begin to set small, step-by-step goals.

# Child – Nature

Archetypal Nature Children are the wanderers, explorers, shamans, pioneers, and outdoor adventurers. They adore all geographical landscapes from the mountains to the rivers, forests, and beaches. These environments are their second home. They are comfortable in these surroundings. They live for the freedom the outdoors offers and are often stifled by the confines of houses and classrooms. They develop a passion for and an understanding of nature. Plants and animals become their friends and companions. The more unusual the species of plant or animal, the greater fascination, intrigue, and affection is. Carnivorous plants are often a favourite. So too are animals, such as axolotls. The Nature Child often carries around a pet rat, tortoise, or parrot. There is an understanding and affection on both sides of this relationship.

The Nature Child energy is also an athletic energy. These children will participate in sport provided the rules of the games are not too confining. Extreme sports are appealing, as are sports that are individual in nature and loosely organized, like surfing, skiing, and cycling. However, exploring nature is what Nature Children live for. This love of nature is a lifelong affair. Some Nature Children are committed enough to forge careers as marine biologists, volcanologists, environmental officers, and park rangers. Other more radical Nature Children become the fringe environmental protectors and actively work with organizations like Greenpeace and World Wildlife Fund. Nature Children who live in a more traditional and communal home and work environment still explore their passions. They enjoy camping holidays, weekends in a bush retreat, treks through a forest, excursions to wildlife sanctuaries, climbs in the mountains, and walks along beaches. Their essence is the physical and mental stimulus that breathes life into their bodies and joy into their souls.

**Negative Aspects:**

Lost in the wilderness ~ Lack of focus ~ Unaware of time commitments ~ Solitary ~ Unable to handle confinement ~ Radical ~ Fenced in

**Positive Aspects:**

Physical fitness ~ Love of nature ~ Healthy lifestyle ~ Care of the environment ~ Animal friendly ~ Conservationist

**Archetypal Energy:**

The strong archetypal energy of Nature Children determines physical fitness, outdoor lifestyle, and the appreciation of nature. Their abilities and attributes demand the care of Mother Earth. We live on a single planet with an ever-increasing human population. We are destroying species of plants and animals at an alarming rate. We are rapidly utilizing the Earth's natural resources. We are progressively filling the land, oceans, and atmosphere with pollution. The day must come when humanity realizes we live on a planet with finite resources, and there is a limit to how much stress we can place upon the earth. Something has to be done, if for purely selfish reasons, that is, to save the human race. The Nature Child is the one to take on a leadership role. Nature Children have an energy that is altruistic. This energy is the protection of Mother Earth, and they are determined to defend her with vigour and endurance.

Unfortunately for Nature Children, their protective energy and influence is constantly fighting an uphill battle. Modern society is based upon urban development and economic growth. This energy is so much stronger than the conservation and environmental energy. This has to change but only in the future when we have reached the point of critical mass. The development of cities and suburbs, the transport system, education system, and the degradation of pristine wilderness areas place Nature Children at such a disadvantage. So much of their days are spent indoors under artificial lighting. Nature Children crave time outdoors with the freedom of movement and exploration. This is difficult in an urban environment with a modern culture that imposes completely the opposite structures. Still, if you are a Nature Child, you are strong physically, with plenty of determination and endurance. It is important to maintain that persistence and organizational skills to defend your lifestyle and Mother Earth.

**Archetypal Combinations:**

The archetypal energy of the Nature Child combines well with the energy of:

Knight * Explorer * Athlete * Warrior * Pioneer * Shaman * Adventurer * Wizard * Wanderer * Hermit * Hero * Witch * Priestess * Scientist

**Effective Use of Nature Child Energy:**

- Be strong and true to your energetic nature to protect Mother Earth and her treasures.
- Your health and physical fitness are the keys to sustain your positive energy level.
- No matter how stressing your commitments, organize yourself to spend time in a natural environment.
- Remember, your family may have different archetypes, so be aware of their choices too.

# Child - Wounded

For the sake of simplicity, I call children who have been orphaned, abandoned, neglected, or abused the Wounded Child archetype. The same energy resides in these children, although it may differ in intensity.

**Orphans** have been left without knowing the energy of their biological parents. They may still experience the positive energy of a Mother or Father archetype. This depends on who takes responsibility for their upbringing. However, they still may miss emotional bonding and belonging that flows between a parent and child.

**Abandoned children** may have been placed for adoption. They may be orphans raised under the guidance of the State. They may have been taken from their parents and placed in foster homes or with foster parents. However, the emotional deal is still the same.

**Neglected children** may be left totally to their own devices. They often have parents who are drug addicted, psychologically unstable, or grossly immature with their parenting skills. This leaves them with the responsibility to fend and establish their own routines.

The **wounded children** have often been abused physically, sexually, emotionally, verbally, or psychologically. This abuse may come from within the family or outside of the family, or alternatively, there may be changes in the family or social environment that cause deep emotional wounds.

The energy for all of these children is similar. It is the energy of the Wounded Child. The intensity may be different, and the positive/negative balance will be different, but each case relates to the same archetypal energy.

Wounded Children have deep emotional and psychological issues. They can experience severe guilt and anger. These are two of the strongest and most debilitating emotions. Wounded Children feel guilt, as if somehow they are to blame for the circumstances of their neglect, abandonment, or abuse. This, of course, is far from the truth, but they are young and vulnerable children. These children have no power in abusive situations and no authority. They can be easily manipulated or threatened and possess little understanding of the overall motives and circumstances that drive some adults. Their self-esteems are like yo-yos; continually up and down. Logically, and even intuitively, they know what is happening to them is wrong and abnormal, as it doesn't happen to their friends. Therefore, they must be to blame. Hence the guilt!

The anger soon follows. There may be anger over their circumstances, anger at the perpetrators of the injustice, or anger with themselves for not being strong enough to stop or deal with the issues. Personal anger encourages further guilt. These emotions fuel a vicious cycle.

These emotional scars are carried through teenage life and into adulthood. For the teenager and the adult, the wounds of abandonment, abuse, or neglect will often be the cause of debilitating patterns of behaviour. Rebellious or risky behaviours, social isolation, introspection, mistrust, sexual aversion or imbalance, emotional dependence, eating disorders, and addictions are some of the likely consequences.

If you are an adult with the Wounded Child archetype, moving from the past may be difficult, but there are a number of steps you can take to process the wounds. The first step is to admit that neglect, abuse, or abandonment took place. Tell a person you trust. This will be the most difficult part of the process and requires a leap of faith in yourself and in your confidant. Then, if you have the courage, tell the world. Get that dark secret out of your inner self, and pass the energy into the world to be diffused among other energies. You might find support is even offered because of your courage in coming forward.

The second step is to define the emotions. Determine what they are. Recognize their cause, and understand the reasons why you felt that way then and why you have no need to feel that way now.

Thirdly, look at your behaviours and patterns. What do you want to change? This is where knowing your archetypal energies are your greatest ally. Examine the energy of your Wounded Child. What negative patterns determine your emotions and behaviour? Work slowly and surely to change to the productive positive energy. Use the positive energy of other archetypes with your transformation. Examine your Victim (self-esteem); your Prostitute (worthiness); your feminine archetypes from the range of Mother, Queen, Princess, Damsel, Goddess, Priestess, or Heroine; and call upon their courage, strength, and nurturing. Examine your action archetypes from amongst the Rebel, Addict, Martyr, Rescuer, Healer, or Saboteur. Summon their knowledge, intuition, strong will, and stubbornness to make you the worthy cause of redemption.

Fourthly, do not forget the past. History reminds us to never fall into that situation or pattern again. Remembering the past is not the same as blaming the past. It is finished with, done. What happened to you cannot be changed. Your Wounded Child is what determines that the time has come to move on to better days.

Finally, take your program of change one step at a time. Most importantly, seek a good friend or healer to assist you with your transformation. Deep-seated emotions and scars take time, effort, and positive and constructive thinking to overcome. You need to be able to share both the darkness and your new and positive achievements. Remember that there will be lapses in your progression towards change. Ignore the guilt. Never dwell on frustration, but focus on your achievements. This is your life. As an adult, you are responsible for your attitudes and actions. Keep them positive, and the Wounded Child energy can be a great friend and stimulus for remarkable achievement.

**Negative Aspects:**

Bitter ~ Self-doubt ~ Anger ~ Eating disorders ~ Inhibited ~ Low self-esteem ~ Risky or rebellious behaviour ~ Traumatized ~ Internal guilt ~ Acquiescence ~ Mistrust ~ Shame

**Positive Aspects:**

Determination ~ Overcoming all obstacles ~ Struggle ~ Enlightenment ~ Inspired ~ Strength ~ Endurance ~ Light at the end of the tunnel ~ Strong convictions ~ Courage ~ Guiding light

**Archetypal Energy:**

The negative archetypal energy of the Wounded Child carries feelings of guilt, anger, and self-doubt. This can lead to self-defeating and debilitating patterns of behaviour. There are many examples of people who suffered badly as children but found success and achievement as adults. Helen Keller and Ray Charles come to mind. Choose one of these, and use their lives as inspiration for your personal transformation.

The Wounded Child has such a strong and valuable energy. Overcome the negative experiences, and focus on the positive achievements. Wounded children make remarkable healers, teachers, and counsellors. They have had the true and gritty experiences and understand the depths of guilt and anger. They know what it is like to have their self-esteem battered into submission, and they know how it feels to be powerless. They understand loneliness and isolation, but they also know the depth of courage, strength, and determination that it takes to turn around a situation. They have the ability to inspire not only other Wounded Children but also others who operate on any negative archetypal energy. They can show you a way out of the wilderness. So, if you know you are a Wounded Child, take up the challenge to keep your energetic levels positive, and inspire others to rise up and conquer their demons.

**Archetypal Combinations:**

The archetypal energy of the Wounded Child combines well with the energy of:

Artist * Hero * Heroine * Healer * Peacemaker * Alchemist * Pioneer * Addict * Rebel * Carer * Wizard * Witch * Teacher

**Effective Use of Wounded Child Energy:**

- Transform the emotions of guilt and anger into feelings of freedom and determination.
- Use the energy of your strength and determination to acknowledge the past, share and release the negative emotions, implement a plan for change, and achieve transition one step at a time.
- Work consistently on your self-esteem.
- Be kind to yourself.
- Surround yourself with family and friends who are empathetic, beneficial to your transformation and exude positive energy.
- Inspire others with your teaching, counselling, healing, and leadership.

# Clown

Clowns are ultimate entertainers. They are often the subject of their own humour, but they are just as capable of making fun of others. Their antics can make us laugh and make us cry. They can even terrify us. The person with the Clown archetype has this innate urge not only to entertain but also to release a build-up of personal emotional energy.

This is one of the reasons performing Clowns wear the made-up faces. Often they will depict an exaggerated emotion, something that is obvious and easy for the audience to identify. There may be tears sliding down their faces, and we realize that life for these Clowns is difficult. Other Clowns will wear the happy, smiling face. They wish to express the fun and joy in their lives. There are Clowns with mischievous faces, and we know they will be up to all kinds of tricks and full of fun and slapstick. This is the Clown and the humour that children love. This is also the Clown that activates the inner Child within an adult.

Finally, there is the Clown that terrifies us. The type of made-up face is not really important, for it is the costume and disguise that elicits terror from an audience. This is the pretence and the hypocrisy that revives the fear of previous experiences. Think about those groups throughout history who have disguised themselves with masks and hoods to rein terror upon their victims. The Klu Klux Klan is the perfect example. Their members pretended to be fine, upstanding citizens yet committed heinous acts of terror and destruction. This is the negative archetypal energy of the Clown that is universal in nature. This energy elicits fear. Individuals who fear clowns tap into this negative energy. They see through the disguise. They recall the fear of previous incidents when they were betrayed by those they trusted, who masked and disguised their real intentions.

To join the circus and become a clown takes a very strong Clown archetypal energy. These are professional clowns, but people from all walks of life can have the Clown archetype. They are the amateur clowns. Many of these people will find an opportunity to display their abilities. You may find them at local markets, children's parties, holiday entertainment venues, schools, shopping centres, amateur circus performances, and so on. They will dress to entertain, especially in drag, at parties, revues, farewell send-offs, roasts, and end-of-year celebrations. The driving force behind each Clown is an emotional need to express his or her individuality, and to that end, he or she will always find an opportunity to perform.

**Negative Aspects:**

Hurtful ~ All of life is a joke ~ Impractical ~ Poor timing ~ Bad taste ~ Foolish ~ Irresponsible ~ Not taken seriously ~ Low self-esteem ~ Deceptive ~ Lack of focus ~ Heckler

**Positive Aspects:**

Entertaining ~ Teaches us not to take ourselves too seriously ~ Funny ~ Witty ~ Holds a mirror to life ~ Light hearted ~ Exposes the truth ~Element of courage ~ Insight

**Archetypal Energy:**

The archetypal energy of the Clown is extremely complex. It exists on two layers. There is an external layer of fun, laughter, and jocularity. Clowns appear to be genuinely jovial people. They are quick-witted and can turn serious situations into a more relaxed and comfortable environment. Clowns are often the subject of their own jokes. People are drawn to them because of the self-directed and non-threatening nature of the humour. Alternatively, the humour will be directed towards a third party with an ease that offends no one.

There is, however, an imaginary line with humour that should never be crossed. This line changes with the type of humour and the type of audience, so the Clown needs to be fully aware and cautious of each situation. The thin line between negative Clown energy and positive Clown energy is somewhat distinctive. Negative Clown energy is being aggressive, self-righteous, abusive, or deliberately pointed at an individual or group in a weakened position. The positive Clown energy is slap-stick, fun-loving, witty, and pointed at hypocrisy and double standards. If you have the Clown archetype, you may need to examine your humour and who's the target. Remember the imaginary line should never be crossed.

Clowns need to express humorous energy to share the burden of their emotional selves. Clowns can be the butt of their own jokes because of low self-esteem. But by entertaining and making people laugh, Clowns can raise their self-esteem to a more positive level. This is done on a regular and sometimes continual basis by some Clowns. The negative archetypal energy is expressed when Clowns raise their self-esteem by putting others down and lowering others' self-esteem. Individuals deal with emotional needs in many ways. The energy of Clowns suggests that entertainment is the best medicine. It is their cure for their hidden emotions, to lighten their emotional burdens, and to trigger positive emotional responses from their audiences.

**Archetypal Combinations:**

The archetypal energy of the Clown combines well with the energy of:

Storyteller * Peacemaker * Court Jester * Joker * Actor * Rebel * Peter Pan Child * Adventurer * Saboteur * Victim * Companion * Wanderer * Prophet

**Effective Use of Clown Energy:**

- The Clown archetypal energy is there to entertain. Your role is to bring joy, laughter, and pleasure into the lives of your audience.
- Always keep in mind that imaginary line of good taste. Be aware of abusive, aggressive and exploitive humour. It degrades your integrity and your craft.
- Monitor your emotions. Are they under your control, or are they under the influence of external factors?
- Examine your self-esteem. Your Victim archetype (self-esteem) should receive constant positive reinforcement from you and others.

# Companion

The Companion archetype is perhaps the most valuable personal archetype of all the archetypes in this book. The Companion archetype allows for the greatness of others to be expressed. These individuals are the solid foundation of relationships, upon which their partners are permitted and encouraged to grow and prosper. If your partner in a relationship or business (or even a family member, friend, or colleague) has the Companion archetype, then treasure him or her with all your trust and goodwill.

The Companion archetype has the assets and energy of both the Rescuer and the Carer. The Rescuer saves others from perceived dangers or neglectful or harmful situations. The Rescuer is about change—change often at the behest of the Rescuer. The Carer looks after those who are incapable or disadvantaged and unable to look after aspects of their own lives. The Companion archetype differs from the Rescuer and the Carer. The Rescuer and the Carer are more proactive in their behaviours. They need to take on a more leadership role. They offer support, encouragement, and loyalty. So does the Companion. However, the Companion's partner is usually the action person, the initiator of change, and the one able to manage his or her own desires and actions. The Companion is the rock upon which the action person can stand above the crowd.

The greatest asset of Companion archetypes is their loyalty. They support a relationship through thick and thin, good times and lean times, success and failure. They offer mental, physical, psychological, and emotional support. They do not interfere with major decisions and leave those to the major players in their partnerships. However, they always offer independent and valid advice. The Companion archetype is the perfect sidekick. Consider Batman and Robin, Robin Hood and Little John, Don Quixote and Sancho Panza. The Companion archetype is present in all three relationships with varying degrees of independence. Watch a film titled *Sky High*. It is predominantly aimed at children, but it expresses the Companion or sidekick archetype perfectly for those looking to understand the Companion better.

Those with the Companion archetype are not restricted in their loyalty. They may be the support base for their partners or businesses, but they may also show the same loyalty to a cause, company, product, or way of life.

If you have the Companion archetype, it is important to remember that you also have a life with independent thoughts and actions. It is a wonderful trait to support another with faithful devotion and loving encouragement, but this support should not interfere with your independence. A healthy relationship encourages the support of both parties to work together on matters of importance yet still retain the independence to allow each individual the freedom to pursue his or her own interests. Companions have to be wary of living vicarious lifestyles that are not their own.

**Negative Aspects:**

Never become their own person ~ Restricted ~ Co-dependent ~ Smothered ~ Unable to make a decision ~ Betrayal ~ Lacking self-confidence ~ Used ~ Low self-esteem ~ Denied

**Positive Aspects:**

Faithful ~ Loyal ~ Supportive ~ Loving ~ Responsive ~ Tenacious ~ Strength ~ Independent ~ Caring ~ Crisis management

**Archetypal Energy:**

The archetypal energy of the Companion is all about support and loyalty. It is an energy filled with grace and love. It is not the energy of the adoring fan. That energy is primitive in nature and extremely physical and emotional. Companions certainly have pride in their partners' or associates' achievements, but this is not the adoration associated with a sports fan, the fan of a pop idol, or a movie star. There is no yelling, screaming, or hysteria by Companions, only quiet humility with the knowledge that they've been a part of great achievement.

The Companion energy is not associated with tribal or cult relationships. That particular energy is of obedience, blind faith, and devotion. That is the negative energy of the Disciple. The Companion is devoted to support a relationship, yes. However, in tribes or in a cult, the individual is supported by the group structure and dynamic afforded by the negative Disciple traits. This is the opposite of the positive Companion energy.

The challenge for those with the Companion archetype is to find balance in their lives. Total loyalty and support to another does not mean a denial of individual expression. Companions may also have lives with or without energetic support and loyalty of their partners or associates. They may have involvement in another outlet; have devotion to a different cause or way of life; or have broader considerations than a personal or business relationship. As an individual, it is important to be mindful of your own independence. Margaret Whitlam, wife to former Australian Prime Minister Gough Whitlam, is the perfect example. She was a loyal, true, faithful companion, but she was more than a Prime Minister's wife. She established herself as an author, social reformer, and cultural ambassador. She was a woman of influence and was respected in her own right.

If you have a Companion archetype, always remember that you have your own life and your own individual journey. You also have other archetypes that will lead you to experience your own areas of personal development and to achieve your own success. As always, it is a question of balance.

**Archetypal Combinations:**

The archetypal energy of the Companion combines well with the energy of:

Heroine * Peacemaker * Advocate * Hero * Seeker * Pioneer * Servant * Entrepreneur * Explorer * Adventurer * King * Queen * Magician * Warrior

**Effective Use of Companion Archetype:**

- Direct your support and loyalty to individuals and causes in harmony with your ethical and moral views.
- Consider what is truly worthy of your support.
- Monitor your self-esteem. You are not there to be used and abused. You are loyal, trusted, and supportive. Expect respect on all occasions.
- Maintain your independence. Develop your personal interests and pursue your own journey.
- Remember to maintain balance in your life.

# Computer Nerd

The Computer Nerd is a modern archetype. Nothing is static, and everything changes. Archetypes are no different. The energy of an archetype may be in use for centuries and then slowly disappear as the world changes. The Scribe and the Mentor are two archetypes that are slowly fading away. With the dramatic changes in civilization and technology, new archetypes are born and those such as the Computer Nerd grow in strength. This archetype has been born out of the computer age. The Computer Nerd is an energetic combination of an old archetype, the Hermit, and a new archetype, the Networker. The Engineer and Pioneer also contribute to this new energy.

The Computer Nerd is the individual who constantly sits in front of a computer. It is often for both work and recreation, as Computer Nerds will generally seek employment in the computer industry. Computers and computer technology are not only their love and passion but also their area of expertise.

Many businesses and individuals now depend on computer technology. It is no surprise that Computer Nerds are such valuable employees. Traditionally, Computer Nerds have been in the fields of technical development—software, hardware, or both. Or they may hold a role in communications. This is where Computer Nerds access different energies from other archetypes. If they are in the technical development area, they use the energy of the Engineer and sometimes the Pioneer. Bill Gates is the perfect example here, but if they are in the field of communications, they will use the energy of the Networker. Computer technology and computer use has developed a whole new language for that aspect of communication. Look at the language of your text messages. Better still; look at the language of your children's text messages. It is a whole new language that linguists are now acknowledging as an evolution of our base language.

The Computer Nerd also uses the computer as recreation. Information, entertainment and trade are all accessed via the computer. This is the perfect guise for the Computer Nerd to utilize the Hermit energy. The energy of a nerd gives us the stereotype picture of a brainy academic lacking social skills and fashionable dress sense. Hermits are individuals who withdraw from conventional society to live singular lifestyles, limiting their social skills and inhibiting dress sense. Hermits are said to have locked themselves away in their caves, and Computer Nerds lock themselves away in isolation with their computers. It is the perfect energetic transformation. Computer Nerds are still clever. Computer Nerds have their own language. However, best of all, they have the isolation they desire, just like Hermits.

**Negative Aspects:**

Obsessed ~ Limiting ~ Restricting ~ Addictive ~ Antisocial ~ Dependence ~ Unbalanced ~ Energy draining ~ Lack of physical exercise ~ Lack of trust

**Positive Aspects:**

Technological ~ Expertise ~ Expanding your horizons ~ Increases knowledge ~ Knowledge is power ~ Creative ~ Logical ~ Creates communications channels ~ Inventive ~ Entrepreneurial

**Archetypal Energy:**

In the social and economic structure of a modern society, the archetypal energy of the Computer Nerd is a profitable commercial asset. Computer Nerds are no longer seen as just unsociable geeks but as worthwhile acquisitions to social and economic development. Their unique combination of various energies and the emergence of regularly updated computer technologies make Computer Nerds not only acceptable but also extremely valuable.

Computer Nerds are especially valuable when they have engineering precision or pioneering spirits. The Engineer energy is called in to design and develop new hardware and software. As an exercise in awareness, count how many items you use on a daily basis that have a computer chip. Just about everything we use is computerized or going that way in the near future. The opportunities for the Computer Nerd are exciting and expanding. For the ambitious or entrepreneurial Computer Nerd, pioneering development is a worthwhile consideration for a career opportunity.

If you are a Computer Nerd, consider your lifestyle. Do you use the negative energy of the Computer Nerd to disguise low self-esteem and a lack of social skills? Is the avoidance of people and social occasions a considered choice or a choice decided by perceived personality flaws? If it is the latter, you are using the negative Computer Nerd patterns of behaviour. Consider your personal balance. The Computer Nerd is only one of many personal archetypes. Does the computer dominate your lifestyle? Are you addicted to its use?

There are a variety of aspects to our nature. Archetypal energy flows and intersects, and we are capable of involving ourselves in multiple fields of endeavour. Our lesson is to strive for personal growth and well roundedness. Be wary of following a one-dimensional life pathway, of pursuing singular objectives and maintaining personal inhibition.

**Archetypal Combinations:**

The archetypal energy of the Computer Nerd combines well with the energy of:

Hermit * Servant * Seeker * Teacher * Scientist * Scholar * Scribe * Storyteller * Detective * Engineer * Pioneer * Networker * Entrepreneur

**Effective Use of Computer Nerd Energy:**

- Utilize your skill and interests not only for recreation but also for employment.
- Consider the ethics of the computer industry and your personal ethics when utilizing your expertise.
- Is your life balanced? Are you in control of your computer use or is it in control of you? Remember to put energy into all areas of your life.
- Do you use your Computer Nerd lifestyle as an excuse to hide a lack of social or personal skills? Becoming a well-rounded personality is worth striving for.

# Court Jester

The Court Jester is the combination of various archetypal energies that merge into a personal archetype on a mission of intrigue and investigation. The Court Jester is maybe a Clown, sometimes a Fool, always a Joker, and the ultimate Detective. The Court Jester is the personification of the entertainer and spy. If you really wish to understand the qualities of this archetype, then watch a film titled *The Court Jester* starring Danny Kaye. It is not only an entertaining movie but a great illustration of the perfect archetypal Court Jester.

The days of Kings and Queens ruling as governments are mostly gone. Back in the days when the rulers had royal guards to protect their sovereignty and the castle was the city fortress, the courts were filled with family, protected courtiers, honoured guests, and vassals, all loyal to the throne and desiring protection. The King or Queen had the throne to protect, but history shows us there was always someone lurking in the shadows planning to usurp the incumbent. The King and Queen employed spies, as their very lives and existence depended on the information they received. The Court Jester, traditionally, was the perfect spy. Playing the fool, the Court Jester could never be taken seriously. As the entertainer, the Court Jester would be the ears of the King or Queen, when wine loosened their guests' tongues, and their guards would drop. The Court Jester could make light of honoured guests to test their reactions and gauge the seriousness or purpose of their visitation. Court Jesters were clever entertainers, informed detectives, and perfectly concealed spies. They were invaluable trustees and confidants of their Kings or Queens.

Court Jester archetypes are still alive and well in modern society. They are a person at work, in your social or sporting set, or in your family. They will tell the jokes, take "the mickey" out of the boss or coach, and make fun of their own inabilities. They definitely entertain you. They certainly amuse you. They may even annoy you, but the whole time, they are judging your reactions, assessing your personality, and storing the information for future reference. They are still the ultimate spies; only these days, they are generally spying for their own records. Court Jesters are especially good at hiding their thoughts and emotions. We all know those who say something and leave us standing there wondering whether they were serious or joking. Those are Court Jesters at their very best.

**Negative Aspects:**

Foolish ~ Deceptive ~ Mimic ~ Low self-esteem ~ Heckler ~ Delusional ~ Humour in poor taste ~ Dreary ~ Misunderstood

**Positive Aspects:**

The King or Queen's spy and confidant ~ Insight ~ Wisdom ~ Light hearted ~ Integrity ~ Exposes the truth ~ Influential ~ Element of courage ~ Entertaining ~ Funny

**Archetypal Energy:**

The archetypal energy of the Court Jester is a mixture of entertainer and spy. As entertainers they may be totally out there or hold steady with dry wit. The Court Jester loves an audience and finds a stage for performance in the strangest of places. An old teaching colleague of mine used school assemblies to ply his trade. He was absolutely brilliant with his humour, and he captivated and involved both children and adults in his performance. Court Jesters are generally funny, as their very existence depends upon their humour and their ability to disarm, distract, or elicit reactions.

As a Court Jester, you probably love to know what makes individuals tick and what makes them react. You can be an excellent judge of character thanks to your detective skills and intuitive ability to identify character traits. You are able to sum up a situation or an individual and place yourself comfortably into that sphere of influence. But remember to keep it light-hearted and honest rather than collect information for no real reason. Beware the Court Jester who becomes his own personal spy and serves no purpose.

**Archetypal Combinations:**

The archetypal energy of the Court Jester combines well with the energy of:

Detective * Clown * Fool * Joker * Trickster * Storyteller * Actor * King * Queen * Peacemaker * Shaman * Diplomat * Magician * Companion * Gambler * Puck * Prophet * Artist

**Effective Use of Court Jester Energy:**

- Maintain the boundaries of your wit and humour.
- Keep your performance fresh and suitable for the occasion.
- Do not be overwhelmed by the Court Jester energy whereby you lose the essence of your own personality.

# Coward

It may surprise you that the fairy tale of Cinderella is not a story about the Princess archetype but about the Coward archetype. Cinderella was born into wealth and privilege. When her mother died, Cinderella was compensated for her loss by the adoration of her father. However, when he remarried, Cinderella was given a series of difficult challenges. The new additions to her family changed the whole dynamic, and she had to deal with testing situations and new relationships. This became worse with the death of her father. Not only did she have to bear the grief of losing her father but also the neglect and abuse from her stepmother and stepsisters. Cinderella, however, never lost her optimism. She endured every hardship and persisted with her duties, even when they were unfair and unpleasant. She never reverted to the "poor me" syndrome and blamed others for her misfortune. Eventually, she found true love and happiness, and her favoured place in the world was rightly restored.

The Coward archetype is about perseverance. Cowards are given many challenges throughout their lifetimes, and how they are dealt with can turn the Cowards into Heroes. The negative energy of the archetype leads to the road of least resistance. They neglect their responsibilities, become fearful of new situations, turn away from truth, lie, make excuses, or blame others for their decisions and actions. The negative Coward archetypal energy is the expert at procrastination, misrepresentation and subtle justification. This kind of energy may not be seen as cowardice, as it is not an obvious action, such as deserting in the heat of battle. It is more the kind of energy that says, "I'll do that tomorrow." "If I ignore this problem, then it will go away." "I'll stop smoking when the time is right." "What's good for the goose is good for the gander." "I am no good at confrontation."

The negative Coward energy is very subtle, reasonable, and often self-justifying. Repeated often enough, it holds an individual back, as bit by bit, one excuse after another pile on top of what soon becomes a mountain of inaction.

The positive Coward accepts challenges and takes action with determination and endurance. You do not have to participate in death-defying activities to prove you are brave. Your positive Coward energy is all about accepting responsibility, persisting through troubled times, listening to your intuitive self, and making decisions accordingly. Deal with the small issues, and the Divine or greater universal energy will recognize you are capable of dealing with more important issues. Remember there is always light at the end of the tunnel. Keep the Cinderella story close to your heart. Through all her challenges, she maintained a positive outlook on life. She persisted through the trials and tribulations that were thrown her way, and she took her responsibilities seriously. Importantly, she never let anything dent her self-esteem or take away her self-belief.

Some people have difficulty identifying the Coward archetype as one of their own. There are two key questions to help you through this doubt. Were you shy as a child? If the answer is yes, chances are you have a Coward archetype. Confirm this by the second question. Have you ever walked away from a challenge? Those two questions will identify the Coward archetype, though you may not be a coward as such. If you've used the positive Coward energy to show resilience, determination, and perseverance, then your Coward archetype has been a blessing to you.

**Negative Aspects:**

Shy ~ Afraid ~ Fearful ~ Indecision ~ Procrastinate ~ Intimidated ~ Scared ~ Lack of self-worth ~ Inhibited ~ Avoidance ~ Irresponsible ~ Difficulty with taking a chance or a risk

**Positive Aspects:**

Learn the power of courage ~ Perseverance ~ Endurance ~ Determination ~ Facing the unknown ~ Struggle ~ Responsible ~ Risk taking ~ Involved ~ Unshakable self-esteem ~ Maintaining personal safety

**Archetypal Energy:**

The archetypal energy of the Coward can be the most debilitating energy or the most fulfilling energy. It is like the flip of a coin. On one side you have the Hero; on the other side you have the Coward. Just remember, heroes do not have to be champion sportspeople, pop stars, film idols, or combat medal winners. Heroes are ordinary, every-day people involving themselves in ordinary deeds. Do what you know to be righteous, and accept life's challenges with determination and persistence and use your Coward archetypal energy to its full potential.

The most important thing you can do is bring your Coward with you. You cannot lock your Coward away. You cannot ignore your Coward. This is just what your Coward wants. Always take your Coward energy with you. Treat your Coward as another person. Say with authority, "We are going to do this together no matter what you say, no matter what excuse you make, no matter how scared you are, or no matter how much you cry or complain. No discussion! No justification! We are doing this together because I have made a decision." This allows the Coward energy to transform into Hero energy. Allow this Hero energy to strengthen with every courageous and pragmatic decision you make. You can do it. Be persistent. Be enduring. Become action orientated!

**Archetypal Combinations:**

The archetypal energy of the Coward combines well with the energy of:

Adventurer * Heroine * Hero * Peter Pan Child *Warrior * Peacemaker * Explorer * Nature Child *Pioneer * Prophet * Knight * Damsel * Victim * Witch *Wizard * Teacher

**Effective Use of Coward Energy:**

- Take your Coward with you. No excuses!
- Use that determination, resilience and perseverance to assist you through the challenges of your life and to great achievements.
- Remember it is only the flip of a coin from Coward to Hero.
- Beware of the subtle Coward energy. This maintains the excuses, the procrastination, the apprehension, and the inability to act with trust and confidence.

# Craftsperson

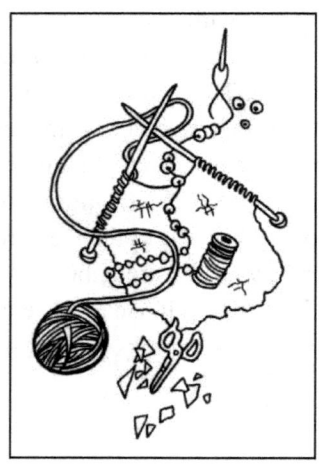

The Artist and the Craftsperson are similar in that they both pursue artistic endeavours. They have an innate desire to express their creativity. To have fulfilling lives and balance, they both need to be working on or planning a project. The energetic difference between them lies in originality and methodology. An Artist is always seeking an original idea, a new method of creative expression, or a product that is unique.

The Craftsperson is more content with replication. The Craftsperson generally follows a pattern and an accepted method of creative production. As examples, you have the porcelain doll maker who reproduces with expert duplication an original doll, the knitter or dressmaker who makes a range of clothing by using a created pattern, and the lead-lighting artisan who uses a process to produce lead-light windows or doors. This does not imply a lack of artistic endeavour. Quite the opposite! Even within the scope of a craft, there is room for creative and artistic manoeuvring. The lead lighter may blend patterns to form a new design. Colour schemes used may be by the Craftsperson's own design. Even a slight variation to technique can be used to enhance or simplify the process. Overall, the key difference is the Craftsperson produces a known product and follows a designated procedure.

The Craftsperson is usually involved in some kind of project. If you enjoy knitting, sewing, weaving, mosaics, lead lighting, doll reproductions, decoupage, macramé, folk art, cooking, beading, needlework, flower arrangements, producing jewellery, or cabinet making and other woodwork crafts and metal work, you are a Craftsperson. Craftspeople tend to move from one craft to another. When they have reached the limit of their expertise in one craft, they invariably begin another. It is not in the nature of the Craftspeople to be idle in creative expression.

**Negative Aspects:**

Pale imitation of art ~ Time wasting ~ Lack of purpose ~ Limited ~ Mass production ~ Tunnel-vision ~ Lack of individuality ~ Frustration

**Positive Aspects:**

Meticulous ~ Copying ~ Creating ~ Love of process ~ Functional ~ Useful ~ Love of finished product ~ Love of materials ~ Love of colour


**Archetypal Energy:**

The archetypal energy of the Craftsperson expresses the love of process, a created product, and the material. It requires incredible concentration, patience, and skill to be a complete artisan. When my wife was making reproduction German antique dolls, she would spend several days perfecting an eyebrow. Her patience and concentration were amazing, and this is one of the many skills that the complete Craftsperson needs. Surprisingly, there's a touch of the Engineer at work here. A process must be followed meticulously to obtain a desired result such as an Engineer would do

Craftspeople are usually most functional persons. They create a product with a purpose, and although it is an expression of creativity, it is often a product that is useful. Walk into a Craftsperson's home, and you will see the functional use of his or her endeavours with objects that simply beautify the home or products of his or her creation necessary for daily living, such as quilts or tablecloths.

Another trait of Craftspeople is their love of the material they use in their crafts. Artisans involved in woodwork love the feel, texture, and pattern of the wood they use. Those involved with cloth often love the texture, feel, colour, and eccentricities of individual materials. Talk to those who work with cloth and they could give you a discourse on fabric. They understand the feel and shimmer of silk, the richness and luxury of velvet, the practicality of cotton, the quality of linen, the natural and insulating quality of wool, and the flexibility of nylon.

If you are a Craftsperson, you probably love colour. There is a whole industry based around colour. Colour therapists; make-up specially designed for different skin tones; aura soma; crystals that reflect colour; and all manner of dyes are used for tie-dye effects, lead lighting, and so on.

Be wary of forms of negative archetypal energy for the Craftsperson. The first is frustration at not being original in design or product. The second is an immovable streak of perfectionism that most Craftspeople possess. Then there are the time-wasting amateurs who won't take their craft seriously. This energy can often be associated with the negative Coward, the negative Dilettante, and negative Hermit energy.

The Artisan or Craftsperson has a rich history of practical achievement in beautification and function, so be proud of your skill, patience, and achievements. Society is the richer for your presence.

**Archetypal Combinations:**

The archetypal energy of the Craftsperson combines well with the energy of:

Engineer * Artist * Servant * Scholar * Pioneer * Addict * Prince * Princess * Knight * Damsel * Actor * Scribe * Diva * Scientist * Teacher * Slave

**Effective Use of Craftsperson Energy:**

- Ply your craft with energy, purpose and dedication.
- Be wary of the frustration caused by perfectionism and the negative Artist's energy of originality.
- Take delight in the process of creation, the materials used and your finished product.
- Your craft may be used as a business and reward you in a monetary sense. Alternatively, your craft may be used as a hobby and reward you in an emotional sense with the beautification of your environment or as gifts for those special in your life.

# Damsel

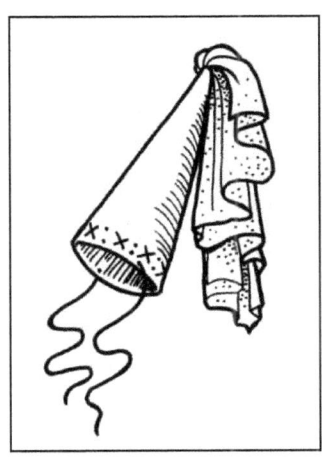

The Damsel is a strong and powerful archetype that vacillates between extremes of behaviour. This can make Damsels difficult archetypes to deal with. They're easily recognized, as they are continually in and out of love. You know them, as they are constantly seeking a Knight in shining armour to rescue them from their daily responsibilities and trivialities. When they are in love, romance and passion fill their every thought and deed. They become obsessive about their physical appearance. They flaunt their charms with bravado and expertise; then, when their relationships die tragic deaths, Damsels become obsessed with independence. They act dramatically alone and muster the strength to tackle all manner of challenges. When that situation becomes unbearable, they revert back to desiring their Knights. Balance is a lifelong lesson for Damsels to learn.

There is an energetic connection between the Princess and the Damsel. Both are looking for love and attention. The Princess, however, is content with being looked after, with security and with living in the confines of a palace (these days more likely a house), but the Damsel is more extroverted, more active and passionate within a relationship. Once the Princess has found her security, she clings to that relationship and situation, but the Damsel often seeks a new romantic thrill or a better way to be independent.

The Damsel, in a free and modern society, has the difficult task of juggling the freedom offered to a woman and the romantic need for love and passion. Teenage girls with the Damsel archetype have the onerous task to stay true to themselves. There is constant and undeniable pressure on teenage girls. Damsels love passion and romance. Teenage girls with the Damsel archetype have to balance that energy with responsible control over their sexual attractions and behaviour. In a constant and unrelenting attack, they have the media screaming indulgence, sex, romance, freedom, popularity, and fashion. It is a challenge for the Damsel to stay true to the positive energy of the archetype. When the barrage of expectation becomes too much, the Damsel succumbs to the negative archetypal energy. This results in defiance, promiscuity, eating disorders, low self-esteem, risk-taking, and irresponsibility. The teenage Damsel who balances this period of her life is one strong individual who benefits enormously from her self-control. Her effort is rewarded with increased confidence and self-assurance.

**Negative Aspects:**

Rescued ~ Co-dependent ~ Lazy ~ Obsessive ~ Dependent ~ Weak ~ Need of protection ~ Unbalanced ~ Waiting for knight in shining armour ~ Easily influenced ~ Disloyal ~ Demanding ~ Possessive ~ Delusive

**Positive Aspects:**

Self-empowered ~ Independent ~ Stay yourself ~ Take care of self ~ Responsible ~ Balanced ~ Practical ~ Strength of character ~ Loving ~ Passionate ~ Beauty

**Archetypal Energy:**

The archetypal energy of the Damsel encourages the extremes of co-dependence and independence. Neither of these is completely satisfactory or fulfilling to the Damsel archetype, as she loves attention, romance, and passion. She often seeks a relationship that offers all of these things, but this sometimes lulls her into co-dependence or, worse, into a state of total dependence. A perceptive young Damsel once told me that being in love was worse than being out of love. She admitted that when she was in love, all she could think about was the romance. Every waking hour, everything she did was designed at fulfilling that dream. Nothing else in her life mattered, and daily duties got pushed aside. She found when she was out of love, she could function again as a responsible person. This was fine until the ache of being alone and out of love became too great to bear, so yet again, she would begin the process once more. When the Damsel is in independence mode, she is willing to take on all responsibilities. This is fine until the load becomes too great a burden, so the Damsel will revert back to co-dependent relationship mode.

Damsels have the challenge of avoiding these two extremes. If you are a Damsel, seek balance in your life. This can be found in a relationship based on interdependency, where both you and your partner have your own interests and duties yet join together in the spirit of sharing and cooperation on mutually agreed responsibilities and activities. There are also other aspects of your life that are equally important and require just as much energy. Balance is a lifelong lesson for the Damsel to learn.

**Archetypal Combinations:**

The archetypal energy of the Damsel combines well with the energy of:

Peacemaker * Warrior * Lover * Diva * Narcissist * Queen * Hedonist * Artist * Seeker * Storyteller * King * Knight * Detective * Craftsperson

**Effective Use of Damsel Energy:**

- The key to a lasting, satisfying relationship is interdependency.
- Balance the Damsel energy with the energies of your other archetypes.
- Be wary of your negative Saboteur's energy. Be aware when you are engaging in activities that sabotage your relationships.
- Damsels are attracted to the Knight archetypal energy. This is great for short-term romance but a challenge for a good long-term commitment. Beware if the Damsel becomes bored or the Knight begins to seek another adventure. Communicate and work together in the joy of a loving partnership.
- Be aware of your emotions. Remember that you are in charge of them. They are not in charge of you.

# Destroyer

Destroyers actively seek the demolition of any person, place, or environment that encroaches into their spheres of influence. At an individual level, the Destroyer may seek to destroy another person's physical assets, dreams, reputation, self-esteem, businesses, or employment prospects. This may be done with subterfuge or outright, open acts of sabotage and vindictiveness. The damage may be physical, psychological, emotional, or verbal. There may even be a third party engaged to enhance the destruction. In the extreme, this archetype can be applied to the psyche of a serial killer.

The Destroyer seeks power. If that power is achieved at the highest level of governance, there may be nationwide or worldwide damage and destruction. The carnage may be of horrific proportions. These circumstances occur at the hands of a dictator, a despot, or theological or dogma-driven junta intent on radical cleansing and destruction. Alternatively, it may be a combination of all of those situations. There are numerous examples scattered throughout history. Attila the Hun, Genghis Khan, Adolf Hitler, Idi Amin, various Emperors from the Roman Empire, the British Empire leaders (especially in Africa), various figures from the Crusades, the heads of the Spanish Inquisition, Joseph Stalin, Pol Pot and his regime, and the list goes on.

There is also the environmental Destroyer. This is often harder to identify, as it tends to be economically driven by a company or a number of companies in league with corrupt politicians or bureaucrats. Alternatively, you may have a government in a conflict situation that destroys an environment as a weapon of war, such as poisoning water wells or laying explosives. Often there is no one individual who can be singled out and labelled as the destroyer, but within that area of destruction, there are a number of individuals with the Destroyer archetype who band together in a like cause. Often, it is not just the environment that suffers.

In modern times, communities are the victims of such collusion. A pharmaceutical company may be responsible for poorly tested drugs that cause irreversible damage. Thalidomide, a drug used in the late fifties and early sixties to treat morning sickness that caused a range of birth defects is the perfect example. The tobacco industry has been responsible for hiding the truth about the harm caused by smoking cigarettes, thereby causing endless cancers and destroying lives for the sake of greed and profit. There are many examples of mining and oil companies guilty of environmental destruction. Consider Shell's environmental record in Nigeria or the BP oil spill in the Gulf of Mexico. At the moment there is the continual questioning of the benefits of techniques such as fracking. The global financial crisis was caused by the lack of regulation, corruption and greed of the financial industry. Irresponsible financial institutions sought government bailouts and caused great suffering to a huge number of people who lost their homes, business, jobs, and retirement benefits.

On the positive side, the Destroyer can be the initiator of change. For example, it may be a government that clears away the slums and shanty towns and replaces them with more modern and efficient buildings. It may be the business that restructures and rids itself of out-dated or harmful practices and replaces them with friendly environmental and more profitable procedures. It may be the individual who works towards the destruction and elimination of negative personal habits and replaces them with positive attributes and behaviours.

The Destroyer archetypal energy can be to the benefit of an individual, a group, and a society. The key is in the intention. Is the destruction for personal, corporate, or national gain and glory? Or is it for the betterment of society? Is the intention to improve the lifestyle of a few at the expense of many? Or is it a win-win situation where all can benefit? The other question that must be asked is the means by which change occurs. The end does not always justify the means. Minimize the harm and maximize the benefits is using the positive archetypal energy of the Destroyer.

**Negative Aspects:**

Destructive ~ Little regard for others ~ Antisocial ~ Despot ~ Dictator ~ Bully ~ Spoiler ~ Power hungry ~ Vandals ~ Graffiti tagging ~ Violent ~ Terrorist ~ Radical

**Positive Aspects:**

Preparing for new life ~ Rebuilding ~ Destroyer of illusions ~ Health conscious ~ Bringing change ~ Creating a win-win situation ~ Social benefactor ~ Personal growth

**Archetypal Energy:**

Fortunately, most Destroyers do not rise to the power of an Adolf Hitler, although when they do, their destruction is widespread and horrific. The negative energy of the Destroyer is powerful enough to ruin lives and degrade environments. Consider your impact on your relationships at work, at home, and with your family, friends, and neighbours. How do you treat people? Do you treat them with respect or with disdain? Do you "white ant" your boss or fellow employees? Do you spread rumours and lies to bring down a person's standing and reputation? Do you bully people with your physical prowess? What is your tolerance towards immigrants, foreign tourists, the disadvantaged or powerless?

Take heed of the negative energy that destroys relationships and puts others down. Examine your attitude to your immediate environment. Do you vandalize, splash graffiti all over town, or trash your neighbourhood? That is the Destroyer at work.

The positive energy of the Destroyer uplifts and encourages people with their words and their actions. They compliment and praise others for both large and small achievements. If a friend is giving up smoking, refrain from mocking but celebrate and give praise to his or her intention and success. Together you are using positive Destroyer archetypal energy.

Be kind to the environment, and assist with the bringing of new life to urban and natural settings. A perfect example of this happens on a regular basis in Mullumbimby, the town where I live. A group of volunteers regularly weeds and regenerates the gardens at either end of the town. Another group preserves the integrity of the local creek environment by destroying the multitude of environmentally damaging self-seedlings and replaces them with native and suitable species.

Many modern-day environmentalists continually and consistently work for the survival and betterment of the environment at both a local and global level. Jacques Cousteau and Steve Irwin are two who come to mind. Break and destroy the illusions that hold you back at a personal level. Change the apathy that can captivate and stifle your local community by becoming a leader in progressive social and environmental developments. Question the accepted social norms and behaviours that are detrimental to our environments and our lifestyles. As an individual, as a community, as a society, and as a people, keep asking, can we do better, and can I contribute to that betterment?

**Archetypal Combinations:**

The archetypal energy of the Destroyer combines well with the energy of:

Pioneer * Adventurer * Explorer * Advocate * Healer * Peacemaker * Nature Child * Martyr * Guide * Warrior * Environmentalist * Entrepreneur * Hero * Heroine * King * Queen * Knight * Politician

**Effective Use of Destroyer Energy:**

- Be positive by building people up and not negative by bringing them down.
- Take care of your home, your neighbourhood, and your immediate environment.
- Examine your self-esteem. Do you gossip, spread lies and rumours, or put people down to build yourself up?
- Do you have a pattern of destroying relationships?
- Do you maintain a healthy lifestyle, or are you a physical wreck and a candidate for self-destruction?

# Detective

All archetypal energy seeks a forum for expression. The Actor seeks a stage for performance. The Clown seeks an audience. The Damsel seeks a rescuer, and the Martyr seeks a cause. The Detective archetype will seek a case. Detectives love mysteries. The ultimate detective is, of course, the fictional Sherlock Holmes.

If you love reading crime or mystery novels or watching a crime television series, then you have the Detective archetype. If you enjoy interacting with people and working out what makes them tick, then you have the Detective archetype. Detectives are keen observers. They notice things others consider trivial. They familiarize themselves with patterns of behaviour. Detectives have a keen eye, a keen brain, and a fine sense of organization. They love a jigsaw puzzle and the finicky task of placing the pieces in the correct position. They also enjoy crosswords puzzles and word games.

Detectives are mostly social people. They mix well, especially in small social settings. They have the ability to be good listeners and maintain the flow of conversation with a small number of pertinent but not always direct questions. The skill of the Detective is to be unobtrusive and allow clients to reveal themselves. Teenage girls with the Detective archetype are brilliant at organizing their social groups. They understand their peers and arrange activities to suit the needs and desires of the whole group. They are able to partner off group members into amiable relationships. There is no need to be alarmed the next time you find yourself having a deep and meaningful conversation with a trusted friend, because, if they have the Detective archetype, then you are in good hands. Detectives are trusted by their peers because good detectives never reveal their sources. This makes them the perfect people to share your secrets and confidences. That's the reason why Detectives quickly earn the trust of their friends and colleagues.

**Negative Aspects:**

Snoop ~ Sticky-beak ~ Spies ~ Busybody ~ Underpaid ~ Voyeurism ~ Falsifying information ~ Selling out to the highest bidder ~ Betrayal ~ Gossip ~ Peeping Tom ~ Subjective

**Positive Aspects:**

Seeking justice ~ Looking for clues to solve the mysteries of life ~ Observant ~ Investigates ~ Look at the big picture and fit the pieces ~ Evolved ~ Intuitive ~ Puts people at ease ~ Trustworthy ~ Friendly ~ Objective

**Archetypal Energy:**

The archetypal energy of the Detective is used in many walks of life. Obviously, there are professions such as private investigators, the police, spy agencies, and investigative journalists. There are those within the legal profession, such as judges and lawyers. There are also the storytellers, such as crime and mystery authors, script writers for film and television, and magazine journalists. There are the performers, such as the actors who play a character role, the comedians who tap into appropriate humour, and the clowns who entertain with their antics. You also find the Detective archetype in dating agencies and matchmakers. (They are people who match other people with similar psychological profiles.)

There is Detective energy in healers and psychologists who investigate patterns of behaviour, the motivations and mental states of their clients, or psychic healers tuning in to the emotions and spirits of their customers (some living, some not). Teachers also use the Detective archetype to judge the needs of their students. Finally, your friends or neighbours may offer you good advice to solve a puzzle or problem that is beyond your understanding. Detectives make excellent friends and companions. Detective energy loves a mystery. Positive Detective energy is calm, concise, unobtrusive, objective, intelligent, and trustworthy.

Negative Detective energy relies on prying, snooping, gossip, betrayal of trust, and mischief making. I am sure we all know a person we cannot trust with our personal details and secrets. We soon learn to be conscious of the information we divulge. Be wary of your own involvement in such affairs. It is a simple matter to join in with the rumour mongering and the spreading of seemingly harmless gossip. Social media is rampant with such information. So too are the pages of popular magazines. Journalism used to be a profession that informed, educated, and created awareness. It seems these days that far too often, journalists are quite prepared to print stories that concentrate and rely on personalities, rumours, and their own opinions rather than the facts and the issues. This is using a privileged position and negative Detective archetypal energy to justify their self-worth.

**Archetypal Combinations:**

The archetypal energy of the Detective combines well with the energy of:

Storyteller * Rescuer * Networker * Seeker * Court Jester * Healer * Diplomat * Advocate * Actor * Philosopher * Judge * Pioneer.* Teacher * Scientist * Servant * Priest * Priestess * Entrepreneur * Wise Woman * Clown

**Effective Use of Detective Energy:**

- Use your power for the greater good and not for gossip or revenge.
- Remember to be objective and to keep a distance between you and the mystery.
- Trust is the key to your ethics and personal integrity.
- Value yourself and your ability. You deserve just compensation for your skill, time, and energy you devote to each case.

# Dilettante

The Dilettante is the amateur pretending to be a professional. It comes from the Italian present participle *dilettare*: to delight. The perfect example of the Dilettante is Hyacinth Bucket (if you please, pronounced "Bouquet," thank you very much), the central character in the television series *Keeping up Appearances*.

Let me tell you about Hyacinth, and you will understand what the Dilettante archetype is all about. As mentioned, her surname is Bucket, but she insists it be pronounced "Bouquet." Hyacinth spends a vast amount of time and energy attempting to hobnob with a social class of people of her own standing and above. She attempts to befriend any person in her community who has a position of perceived importance, such as the mayor or councillors, successful businessmen (especially if they have been on television, if only in an advertisement), or those with titles like "The Major." She refers to one local businessman as "The C. P. Benedict."

Hyacinth is forever seeking this perceived class of people as guests to her candlelight suppers. Her candlelight suppers and other entertaining occasions are regular social-climbing expeditions. Hyacinth is appalled at her sister Daisy and her brother-in-law, Onslow, whose lifestyle is basic and lower class. Her sister Rose is a total Damsel, and her man-chasing and style of dress (miniskirts) are further irksome details that Hyacinth has to deal with. She is much more comfortable with name-dropping her sister Violet, who has a Mercedes and a home with a swimming pool and room for a pony. Hyacinth is continually mentioning her hand-painted china tea set. She visits old homes and mansions to dabble in history and art, but more importantly, it may be an opportunity to meet the titled owners. She displays classy holiday brochures as a pretence to her wealth and status. She overdresses on all occasions, and she is the fanatic when it comes to social graces and etiquette. Hyacinth Bucket is the absolute archetypal Dilettante.

**Negative Aspects:**

Superficial ~ Social climber ~ Amateur ~ Dabbler ~ Pretentious ~ Deluded ~ Jack of all trades, Master of none ~ Illusions of grandeur

**Positive Aspects:**

Adaptable ~ Delighting in the arts ~ Pursuit of excellence ~ Go with the flow ~ Willing to try new ventures ~ Social politeness ~ Consideration ~ Lover of fine things

**Archetypal Energy:**

The archetypal energy of the Dilettante is either a subtle energy that may be hard to recognize or an over-the-top pretence as with Hyacinth. It is prominent in the area of sport. This person plays many different sports and then, after a short period of playing one sport, moves on to another. This is not necessarily good or bad, it is just the way of the Dilettante.

However, the energy of the Dilettante swings to the negative when there is pretence. Lying about one's achievements and abilities, making excuses, drawing comparisons with others that are detrimental to them are all forms of pretence. Bragging about one's achievements or conquests is also negative Dilettante energy. Sledging is another aspect of this energy.

Negative Dilettante energy is also found in the arts. Beware of the envy, the jealousy, the competiveness that often rear their ugly heads at art competitions, local fairs and shows, eisteddfods, and similar events. Remember that beauty is in the eye of the beholder. If you engage in these pursuits, remember your opinion is just that. It is the opinion of the judges that decides these competitions, and you should accept this as the first premise of your involvement.

It is a good thing to pursue excellence and improve all aspects of our lives. However, the philosophy of "keeping up with the Joneses" has its risks and its consequences.

Positive Dilettante energy is being truthful and modest about your accomplishments. Take delight in your creations, your achievements, and your accomplishments. Celebrate your involvement. Strive to improve. Look for new and innovative ways of achieving your goals. Be proud of your physical abilities and your creative skills. However, above all, be content. Contentment is not being happy with second best. Contentment is being happy knowing you have done your best at a particular time and in particular circumstances.

**Archetypal Combinations:**

The archetypal energy of the Dilettante combines well with the energy of:

Hedonist * Lover * Wanderer * Athlete * Explorer * Pioneer * Diva * Narcissist * Prince * Princess * Adventurer * Pilgrim * Companion * Artist * Craftsperson * Divine Child

**Effective Use of Dilettante Energy:**

- Life is a journey, and we are all at liberty to follow the many paths and to taste the variety of experiences that life offers.
- Discover who you are, and be true to yourself.
- Avoid pretence. It leads to the accumulation of self-importance, ego enhancement, and a trail of deceptions.
- Happiness is a state of mind and an attitude of enjoying all that you are given. Embellishment does not guarantee greater pleasure.

# Diplomat

The Diplomat is a representative of a group that negotiates with others who represent a different group or belief system. The positive energy of the Diplomat is shown as the peacemaker, while the negative energy is that of the spy and saboteur. The Diplomat archetype finds a home among the Foreign Affairs Departments of various countries, other government officers in sensitive departments, international organizations under the auspices of the United Nations, non-government organizations such as Greenpeace and World Vision, business advisors, customer service departments and lobby groups, principals and heads of educational institutions, and agents of sporting professionals and performing arts individuals.

Communication is the art of Diplomats. They are well-skilled in the art of saying exactly what needs to be said to their particular audience. They are well-versed in the background of the individual or organization they represent and have in-depth knowledge about the individual or organization they are negotiating with. Diplomats have the remarkable skill of remembering names, places, dates, and conversations. Their minds are trained to operate in well-ordered patterns, and they are often fluent in several languages and aware of cultural differences and customs. Diplomats have to be good listeners and keen observers.

The skill of the Diplomat operates at two levels. The public level requires the Diplomat to be effective and sensitive. The effectiveness is judged by how well the message is received and accepted by the public. The sensitiveness is judged by what is inferred in the message but not necessarily spoken in public.

Communication that is out of the public eye but exchanged through diplomatic sources or agents is often a frank and open form of communication, usually between agencies willing to reach an agreement. It could also be private negotiations between public enemies. This always requires a delicate balance. If you appear to be so tough and critical with another party yet, at the same time, hold private negotiations, there can be justifiable accusations of hypocrisy. Often the art of diplomacy is a fine balance.

**Negative Energy:**

Sabotage ~ Spy ~ Impolite ~ Insensitive ~ Aggressive ~ Inconsiderate ~ Knows best ~ Paternalistic ~ Racist ~ Bully ~ Bigot ~ Holier than thou ~ Hypocrite ~ Gossip

**Positive Energy:**

Articulate ~ Peacemaker ~ Sensitive ~ Considerate ~ Good listener ~ Relaxed ~ Able to see both sides ~ Multilingual ~ Multicultural ~ Calm ~ Understanding ~ Frank ~ Good communicator ~ Tactful

**Archetypal Energy:**

The archetypal energy of the Diplomat is about compromise and peacemaking. The trick is to find the common ground between two different and sometimes competing points of view. This requires negotiating skills that obtain the best results for a client while satisfying the needs of the opposing point of view. The Diplomat has to be a master of tact.

The positive energy of the Diplomat is a highly sought after commodity in our modern world of globalization, networking, communications, internationalization, and travel accessibility. The negative energy of the Diplomat surfaces in the form of sabotage, aggressiveness, or paternalism. The world is in a constant state of energy flow, and we cannot help but notice both the positive and negative energy of the Diplomat in our society. From the highest level of the United Nations to the lowest level of local government, Diplomatic energy is at work. As citizens, it is up to us to recognize whether the energy used in negotiation and consultation is positive or negative. Always ask yourself where your Diplomatic energy lies.

The Diplomat archetype can reside in the average citizen too. A primary school teacher who is now a former colleague is blessed with a strong Diplomat archetype. He constantly works with positive energy. He remembers the children's interests. He recalls their parents' names, their occupations, and their concerns and expectations. He is sublime in the art of conversation. He makes everyone feel welcome and special. He has an avid interest in Aboriginal culture. He has learnt sign language and, to my mind, is the ultimate representation of the Diplomat archetype.

The negative Diplomat is the spy or the double agent. The ultimate spy, of course, is the political spy who works for his or her country and seeks confidential information about other countries. Some operate in the corporate field, seeking information about the techniques, operations, and plans of rival companies. Financial spies seek inside information about business decisions to further their own pecuniary interests and advantages. These are all on a fairly grand scale. However, negative Diplomat energy can be used in all kinds of situations. It may be used to "white ant" a boss or a work colleague. It may be used within a social group to ostracize one member or advance another's influence and social standing. It may be used within families to gain favours, both monetary or emotionally. Negative Diplomat energy is used when there is sabotage, the deliberate peddling of misinformation, bullying, and the management of self-importance.

**Archetypal Combinations:**

The archetypal energy of the Diplomat combines well with the energy of:

Peacemaker * Detective * Politician * Hero * Heroine * Carer * Advocate * Servant * Priestess * Priest * Teacher *Companion * Healer * Judge * Princess * Prince * King * Queen * Angel

**Effective Use of Diplomat Energy:**

- Wisdom plays an important role in the effectiveness of diplomatic energy.
- Positive Diplomats use their skills for the advancement of all interested parties.
- Take an objective point of view despite your subjective representation.
- Beware of the subtle negative energy of the Diplomat. The subterfuge, spying and bullying is easy to identify. The patronizing energy of paternalism is more difficult to identify but just as damaging.

# Disciple

The Disciple archetype is not limited to the followers of a church or religious organization. The Disciple is the archetype of personal involvement in any manner of groups. The Disciple is involved in sporting clubs, political parties, business boards, educational committees, recreation organizations, police and defence forces, and so on. The individual with the strong Disciple archetype is likely to hold the position of manager, chairperson, secretary, treasurer, coach, captain, or even the head of a fundraising committee. They hold these positions because they are committed to the group and are trusted by the members. Disciples often belong to multiple organizations or clubs at the same time.

The energy of the Disciple has no boundaries when it comes to commitment and loyalty. Loyalty is a special energy, and there are only two archetypes where loyalty ranks as the number one quality. They are the Companion and the Disciple. The loyalty of the Companion archetype is devoted to a single person or cause. The loyalty of the Disciple is similar in nature but is devoted to the group cause and the group members.

Commitment is the other quality special to the Companion and the Disciple. The commitment of the Disciple subsides only when there is a change of lifestyle or a change in personal or family circumstances. For example, Disciples will move physically and energetically from the committee of a primary school to the committee of a secondary school as their children grow older and change schools. Disciples who have been Secretary of the local football or tennis club may change their commitment to be the Secretary of the local golf or bowling club as age and fitness move them away from an active sport to a more gentle physical activity. The loyalty and commitment of the Disciple archetype never fades away. Ask any type of football fans which teams they support, how long they have followed those teams, and if they have supported anyone else. In almost every case the commitment and loyalty will be for a lifetime.

**Negative Aspects:**

Mindlessness ~ Hand over will power ~ Cultic ~ Into fads ~ Herd mentality ~ Action without thought ~ Dependent ~ Follow the leader ~ Mental laziness ~ Betrayal ~ Blind faith

**Positive Aspects:**

Follower ~ Loyalty ~ Discipline ~ Selectiveness ~ Commitment ~ Autonomy ~ Discernment ~ Self-responsibility ~ Dependable ~ Ardent ~ Devoted ~ Faithful ~ Service ~ Tradition

**Archetypal Energy:**

The archetypal energy of the Disciple poses questions to the individual. What are the reasons behind choices? Disciples have to be aware of why they involve themselves in various groups. Because loyalty and commitment factors are so strong with Disciples, it may lead to them giving away their individual dignity, freedom, rights, and judgment. This is the art of indoctrination. This is when the energy of a group is so strong that it overwhelms the energy of individual Disciples. This is seen in various cults, fads, and religious sects. The commitment of loyalty sometimes overpowers an individual's judgment.

The other factor Disciples have to take into account is self-esteem. Disciples with low self-esteem are often drawn to a cult or religious sect for recognition and companionship. Belonging triggers an emotional response. They feel wanted, useful, and secure. We are social beings. We rely on each other for security, for communication, for respect, for recognition. Belonging to a group gives an individual that security and recognition.

When we join and belong to a group, our personal responsibilities diminish and our group responsibilities increase. The individuals give away many of their rights and decision-making privileges. Group rules are established. Decisions are made by the leadership group. Disciples alleviate themselves of responsibility for many of their own thoughts and actions. This is a prerequisite for the armed forces. Following commands and the security of the group are paramount and override many of the decision-making processes that are the usual concern of an individual. The "just following orders" excuse is a prevalent abdication of individual responsibility.

If you have the Disciple archetype, be prepared and always question your involvement in the various groups and their ventures. Are you enhancing the group with your contribution? Is the group allowing personal growth and development? Do you have the freedom to leave at any moment? Is the emotional bond you have with the group so strong that it takes away your growth, your freedom, or your decision to leave? The positive energy of a Disciple is like gold to the group dynamic. It enhances the group spirit, allows for the growth of the organization, and builds the group reputation beyond reproach.

**Archetypal Combinations:**

The archetypal energy of the Disciple combines well with the energy of:

Servant * Warrior * Martyr * Carer * Knight * Companion * Monk * Nun * Teacher * Pilgrim * Coward * Priest * Priestess * Networker * Slave

**Effective Use of Disciple Energy:**

- Rejoice in your loyalty and commitment, but be aware of taking on so much responsibility that it becomes detrimental to the other areas of your life.
- Be aware of the cult, fad, or sect that takes away your freedom. This is an issue of self-esteem and emotional blackmail. Watch your self-esteem, especially after an emotional upheaval. This is when you are vulnerable.
- Do not be afraid to move on to another group or cause. This is all in your life's journey.
- Use your skill and experience from past group involvement to enhance your participation in the next group. This allows for both personal and group development.

# Diva

In cultural terms, the Diva is the popular, well-loved female performer. She establishes her reputation as a performer of the highest quality. The term Diva is often associated with opera singers and more recently with pop singers. Dame Nellie Melba is the most famous operatic Diva. The term was applied to Madonna in the 1980s. Mariah Carey, Celine Dion, Lady Gaga, and Beyonce are other pop singers classed as Divas.

Diva is Italian in origin and means female deity or goddess. The male equivalent is Divo, and various male opera singers have earned that title. However, in popular culture it is the female Diva that has stolen the limelight. The title of Diva has also been used to describe popular and classical talented ballet dancers. Dame Margot Fonteyn is the best known in this field. However, the correct terminology for the female star of ballet is prima donna.

More recently the term Diva is used to describe a range of female performers. The term not only applies to singers but also includes dancers and wrestlers. In fact, females with well-developed bodies in scantily-clad outfits, who are prepared to perform or just pose for the camera or the selfie, are today deemed as Divas. Realty television shows promote such individuals. Kim Kardashian is an obvious example.

Divas are similar in their independent nature to the Damsel. Both crave the extreme of independence and self-empowerment on one hand. However, at the other extreme, the Damsel is interested in finding a love interest, while the Diva is more concerned with fame and publicity. For the Diva, it is all about being noticed.

With the era of modern technology, the Diva has ample opportunity to strut her stage. The Internet and the various modes of social networking present the Diva with a whole range of public forums. Singing, dancing, and all manner of performance may be involved as the Diva seeks the notoriety to which she feels entitled.

Another personality trait of the Diva is her reluctance to retire. Divas will not fade away gently. There is always once last performance. Dame Nellie Melba had many farewell performances. Madonna is still keen to surprise or shock the audience as she struts across the stage, akin to being in her prime. The term Diva applies to young female performers but be wary if you suggest that concept to an older female performer.

**Negative Aspects:**

Show-off ~ Attention seeker ~ One dimensional ~ Boastful ~ Unedifying ~ Misbehaviour ~ Pretentious ~ Amateur ~ Vain ~ Arrogant ~ Tacky

**Positive Aspects:**

Talented ~ Popular ~ Artistic ~ Beloved ~ Adored ~ Simply-the-best ~ Confident ~ Charisma ~ Noticed

**Archetypal Energy:**

The positive archetypal energy of the Diva is the combination of her talent, popularity, and charisma. For the Diva to earn her title, she has to be talented in her field. This was always the case. The very best in operatic performance was bestowed the title of Diva.

The modern trend of mass media and promotion has made it a little easier for an individual to be viewed as a Diva. Yes, there usually is a great deal of talent associated with the likes of Madonna, Beyoncé, and other popular icons. However, there is always a great deal of promotion, as well as a small amount of controversy often added to the mix. In these cases, popularity is promoted as well as earned.

The other ingredient that is part and parcel in being a Diva is that indefinable element of charisma. Performers either have charisma or they lack charisma. Success does not depend entirely on charisma. However, performers, no matter what field of entertainment, are always guaranteed success if they are deemed charismatic.

The negative energy of the Diva is exposed when there is an obvious lack of talent and an overdose of controversy and self-promotion. Many young females view cheap and tacky as the essential ingredient of becoming a Diva. The title needs earning. There is hard work involved in getting to the top of your profession. It is not only a case of unlimited exposure and massive promotion.

**Archetypal Combinations:**

The archetypal energy of the Diva combines well with the energy of:

Goddess * Lover * Narcissist * Damsel * Dilettante * Queen * Artist * Actor * Athlete * Rebel * Hedonist

**Effective Use of Diva Energy:**

- Work hard at your trade, develop your talent and plan for success.
- Keep yourself fit, well, and energetic through a good diet and a healthy lifestyle.
- Take pride in your achievements, but remain humble. Be grateful and generous to those who contribute to your success.
- Be wary of unethical behaviours and of compromising your principles.

# Engineer

The Engineer archetype is like the nuts and bolts of a well-oiled machine. Engineers hold the manufacturing business in good stead. They are the people who invent, run, and repair all manner of machinery. They are the designers and builders of cities, transport systems, communication networks, and so on. Since the Industrial Revolution, there has been a greater need for the Engineer archetype, and this archetype has increased numerically and in skill level.

The Engineer is the child who takes something apart to see how it works and then put it back exactly as it was. The Engineer is your mechanic, maintenance personnel, tradesman, computer technician, architect, city planner, communications technician, and transport engineer. Engineers are the masters of order and process. They have analytical brains that allow for step-by-step procedures in an organized manner. They realize that the process begins at step one and finishes at step one hundred. They know that each step builds upon the previous step, and they understand that if even one step is omitted or faulty, then the process will have to recommence or the product be repaired. This then, requires more time and energy. The Engineer is always conscious of time and energy. If the project is done correctly the first time, there is no need for it to be done again.

Flexibility is another quality of the Engineer. If the traditional process of construction or repair does not apply, then Engineers are the masters of adaption. They have the awareness to use another application or different process. Check out the construction history of the Millau Viaduct in southern France. This road bridge is slightly taller than the Eiffel Tower and only slightly shorter than the Empire State Building. This is an incredible feat of engineering that required some real lateral thinking. Only someone with an Engineer archetype could have made it happen. On a smaller scale but still a challenge, talk to the Engineer who restores antique furniture or classic cars. They really know how to overcome a challenge.

**Negative Aspects:**

Master manipulator ~ Unrealistic ~ Pie in the sky ~ Egocentric ~ Staid ~ Stubborn ~ Dreamer ~ Grand illusions ~ Reckless ~ Disorder

**Positive Aspects:**

Grounded ~ Orderly ~ Using creativity for practical expression ~ Creative ~ Everyday solutions ~ See the big picture ~ Respecting the process ~ Handy ~ Practical ~ Understanding the step by step process ~ Careful

**Archetypal Energy:**

The archetypal energy of the Engineer is based around order. Engineers understand everything in life is a process. When they move through that process in an orderly fashion, they achieve everything they set out to accomplish. When steps of the process are ignored, mismanaged, or half-completed, chaos reigns and the desired result is not achieved.

The positive Engineer energy is a mixture of both creativity and practicality. The Engineer sees the big picture and has a complete understanding of the final product. There is a fair proportion of Networker energy within the Engineer archetype too. It is important for the Engineer to have access to others who can assist in the engineering process. Another trait of the positive Engineer is the collection and maintenance of appropriate tools and machinery. You can always tell a person with an Engineer archetype by looking in his or her work shed. If all the tools are well kept and appropriately housed with easy access, then that person has the Engineer archetype.

The negative energy of Engineers takes over with delusions of grandeur. This energy is ego driven. These are the projects pursued for the glorification of the instigator, creator, or designer. They disregard the practical purpose for which they are constructed and become monuments of folly. The energy that drives the idealist to construct the world's tallest building is negative Engineer energy. This will always be an ego-driven project. There is no practical purpose in having buildings that tall. There are a number of cathedrals that also fit into the category of ego driven constructions. They were built for the glorification of the men who raised the capital and oversaw the project. The men who taught the Word of God did so by the rivers and lakes, on the hills and plains, in the towns and villages, and in simple houses and buildings. They did not seek or need vast monuments for their glorification.

**Archetypal Combinations:**

The archetypal energy of the Engineer combines well with the energy of:

Pioneer * Networker * Craftsperson * Servant * King * Queen * Entrepreneur * Scientist * Teacher *

**Effective Use of Engineer Energy:**

- Remember the boundaries that separate practicality from illusion.
- Your sense of achievement is through ordered process.
- Beware of frustration, especially with those who do not understand the Engineer energy.
- Be humble and share your skills. Your talent is always appreciated by those who are your true friends.

# Entrepreneur

The Entrepreneur is the archetype for making money. Where there are high-risk investments, lucrative business ventures, niche market opportunities, or short-term, highly rewarding fads, you find Entrepreneurs. They have a sixth sense when it comes to making money. They are high gamblers where the rewards are big and the losses just as great. It is often the case that Entrepreneurs not only make a fortune quickly but also lose it just as fast. It is their belief and confidence that lead to success and it is the same belief, but over-confidence, that leads to failure. Success for the Entrepreneur is like a drug. The hits need to keep coming.

Both the Entrepreneur and the Banker make money but the energy and methodology is different. The Banker is far more cautious and plays a more secure numbers game. Entrepreneurs are adventurous, take risks, and use intuition and gut feelings. Occasionally Bankers, usually investment bankers, gain a deal of notoriety when they decide to push the limits of the banking industry and act like Entrepreneurs. To their shame and disappointment, and to the detriment of Banks and their shareholders, comes the realization that failure is inevitable. Why? Because the Banker energy and the Entrepreneur energy is different! The Banker relies on safety and security. The Entrepreneur relies on opportunity and risk-taking.

Entrepreneurs trust their intuition and judgment and go full tilt. The Entrepreneur is happy to be involved in any kind of venture, and if it is a deal that will make easy money, the Entrepreneur is there. Real estate, mining, construction, transportation, computer technology, fashion, service industries, and entertainment are all lucrative areas for Entrepreneurs. The key for continued success is to trust their judgment and recognize what industry or sector will work and for how long. Some well-known entrepreneurs are Dick Clark, Alan Bond, Rupert Murdoch, Bill Gates, and Richard Branson. The Entrepreneurs on this list provide an interesting mix of the archetypal energy, both positive and negative. If you read a little of their biographical histories, you learn a great deal about the Entrepreneur archetype.

**Negative Aspects:**

Corrupt ~ Fanatical ~ Self-delusion ~ Ideas of grandeur ~ Self-importance ~ Take advantage of ~ Over-confident ~ Reckless

**Positive Aspects:**

Risk taker ~ Organized ~ Networking ~ Midas touch ~ See the big picture ~ Seize the day ~ Wealth ~ Intuitive ~ Confident ~ Self-assured ~ Understand the market

**Archetypal Energy:**

The Entrepreneur is the person with the Midas touch. The energy is similar to that of the Alchemist, who can turn lead into gold. The Entrepreneur is a gambler, but the energy of the Gambler is different from the energy of the Entrepreneur. The Gambler expects to win with little or no effort. Entrepreneurs are willing to work for their rewards. Entrepreneurs are very much workaholics Their whole lives revolve around their ventures and successes.

Business and pleasure are welded together in the archetypal energy of the Entrepreneur, and that's why the Entrepreneur is happy to finance lavish social occasions. This attitude and behaviour sends out a message that displays the energy of success. It brings into operation the Law of Attraction. The Entrepreneur is also the master of networking. If there is a source, a contact, an opportunity, or a need that is necessary to gain an advantage, then Entrepreneurs have a networking web and knowledge at their disposal.

Addiction is often part and parcel of the whole deal. The Entrepreneur lives for the adventure and the success of a venture. The negative archetypal energy takes control when the addiction is too great, and the Entrepreneur's judgment is impaired. This is when the ego comes into play. Delusions of grandeur, over-confidence, and corruption come to the fore. Corruption is generally the final card that negative Entrepreneurs deal and that often brings about their downfalls.

**Archetypal Combinations:**

The archetypal energy of the Entrepreneur combines well with the energy of:

Alchemist * Pioneer * Addict * Indulged Child * Explorer * Gambler * Networker * Saboteur * Visionary * Warrior * King * Queen * Hedonist

**Effective Use of Entrepreneur Energy:**

- Set yourself goals, and stay within the set limitations.
- Use your intuition and business acumen to achieve your goals.
- Use your networking skills effectively and remember to pay tribute and just compensation to those who assist you with loyalty and know-how.
- Beware of the ego. Keep your self-esteem under control.
- Be civil, legal and just with all of your business dealings.
- Maintain balance in your life. There is more to you than just an Entrepreneur.

# Explorer

The Explorer discovers and investigates new territories. With the expansion of the New World, the Explorer archetype came to the fore. Europeans spread their influence throughout the Americas, Australasia and the Pacific Islands, Asia, and Africa. This was the era of the famous European explorers such as Vasco da Gama, Christopher Columbus, Sir Francis Drake, Captain James Cook, Ferdinand Magellan, John Cabot, Sir Walter Raleigh, and Hernan Cortes. These explorers were preceded by others like Marco Polo.

Mention the word Explorer and what generally comes to mind are journeys of heroic figures in wooden sailing ships. Their journeys, which covered vast oceans, concluded with landing on foreign soil and conquering indigenous resistance for the glory and wealth of their mother countries. They were certainly brave, courageous, and dedicated Explorers using the positive archetypal energy. In many cases, however, they were, in reality, ruthless, arrogant, and rapacious, making full use of all the negative aspects of that archetype.

Since the European wave of exploration, Explorers have gone into the heart of Africa, the depths of the Amazon basin, and the frozen wilderness of the Arctic and Antarctic. They have examined volcanoes and the vast ocean floor, and who can forget the famous trip to the moon. All of these expeditions have called upon the Explorer archetypal energy.

The Explorer energy also explores human anatomy, mental states and capabilities, philosophies, and spirituality. It is responsible for new inventions. In these cases, the Explorer archetypal energy is very much linked to the energy of the Pioneer, Scientist, Seeker, and Philosopher.

Any one individual can possess the Explorer archetype. Many seekers, travellers, or tourists who wander off the beaten track are using the Explorer archetype. They are on their own personal voyage of discovery. Explorers may be Wanderers, but Wanderers usually move from place to place, from job to job, or from relationship to relationship in an indiscernible pattern. Usually the Explorer has some goal or destination in mind or is fulfilling a commission from someone else.

**Negative Aspects:**

Going around in circles ~ Isolate ~ Introverted ~ Inflexible ~ Lost ~ Abandon the present ~ Unsettled ~ Seeking glory ~ Rapacious ~ Arrogant ~ Never contented ~ Ruthless

**Positive Aspects:**

Risk taker ~ Trail blazer ~ Brave ~ Intuitive ~ Strength of character ~ Flexible ~ Visionary ~ Faith in self ~ Hardened ~ New horizons ~ Experiences ~ Courage ~ Commitment ~ Rewarded ~ Inquisitive

**Archetypal Energy:**

The archetypal energy of the Explorer is based around the quest for the unknown. There are questions to be answered, places to be identified, ideas seeking enlightenment, and challenges seeking solutions. This is the realm of the Explorer. Generally, the Explorer is the archetype that asks the big questions and is prepared to go to extraordinary lengths to find the answers. The Explorer has to have vision, courage, and commitment. Watch a few episodes of the television show *Globe Trekker*, and you will gain a good understanding of what it is like to be a modern day Explorer. Push yourself further into the realm of adventure, and imagine what it is like to climb Mount Everest, trek to the North Pole, spend time in Antarctica, dive to great ocean depths, sail solo around the world, fly an air balloon across continents, and explore space. Vision, courage, and commitment are the necessary components to the Explorer archetype.

The negative archetypal energy of the Explorer revolves around exploitation. The stories of death, destruction, and plundering are the legacy from many of those European explorers mentioned earlier. There are still tales today of such exploitation. Check out the recent history of the Congo region in Africa to understand what exploitation is all about. The negative energy is found in the Explorer who is seeking self-glorification, or is responsible for the exploitation of the conquered.

The Explorer seeking self-glorification is a victim of the ego. You see this daily, especially in the fields of art and entertainment. Those individuals who push the boundaries more for the notoriety than for their pursuit and satisfaction of their creative expression are prime candidates. At the risk of offending some people, although I suspect they are young males, I use the *Jackass* movies as an example.

There are also the lost Explorers who have no vision, no purpose, and wander aimlessly through life. There is no learning in their adventures, and they often go in circles, repeating the same mistakes over and over again.

If you have an Explorer archetype, follow your vision and enjoy the journey for what it is. Exploration is fine for personal development, but be wary if it is for personal advantage and glorification.

**Archetypal Combinations:**

The archetypal energy of the Explorer archetype combines well with the energy of:

Nature Child * Wanderer * Entrepreneur * Engineer * Healer * Saboteur * Shape Shifter * Teacher * Addict * Adventurer * Seeker * Pioneer * Scientist

**Effective Use of Explorer Energy:**

- Understand your vision and your goals, and accept the journey that may differ from your expectations.
- Stay firm and positive with your commitment.
- Beware of grandiose plans that have no significance, no definition and no resolution.
- Use your vision, intuition, courage and loyalty in all aspects of your life

# Fairy

Individuals with the Fairy archetype have a daintiness and fragility about them. They are light on their feet and find it difficult to cope with the intense physicality of this world. They love nature. They enjoy the small, simple pleasures, such as rocks and stones, flowers, bubbling creeks, butterflies, insects, and small birds like wrens and finches. They also like to spend time amongst the trees, visit mountain landscapes, and explore lakes. It is the size and magnificence of these features that attract the Fairy archetype. The Fairy person enjoys the company of animals, especially those associated with mythology. Fairies love wandering through nature. Here, they are comfortable and at home.

The Fairy archetype is attracted to the simplicity and honesty of children. Those with the Fairy archetype enjoy raising children, especially girls, as they love feminine energy. These people are attracted to jobs such as primary school teaching, childcare, and nursing. Here they can express their tenderness, show their love of nature and animals, dabble in artistic and creative pleasures, and revel in the art of storytelling and fantasy. Individuals with the Fairy archetype are often found at markets and shows, all dressed up in complete fairy costume. They are likely to sell fairy paraphernalia, such as costumes, wings, illustrations, music, and wands. They delve into face painting or body tattooing. They tell stories and dance with freedom and lightness of being.

Those with the Fairy archetype are usually pleasant to be around except when they become frustrated at the complexity of the world. Fairy archetypes encourage a trusting nature, and individuals with this archetype can display a great deal of anger and disappointment when that trust is broken. Similarly, if things in this world become too complex and unmanageable, the Fairy will be prone to attacks of temper tantrums. However, it is never too serious and passes quickly. Fairies have forgiving natures and are not bound by the psychological or emotional rules of this world.

**Negative Aspects:**

Living in a fantasy world ~ Fragile ~ Easily frustrated ~ Unrealistic ~ Dreamer ~ Prone to wander ~ Simplistic ~ Temper tantrums ~ Impractical

**Positive Aspects:**

Fantastic ~ Lover of nature and animals ~ Enjoys simple pleasures ~ Storyteller ~ Relates to children ~ Caring ~ Delicate ~ Creative ~ Imaginative ~ Artistic

**Archetypal Energy:**

The archetypal energy of the Fairy is soft. It is the energy of delicacy and affection that appreciates the simple things the world has to offer. It is an energy that has an affinity with nature and animals and has special appeal for children. Those with the Fairy archetype love to be around the joy that children possess. How many young children love being fairies? When they grow older and the world of materialism and responsibility takes over from the world of fantasy, it becomes more of a challenge to enjoy and express that Fairy archetypal energy. If you have the Fairy archetype, savour and treasure that Fairy energy and spread it throughout your sphere of influence. Be brave! Be adventurous! Be fantastic! There are many occasions and many demands when responsibility is required. It is fine to leave a little time to indulge in fairy magic, no matter what others may think or say.

The negative Fairy energy is seen in the person who is lost in fantasy and has trouble adapting to the physicality of this world. There is a fine balance between fragility and delicacy. The other challenge for someone with the Fairy archetype is finding a venue for the creative and feminine energy associated with the Fairy energy. It is important for the individual with the Fairy archetype to express themselves. As an adult, striking the balance between daily responsibilities and fairy fantasy is crucial.

**Archetypal Combinations:**

The archetypal energy of the Fairy combines well with the energy of:

Storyteller * Teacher * Nature Child * Artist * Clown * Angel * Peter Pan Child * Wanderer * Adventurer * Mother * Carer

**Effective Use of Fairy Energy:**

- Be aware of the ways of this world. Control any frustration by channelling energy into your creativity.
- Remain true to your love of nature, freedom of spirit, enjoyment of simple pleasures, creativity and fantasy.
- Seek employment or activities that involve children and those young at heart.
- Express your creativity through storytelling, writing, drawing, painting and intuitive games.

# Father

The Father archetype is the male energy concerned with the raising of children. Fathers are role models for their sons and surrogate male energy for their daughters. The person with the Father archetype usually has children. However, some go through life without their own biological offspring yet still possess the energy of the Father archetype. These people utilize this energy with extended family, relatives, friends, or organizations devoted to young children or teenagers.

Young children learn from modelling their parents' language, behaviours, and attitudes. As they grow, they learn to combine those learnt behaviours with those of the wider society. Children are influenced by their relatives, peers, education, social norms and expectations, and mass media. Many of these influences reinforce previously learned attitudes, while a few of them offer a change in direction. It is, however, the Father and Mother who are the prime motivators behind their child's patterns of behaviour. There is great responsibility attached to the parenting archetypes.

The Father archetype has an energy that is powerful around children. It is important those with the Father archetype use the positive aspects of this archetype at all times. It is so easy, when working with children, to fall into negative habits. Children are still learning to control their behaviours and emotions while discovering the wider world. From time to time, their behaviour can be a cause of frustration. How easy it is for a Father to react with anger, bribery, abuse, neglect, and negativity! How often do you hear yourself repeat the negative phrases of your own father? Parenthood is a joy, but it is not easy. You often make up the rules as you go along because you are faced with situations that are new and different to your own experience.

Individuals with the Father archetype may be found in various jobs and positions. Male teachers often have the Father archetype. Those, who coach sport or who are involved in the creative arts, use the Father archetypal energy. Organizations devoted to young people, such as Scouts, youth groups, and so on will have leaders with the Father archetype. These people may or may not have their own children, but they use the Father archetypal energy in exercising their duties.

Often they use this energy in a more positive fashion with other children than with their own. This is because they are slightly removed from the personalities and the expectations of home. Many of these leaders make excellent teachers and model fathers.

Good male leaders are important in all levels of society. They exhibit behaviour modelling that is both positive and consistent. They communicate on a level that everyone can understand. They are able to work with both adults and students towards common goals.

For daughters, the Father energy provides them with an introduction to masculine energy. This energy is strongly imprinted in a girl's formative years. Generally, those who have the Father archetype offer boys a way of thinking and behaving. The Father archetype expressed in its positive form offers girls strength, independence, comfort, and protection. It also supplies an attraction to males with similar energy. The strength of this energy varies depending on their other archetypes. Think about the bond between the Princess daughter and the King father. This can be considered a bond of positive energy. Now think about the bond between the Rescuer daughter and the Addict father. This can be considered a bond of negative energy. This is the daughter continually rescuing her father from all kinds of addictive behaviours. This pattern is likely to be repeated as the girl grows into womanhood and keeps rescuing males with a similar energy to her father. This continues until she realizes she cannot sustain the Rescuer energy on lost causes. Grounded, well-rounded individuals with a positive Father archetype never encourage their daughters to develop negative patterns of behaviour. They encourage patterns of behaviour that are productive, offer security, and encourage individual development.

**Negative Aspects:**

Conditional love ~ Neglect ~ Abandonment ~ Abuse ~ Smother love ~ Control ~ Selfish ~ Bribery ~ Do as I say and not as I do ~ Emotional blackmail

**Positive Aspects:**

Provider ~ Protector ~ Nurturing ~ Caring ~ Mentors ~ Teaching ~ Leadership ~ Guide ~ Selflessness ~ Positive modelling ~ Good example ~ Empowering

**Archetypal Energy:**

The archetypal energy of the Father (and the Mother) is the prime influence on the behaviour of their children and an effective influence on other children that come within the immediate environment of that energy. The Mother and Father energies are most likely the first energies that interact with a child. The archetypal energy of the Child is fresh and eager to intermingle with other energies, so those first encounters have lifelong consequences. You have a combination of the physical attributes of both your mother and father and their joint lineage. Think of all your personality traits you have picked up. Patterns of speech, attitudes, mannerisms, emotional reactions, likes, and dislikes are all handed down via parental influence. Whether you love and respect your father or feel bitterness towards him, he has been an undeniable influence on your life.

In cases where children are separated from the influence of their biological fathers, they generally gravitate to surrogate Father archetypal energy. The Child energy always seeks some form of guiding or parental authority. Male primary school teachers are a rich source of Father archetypal energy, especially for girls, as is the local sports coach for boys.

It is up to people with the Father archetype to be aware of their responsibilities. When they operate on a positive energetic level, they have a lasting and beneficial influence on the lives of many young people. The archetypal Fathers may never know the breadth and strength of that positive influence over the course of their student's lives, but it will be there. Think back to all the positive male role models you've had in your lifetime. Now think back to all the times you told them how good they were and what valuable skills or lessons they taught you. Can you count them on one hand? We touch so many people on an energetic level yet have so little knowledge of our victories and our influence.

**Archetypal Combinations:**

The archetypal energy of the Father combines well with the energy of:

Mentor * Teacher * Carer * Healer * Victim * Mother * Peacemaker * Saboteur * Servant * Child * Guide * King * Knight

**Effective Use of Father Energy:**

- Remember that you do not own your children! They are individuals who grow and mature under your care and guidance.
- You have a duty of care for your children. Live up to that duty and allow your children to be who they wish to be.
- Always be positive in the relationships with your children. Trust and respect them and expect trust and respect in return.
- Be aware that your Father archetypal energy is powerful and influential.
- Remember that your influence extends way beyond your immediate family, so be aware of the children you come in contact with. They may be locking-in to your archetypal energy, both the positive and the negative.

# Fool

Fools behave in foolish ways. Their behaviour may be clever or it may be just plain silly. The Fool does not necessarily mind how his behaviour is judged, just as long as there is the opportunity to be on display. The Fool may have some of the Court Jester energy, some of the Clown energy, some of the Joker energy, and some of the Trickster energy. Fools differ from Court Jesters in that Jesters play the fool to endear themselves to their audiences or to lull them into a false sense of security.

Clowns love to entertain and elicit an emotional response. Jokers tell jokes and make fun of people, especially themselves, to put everyone at ease. Tricksters play tricks and practical jokes on people for personal and peer-group entertainment. The Fool plays the fool because there is an audience. There is no other reason. The Fool is not concerned with entertainment. The Fool just loves to do foolish things.

If Fools use the positive energy of their archetype, they are entertaining. However, the negative energy of the Fool archetype may result in actions of bad taste and annoyance. The Fool loves slapstick. The "crash into things," "knock 'em down," "pie in the face," and "slip on banana skin" routines are all part and parcel of the Fool's behaviour. Fools generally make fun of their misfortune. They are often the victims of their slapstick. They have no need to bring others in on their routines, as they enjoy being the centre of the foolishness. If others do join in the antics, they quickly become props and appendages to the main show.

Fools do not endear themselves to people with certain archetypes. Those with the King and Queen archetype have an especially low tolerance of the Fool archetype. As the saying goes, "Queens do not suffer fools lightly." To those individuals who possess a royal monarch archetype, Fools have no purpose. They are generally not entertaining enough for their tastes, and they are incapable of spying: the two favourite attributes of the Court Jester, who is much prized by the King and Queen. Other archetypes that have a serious and ordered side will also find the Fool both trifling and annoying. These archetypes include the Teacher, Servant, Engineer, Scientist, and Judge.

**Negative Aspects:**

Foolish ~ Silly ~ Mimic ~ Low self-esteem ~ Heckler ~ Nonsense ~ Juvenile ~ Irresponsible ~ Pathetic ~ Not taken seriously ~ Senseless

**Positive Aspects:**

Light hearted ~ Funny ~ Entertaining ~ Element of courage ~ Surprising ~ Self-expression

**Archetypal Energy:**

The Fool thrives on foolishness. There is nothing more thrilling and involving for the Fool than to just be doing foolish things. There is very little purpose to the Fool's behaviour. It is just a natural way of acting. Children are excellent at playing the Fool. Eight or nine year old boys seem to tap into the archetypal energy of the Fool with ease. They only need one true archetypal Fool in their peer group, and suddenly all of them tap into that energy. It then becomes a case of who can do the silliest, most foolish of actions or pranks. Given the right circumstances, this type of behaviour can also be adopted by men of any age. Check out what can happen at a Buck's party or the celebration of a sporting victory.

If you are a Fool and this energy remains positive, then all involved can have an enjoyable and fun-filled time. It is when the negative archetypal Fool energy comes to the fore that irresponsibility and dangerous actions take place. Most accidents occur when people behave recklessly and foolishly. This is the Fool archetype at its most harmful and dangerous, not only to yourself but to your peers or even unsuspecting bystanders.

**Archetypal Combinations:**

The archetypal energy of the Fool combines well with the energy of:

Storyteller * Clown * Trickster * Hermit * Joker * Fairy * Peter Pan Child * Dilettante * Rebel

**Effective Use of Fool Energy:**

- Entertain yourself and your audience with antics that are suitable for the occasion.
- Beware of dangerous and reckless behaviours.
- Be conscious of your other archetypes. Do not confuse responsible and serious situations with occasions that demand the archetypal energy of the Fool.
- Avoid using the archetypal energy of the Fool around people who have the King, Queen, Teacher, Judge, Engineer or Scientist archetype. You may not be appreciated, and your relationships may be at risk.

# Gambler

The popular picture of a Gambler is a person who spends money on the chance of making a larger sum of money. It is of little consequence as to which form of gambling is chosen. That is up to the individual Gambler. Each has his or her favourite, whether it is the pokies, horse racing, sports betting, casino, or lottery. The choice will often come down to convenience, past successes, and the chance to win a large amount on the calculated odds. Most Gamblers are concerned with the winning of money. There may be other prizes on offer, but generally, cold, hard cash is the attraction.

For most Gamblers, their activities are forms of entertainment. For others, it is serious business. For some, the activities are an addiction. If those with the Gambler archetype view gambling as an entertainment, gamble within their means, and are able to refrain from gambling at their choosing, then they are capable of using the positive energy of the archetype. When gambling becomes an addiction, the Gambler is under the control of the negative archetypal energy.

Some individuals with the Gambler archetype may also gamble with their relationships, emotions, business ventures, material possessions, and even their lives. Insurance is a subtle form of gambling. You pay a certain amount of money to alleviate the risk of having an accident or having your possessions broken or stolen. In many cases, this type of gambling is enforced by law. Governments of all persuasions rely on gambling for income or to manage the risk of loss of income. In Australia, over eleven percent of State taxation revenue comes from gambling. It is little wonder that the Gambler archetype is alive and well in modern society when our governments depend on it as much as the gambler does.

**Negative Aspects:**

Addicted to risks ~ Need for a high ~ Something for nothing. ~ Pathological ~ Delusion ~ Self-centred ~ Self-destructive ~ Thrill seeker ~ Reckless ~ Weak ~ Irresponsible ~ Living in hope ~ Dreamer ~ Unbalanced work/reward ethic

**Positive Aspects:**

Healthy risk taker ~ See the big picture ~ Planner ~ Trusting the process ~ Faith in oneself ~ Understanding risk ~ Calculating ~ Statistical ~ Balanced

**Archetypal Energy:**

There is a laziness connected to the energy of the Gambler. In many cases, it represents the notion of getting something for nothing. There is no work and little effort involved. In reality this is not the case, as the vast majority of gamblers lose. However, it is the hope that one day "lady luck" will smile on them and not on someone else. This laziness is modelled from the top, as governments reap the reward of the Gambler's folly. This is such a lazy way of collecting what amounts to a tax on weakness and false promises. This energy filters down through society and encapsulates our value of a free ride, and as we all know, there is no such thing. Somebody must pay, but the promise of instant reward and the attitude "a gambling addiction won't happen to me" obliterates the obvious. Taken to the extreme, the negative energy of the Gambler is harmful, not just for individuals but also for those who depend on those individuals, such as family and business partners.

There is a positive side to the energy of the Gambler. The successful Entrepreneur is the best example of the positive energy of the Gambler. However, all of us use Gambler energy every day. We purchase houses, cars, and household and personal items. We insure for logical risks but not for illogical risks. We send ourselves to work or change jobs in the hope of better achievements and financial rewards. We send our children to be educated in the expectation they achieve socially and academically. We change political parties with the expectation they are likely to reward us financially at tax time or meet our social expectations. We risk our health and safety with our diet, exercise, or the leisure adventures we participate in.

The Gambler archetype relies on judgment. Whether that judgment be intuitive or calculated is not important. Remember, though, if you are a Gambler, it is important to keep everything in perspective and balance all of life's risks and challenges by remaining focused on the positive aspects of everything you hold important to you.

**Archetypal Combinations:**

The archetypal energy of the Gambler combines well with the energy of:

Entrepreneur * Pioneer * Seeker * Warrior * Hero * Heroine * Politician * Alchemist * Explorer * Court Jester * Adventurer * Indulged Child *Rebel

**Effective Use of Gambler Energy:**

- Use your intuition or gut feeling when making major decisions. Deep down inside you know what is right. Trust yourself.
- If you gamble as a form of entertainment, then do so with control and within your means.
- If you are out of control with your gambling, admit you have a problem. Do not delude yourself. There can be no action without admission.
- What is your attitude to monetary wealth? If you cannot handle small amounts of money, why would the universe grant you large amounts?
- Wishing and hoping is just that. This is the energy of the negative Gambler.
- The positive energy of the Gambler calls for a good work ethic, a changed attitude from hope to belief, and action to achieve results.

# God

The God archetype is the epitome of strength and masculine power. If you know someone with a God archetype who does not have physical strength, then that individual is bound to have strength of personality and character. In this aspect, Stephen Hawking is a good example. All that is masculine is represented by the God archetype. From his physicality to his forthright convictions, the God archetype wields power. This power can be used to create wealth, protect all in his sphere of influence, and forge a path of distinction in this physical world. On the flip side, this power may also be used to abuse and denigrate.

The archetype of God is found in people who have an answer to everything. You may be the most knowledgeable or best qualified physicist in the world, yet people with the God archetype still insist they know better than you. It is fruitless and pointless to argue with God archetypes. Their self-esteem is important. If people with a God archetype have a low self-esteem, then the process of boosting it is continual and never-ending. If these individuals have a high self-esteem, and their egos take control, then they never admit defeat or become convinced of making an incorrect decision. The character of Sheldon in *The Big Bang Theory* is the perfect example of an individual with the God archetype.

Those with the archetype of God are extremely persistent. Since they feel they are incapable of making a mistake, they often go to any lengths to prove they are correct. For individuals with the God archetype, time and expense are never a problem when proving they are right. It is the process and satisfaction of winning the argument that is important. This character trait creates a good deal of inflexibility and stubbornness within the person with the God archetype.

If those with the God archetype can be shown conclusively they are incorrect, they find ways around the contradiction. They often blame others for their mistakes and are content to divert discussions into irrelevant side issues to distract from their errors. They never make a verbal or written admission of their mistake, but what they do is make some form of recompense. This may be in the form of a bonus, a gift, or a positive change in a working relationship. This is a subtle form of recognition to the other party, but rarely is an apology forthcoming. Remember, God never makes mistakes, so how could a person with the God archetype make a mistake?

The other trait a person with the God archetype has is the art of projection. This is an excuse for negative behaviour. Those with the God archetype never admit to making mistakes. Therefore, according to them, they never participate in dubious behaviour. If this is the case, and the person with the God archetype is involved in dodgy business transactions, then that behaviour is justified by the excuse that everyone else does the same thing. If a person with the God archetype is having an affair, then it is acceptable because all his friends do the same thing. This projection of negative behaviour is deemed acceptable because of the delusion that it is common practice. Children often excuse themselves with this tactic. The person with a God archetype does exactly the same thing.

Individuals with the God archetype have many positive characteristics. In many cases, their assets are physical prowess. Often their personalities are larger than life. They have a charisma that draws people to them for protection, for knowledge, for power, for opportunity, and for a quest. Many of these individuals are treasured for their wisdom and knowledge. They are generous and often give handsome rewards to those in their service.

**Negative Aspects:**

Despot ~ Autocrat ~ Misogynistic ~ Seducer ~ Self-indulgent ~ Abusive ~ Arrogant ~ Full of himself ~ Hurtful ~ Stubborn ~ Inflexible

**Positive Aspects:**

Working with the power of the masculine spirit ~ Powerful ~ Magical ~ Protector ~ Wisdom ~ Sensuality ~ Embracing ~ Generous ~ Confident

**Archetypal Energy:**

The energy of the God archetype is all about power. People with this archetype see no distinction between God and themselves. They are in charge, not just of their kingdoms but of all realms. They believe their knowledge has no end and their influence has no boundaries.

There are positive aspects to those with this archetype. When their power and wisdom is used with respect and liberal forethought, those with the God archetype are a joy to have in your life. They are generous, protective, and extremely caring. They have the power and the connections to make things happen. They care about their bodies and are especially pleasant to the female who exudes feminine energy.

The negative energy with the God archetype is prevalent with an abuse of power. These people can be prone to anger, sarcasm, denial, bribery, and stubbornness. They cannot be reasoned with for they are never wrong. When confronted with a person in this situation, there is only one effective method. You state your point of view or your course of action and then remain silent. There is no value in any prolonged argument or discussion. On the second occasion for you to speak, you agree with aspects of the God archetype that align with your views, and then reiterate your point of view in a sensible and reasonable fashion. You play politics and keep repeating the same thing over and over until the discussion finishes. There is no point in arguing with the individual who has a God archetype. You can only say what is important to you and maintain that as your authoritative course of action.

**Archetypal Combinations:**

The archetypal energy of the God combines well with the energy of:

Goddess * Queen * Servant * Pilgrim * King * Seeker * Philosopher * Divine Child * Hero * Monk * Priest * Shaman * Angel

**Effective Use of God Energy:**

- Use your power and position for the protection and benefit of those in your sphere of influence.
- Patience, humility and tolerance are all qualities of the highest order and befitting one with strength and might.
- Beware of arrogance. We are all human and have human frailties.

# Goddess

Goddess archetypes are the female equivalents of the male God archetypes. Their energies do differ somewhat. The person with the God archetype is all about masculine energy, physical strength, control, and power—power that is often put to use for admirable causes but power that can also be used for dishonourable causes. Those with the archetype of Goddess are all about the expression of feminine energy. This is a much softer energy than the masculine physical energy. However, the Goddess may also use and abuse her power. Her abuse usually comes in the form of a verbal rage—short, sharp, and to the point.

True feminine energy is about beauty, love, understanding, nurturing, and spiritualism. The Goddess archetype is concerned with all of these energies. Beauty is important for the Goddess. Find a friend with the Goddess archetype, and look at her style of dress (often long and flowing). Look at her physical appearance, and check out how she moves (her walk is more of a glide), and notice how she cares for her diet, her skin, and her hair. She often wears glamorous clothing and takes the time to show others how she respects herself.

Finding love and giving love is important to the Goddess. She enjoys close personal relationships and can move between the extremes of a soft and a fiery temperament. Remember that she has the energy of a supreme being as well as the energy of the feminine spirit. The Goddess archetype favours certain chosen individuals with her attention. She is kind, generous, and caring to these friends and acquaintances. Individuals who are out of her favour are generally berated and ignored.

A source of confusion to the person with the Goddess archetype is her spirituality. Being a Goddess, she has access to the Divine, yet she has chosen to reside in this physical plane. There is frustration with worldly inventions and impatience with the notion of time. This occurs because in the divine world, the Goddess has access to all that she desires, instantly and with merely a thought. On Earth, the Goddess is often dreamy and can be far away on a spiritual plane. She may ponder the pursuit of a spiritual quest on Earth. In the divine world, she has access to all paths. But she is here to experience life in the world of the physical, a life where energy is slow moving and filled with myriad events and personalities.

**Negative Aspects:**

Dreamy ~ Self-indulgent ~ Seductress ~ Autocratic ~ Confused ~ Fiery ~ Selective ~ Extreme ~ Unable to cope with the physical ~ Abusive

**Positive Aspects:**

Working with the power of the feminine spirit ~ Physical grace ~ Sensuality ~ Wisdom ~ Protector ~ Magical ~ Feminine ~ Nurturing

**Archetypal Energy:**

The archetypal energy of the Goddess is of pure feminine energy. People with the Goddess archetype exude sensuality. They are noticed and noticeable, and they have energy that stands out here on the Earth plane. They have knowledge of beauty that radiates through their entire being and spiritual awareness that connects directly with the Divine.

The challenge for the Goddess is to integrate her energy into the mix of other archetypal energies. The Goddess energy is so feminine, and a great deal of the energy on earth is masculine. There are few points of conversion and plenty of points of confusion and diversion. This results with the Goddess having extremes of temperaments and extremes of interests. She can be hard to know. When this frustration builds, the individual with the Goddess archetype can resort to using negative archetypal energy. There may be a torrent of rage, although this is usually short in duration. More likely, though, the Goddess will display her feminine energy and fall into a state of emotional turmoil and self-pity.

If you know you are a Goddess, use your energetic charms for sensual experiences to nurture those around you, to impart wisdom, and for the protection of the feminine spirit. The Goddess is the perfect blend of earthly beauty and spiritual wisdom. As I am sure you know, those with the Goddess archetype love to be treated like a Goddess! In return, they are happy to reward all in their favour with their grace, charm, and spiritual connection.

**Archetypal Combinations:**

The archetypal energy of the Goddess combines well with the energy of:

Princess * Pilgrim * Guide * Lover * Angel * Divine Child * Athlete * Wise Woman * Priestess * God

**Effective Use of Goddess Energy:**

- Remember the Goddess is the perfect example of feminine energy and provides the balance to masculine energy.
- You are the protector of feminine energy. This is your birth right and duty.
- Spread your feminine energy to all those in your sphere of influence.
- You are here to experience the physical nature of this earth. Do not be confused or seduced by it.
- Remember you are a spiritual being with a direct link to the Divine. Assist those who come to you for spiritual guidance.

# Guide

The Guide is the shining light of a spiritual pathway. Those with the Guide archetype have the ability to directly access spiritual knowledge and wisdom. They use this ability to enhance their personal spiritual growth and to teach and inform others. The Guide leads by example. The positive energy of the Guide assists others by making knowledge, information, and guidance available but never infringes upon an individual's free will. Jesus is the perfect example of the Guide archetype. Jesus showed a way to spiritual growth and enhancement. He may have displayed human frailties, yet he never lost sight of his purpose and his ability to radiate the positive energy of the Guide.

Guides, using the positive archetypal energy, are never dependent on the results of their teachings. Their purpose is to tap into spiritual information. The rule is to walk the walk and talk the talk and allow others to use that knowledge freely and without interference. Guides never allow their egos to dictate a position of power or impose on those who come to them for help. The person who takes on guru status without due experience is using the negative energy of the Guide archetype. If a structure or power is condoned by Guides, they are using negative archetypal energy. This action becomes a product of the ego. This is personal glorification.

A common scenario of negative Guide energy is shown with exclusivity and dogma. This happens when the Guide or the Guide's followers form a group that has boundaries, conditions of entry, and strict models of belief and behaviour. This packages spiritual knowledge and belief into a structure. This structure then defines a spiritual club. Religious organizations, churches, cults, and various New Age groups have this structure. The leader is given status. There is a hierarchical structure and a dogma. There are conditions of entry and of belonging, rules of behaviour, and the concept of salvation. This structure is suitable for the Disciple, the Priest and Priestess, the Pilgrim, and the Monk.

The Guide who uses the positive energy of this archetype has no place in such a structure. The Guide's message is free to everyone. It is given unconditionally. It is given without fear or favour.

**Negative Aspects:**

Manipulative ~ Self-importance ~ Tunnel vision ~ Arrogant ~ Intolerant ~ High and mighty ~ Grandiose ~ Controlling ~ Expectant ~ Dependent

**Positive Aspects:**

Channelling ~ Responsive ~ Self-fulfilment ~ Leadership ~ Showing the way ~ Knowledge ~ Informative ~ Example ~ Model ~ Humble

**Archetypal Energy:**

The archetypal energy of the Guide revolves around spiritual connection and setting personal examples. We all have the power to tune into our spiritual selves. The Guide has this power and ability in abundance. This is no different to the elite athlete, the successful entrepreneur, or the recognized artist. These people are all at the high end of achievement, but it is how potential is transformed into achievement and how the following success is handled that determines whether the archetypal energy used is positive or negative.

The positive energy of the Guide determines a strong spiritual connection and continuing spiritual awareness. Those with the Guide archetype have a commitment to utilize that energy. It is important for Guides to be aware they are examples of all spiritual expression. They are the spiritual models who educate others not only through their teachings but also through their roles as guiding spiritual lights. The positive energy of Guides does not seek power or loyalty. They pass on their spiritual knowledge and message and are not dependent on any outcome.

If you are a Guide, you are likely to have a solitary and lonely existence. If you find you have followers, never accept status and adoration, as you will be susceptible to negative patterns from the ego. Negative energy encourages power, authority, exclusivity, rules, and dependence. The person with the Guide archetype has to walk the fine line that encourages independence and not fall for the emotional allurement of attachment and adoration.

**Archetypal Combinations:**

The archetypal energy of the Guide combines well with the energy of:

Martyr * Mystic * Shaman * Hero * Warrior * Healer * Divine Child * Angel * Mentor * Advocate * Goddess * Seeker * Teacher * Storyteller * God * Prophet

**Effective Use of Guide Energy:**

- You are the ultimate spiritual messenger. Develop that ability to communicate with consistency and objectivity.

- Be the example of spiritual independence. You are a spiritual shining light in a world of physical and emotional dominance.

- Be wary of the ego. Avoid the allure of power, control, position and status.

- Avoid the temptation to impose structure, rules, dogma, expectation and obedience.

# Healer

There are many different types of healers, and those with the Healer archetype come from many different walks of life. Within the healing fraternity, there are professionals, semi-professionals, and amateurs. Healers deal with repairing or changing conditions that are deemed to be out of synchronization. Some Healers deal with a combination of the physical, emotional, psychological, and spiritual. Healers could include medical specialists, such as radiologists, anaesthetists, physiotherapists, psychologists, psychiatrists, and general-practice medical doctors. They could also include herbalists, naturopaths, masseuses, spiritual therapists (using techniques such as Reiki and Bowen), and tarot readers.

People with the healing archetype have a pervasive interest in assisting others. They may also have a deep fascination with the human condition and all its multidimensional aspects. When Healers use their knowledge and skill and have the pure intention of assisting their clients, they are fulfilling their archetypal functions in a positive manner. When Healers take advantage of clients or go beyond the realms of their knowledge and skill, they are using negative archetypal energy patterns.

**Negative Aspects:**

Sympathetic ~ False claims ~ Prey on vulnerability ~ Live through others ~ Takes advantage of the client or system ~Abuse of position or power ~ Greedy ~ Pretence ~ Boastful

**Positive Aspects:**

Vocation ~ Calling ~ Mission ~ Empathetic ~ Channel ~ Advocate ~ Gifted ~ Serve others ~ Caring ~ Knowledgeable ~ Skilled

**Archetypal Energy:**

Usually people with the Healer archetype do not deny themselves the opportunity to assist others. It is an intricate part of their psyche. Most Healers have a natural and intuitive ability to detect discomfort and disease. They use their knowledge, training, and expertise to inform and instruct their clients. They suggest the best methods and treatments known to them to change their clients' discomfort and disease. If Healers are not practicing at a personal level, they are likely teaching others their methods. This is also part of the Healer energy.

The knowledge, experience, and skill level of the Healer plays an important role in the well-being and welfare of the patient. However, there are other factors. Another part of the healing process is determined by the intentions and condition of the patient. Some medical conditions heal naturally with only slight intervention. Broken bones, for instance, mend in correct formation after the Healer has realigned them. There are treatments and medicines that can assist with the severity of symptoms for the duration of a disease.

However, the most successful healings are a partnership between Healer and patient. If there are issues not resolved by the patients, then no amount of medical intervention or healing treatments are likely to change their circumstances. As an obvious example, if a patient with emphysema refuses to give up smoking, then the chances of recovery are minimal. From an archetypal point of view, there are many patterns that restrict recovery or growth. If patients have a strong Martyr archetype and continually use the negative patterns of that archetype, there are bound to be physical, emotional, or psychological conditions that will not be alleviated without the knowledge and understanding of how they operate and, more importantly, willingness on their behalf to effect change.

Healers have to be aware of this fifty-fifty partnership. It is important for the Healer to have an understanding of the patients' point of view. The one-size-fits-all approach fails to acknowledge the individual differences, attitudes, and personality traits of each patient. The need of modern medicine to adhere to a rigid system, to limit patient consultation time, or to seek the one miracle drug or treatment is one of the reasons why modern medicine fails many of its clients. It is also a reason why alternative healing is gaining acceptance. The alternative Healer has more opportunity to work with the patient, not only on the symptoms but also the causes of disease.

All Healers have to be aware of their own behavioural patterns that condone arrogance, paternalism, greed, and systemic failure. Various systemic situations may be out of the control of the Healer, but if you are a Healer, it is your responsibility to use all the positive energy of the Healer archetype and bring into balance all factors that operate around your patient. This is not only for the good of the patient, but ultimately, for the good of the Healer.

Another result of this Healer/Patient partnership is awareness by the Healer that all clients may not respond to treatment. The strong negative energy of various archetypes, such as the Martyr, the Victim, the Damsel, the Addict, and the Prostitute, establish such a strong, self-destructive pattern of behaviour that no amount of intervention can bring change. If there is no willingness on the part of patients to change, then Healers must accept this and be prepared to have limited influence with those patients or allow those patients to leave their care.

**Archetypal Combinations:**

The archetypal energy of the Healer combines well with the energy of:

Carer * Servant * Shaman * Scientist * Rescuer * Wizard * Witch * Seeker * Detective * Pioneer * Priest * Priestess * Teacher * Mentor

**Effective Use of Healer Energy:**

- Use your gift, knowledge and skill for the good of the patient and not for the enhancement of ego, position or power.
- Remember that healing is a partnership between Healer and patient.
- Keep in mind your own personal health issues. Be aware that self-neglect can affect your physical, emotional, psychological and spiritual health.
- Do not confuse sympathy with empathy.

# Hedonist

The Hedonist enjoys the finer pleasures in life. People with this archetype seek out the very best that life has to offer. This may be good food, fine wine, the very best in service and accommodation, proper manners and protocol, sensual and sexual gratification, trendy clothes, and the latest technology. Hedonists like to indulge themselves. They delight in a classy restaurant with an exquisite menu and wine list. They stay at five star hotels. They delight at being pampered with massage, beauty therapy, and other services that offer style. They enjoy the protocols of being treated with dignity and respect. Brand labels are a necessity, and they always utilize the latest technical advances, be it in communication, transport, or entertainment.

Please do not have an impression that the Hedonist archetypal energy is only for the rich and famous, although many of these people do have the Hedonist archetype. The Hedonist archetype is alive and well and is represented in all walks of life. Hedonists, perhaps surprisingly, are likely to be next-door neighbours. Their circumstances may dictate various restrictions and limitations with their indulgences, but their priorities always lead them to the very finest of pleasures. They may take their responsibilities and obligations very seriously. However, if there is an opportunity to indulge, it is always done in style and with the finest in terms of quality. In fact, the motto of the Hedonist is "quality rather than quantity."

**Negative Aspects:**

Indulgence ~ Pretence ~ Aloofness ~ Pride goes before a fall ~ Holier than thou ~ Pushing the boundaries ~ Debauchery ~ All that glitters is not gold ~ Unhealthy ~ Snobbery ~ Living beyond your means

**Positive Aspects:**

Quality ~ Striving for the best ~ High standards and expectations ~ Satisfaction ~ Nothing but the best ~ Gourmet ~ Expectation ~ Bringing out the best ~ Enjoyment ~ Lavish ~ Grandeur ~ Stylish

**Archetypal Energy:**

The Hedonist seeks quality in every aspect of life. This quest is natural to the Hedonist, almost second nature. There is never a question of lowering expectations. The Hedonist expects quality, demands it, seeks it out and participates only when that quality meets expectations. There is no "second rate" for the Hedonist. Those with the Hedonist archetype have to remember that we all live according to our incomes. From the very rich to the relatively poor, the energy of the Hedonist still dictates style, taste, and indulgence. Income will dictate the extent and opportunity of that indulgence.

The Hedonist likes to be in control. To achieve such high expectations, one needs to follow an ordered path. There should be nothing haphazard and nothing should be left to chance. Adaptability is a dilemma to the Hedonist, and structure is considered a much better option. This is not to indicate that the Hedonist is not into fun times, quite the opposite. Hedonists seek out pleasure and good times, but it is important to them that there is no distraction to divert them from the path of these good times. Order, position, and hierarchy lead to applicable standards and the delivery of quality, which is there to be enjoyed. Life for the Hedonist should be like the service at a five-star resort or an exclusive club. The structure is in place. The hierarchy of personnel and services is established and can be relied upon. The very best is offered. If there is a service that you want specifically for your needs or indulgence, it is usually accommodated. When order and quality is the norm, the Hedonist is satisfied.

**Archetypal Combinations:**

The archetypal energy of the Hedonist combines well with the energy of:

Lover * Dilettante * King * Queen * Prince * Princess * Damsel * Servant * Indulged Child * Politician * Actor * Diva * Narcissist * Craftsperson

**Effective Use of Hedonist Energy:**
- Be discerning and selective.
- Live within your means.
- Enjoy the energy of the Hedonist. Do not feel guilty by the jealousy of others.
- Never flaunt or preach.
- Use the positive energy in as many areas of your life as possible.

# Hermit

People with the Hermit archetype have the burning desire to have time by themselves. They are content with their own company. They are not always anti-social. They may be active in their communities, yet there are times when they yearn for the solace of their own space and the company of their own thoughts. Hermits have their special "caves." Often this is within the home, probably a bedroom or study. This becomes a private place, away from other family members and friends. Difficulty may arise if Hermit children share a bedroom. If one of them has the Hermit archetype, then other special places have to be found. Often, if the Hermit child's sanctuary is not within the home, they find a special place outdoors such as a cubby house, the branch of a favourite tree, the chook shed, the vegetable garden, the bank of a creek, or even a drain.

There are several reasons why Hermits desire time in their sanctuaries. Safety is a prime consideration. They feel safe within the confines of their own space and company. They are free from social obligation and duty. There is no need to please others or compromise beliefs. They are safeguarded from listening to and taking on the opinions of others. They are released from the emotional binds of relationships. They can be at peace with their own thoughts and habits without fear of judgment.

A person with strong Hermit archetypal energy seeks solitude. These people are usually homebodies. They often find employment and entertainment that can be done at home. Modern technology is a real bonus to these Hermits. There are many ways of using computers to generate an income from the home or place of residence. The modern world has provided Hermits safety in their sanctuaries and the means to communicate at their convenience.

Hermits are not necessarily antisocial. Often they seek isolation to recover and regenerate their energy. Some Hermits may lead busy lives, and their time alone allows them opportunities to recharge their batteries, contemplate their direction, and review relationships. At different stages of our lives, the process of taking time out is important for all of us. For Hermits, it is a most normal and essential part of their lives.

**Negative Aspects:**

Fear ~ Introvert ~ Antisocial ~ Alienate ~ Eccentric ~ Paranoid ~ Lonely ~ Lack of Fulfilment ~ Lacking social skills ~ Isolated ~ Self-absorbed ~ Intimidated ~ Self-obsessed ~ Inhibited

**Positive Aspects:**

Choice ~ Reflective ~ Working with the creative energy ~ Solitude ~ Selective ~ Self-sufficient ~ Illumination ~ Regenerate ~ Peace of mind ~ In control

**Archetypal Energy:**

The archetypal energy of the Hermit represents the satisfaction of being in control. Hermits seek control over their environments and lifestyles. This gives them safety and security in the pursuit of relaxation or regeneration. It shuts out the external world and the myriad complications that come with it. It simplifies relationships. It allows Hermits to focus on single issues rather than having to deal with a multitude of tasks. It allows the physical to rejuvenate. It allows peace to form spiritual connections.

There may be a social disconnection on the part of the Hermit, such as a social immaturity or other conditions. We live in a complex society. The demands placed upon each individual are ever-increasing. We all have mechanisms to help us maintain our composure and keep us mentally healthy. If social disconnection occurs, it may represent a balanced course of action. The Hermit archetypal energy demands time alone. It demands time where social demands are minimized. The key is to understand that this disconnection is a positive action. It may be rewarded with improved mental stability and enable the individual to refocus. The challenge is to maintain balance. Time alone is used to generate greater self-esteem and not be overwhelmed by obsession, self-absorption, and introspection. If the latter persists, it may lead to a state of depression. Depression is a lonely place and not a recommended mental condition. It is important to realize we are social beings, and on many occasions, we are reliant on the support of others.

If you are a Hermit, you have probably found a niche in society that allows you to function at full capacity. After the completion of your daily tasks, you probably slip home to peace and quiet to renew and regenerate your energy. Tune in to your intuitive awareness, and find the right time for renewal. There are circumstances in all of our lives when we desire to take a breath. This is when we tune into the Hermit archetypal energy. The regeneration or reflection may be short in duration. It may be in meditation, in losing yourself with a good book, or by taking a walk along the beach or through a park. It may be a longer time, such as a holiday or retreat. However, it allows us that moment in time to "clear the decks" and continue life with vigour and purpose.

**Archetypal Combinations:**

The archetypal energy of the Hermit combines well with the energy of:

Mystic * Monk * Shaman * Scholar * Computer Nerd * Divine Child * Scribe * Philosopher * Prophet * Nun * Priest * Artist * Priestess * Wanderer

**Effective Use of Hermit Energy:**

- Use the Hermit energy to reinvigorate and regenerate.
- The Hermit energy should not be used as an escape from commitment or social interaction.
- Develop that special place and time when you can be at peace and shut out the world.
- Develop the ability to live in the moment, even though that moment may be in the midst of social involvement and activity.

# Hero ~ Heroine

In today's world, the word "hero" is used far too often. The mass media are constantly guilty of this, particularly when applied to sport stars and entertainment icons. Many of these so-called heroes are just doing their jobs, doing what they love and what they have been trained for. Synchronous circumstances and their involvement in popular, cultural activities combine to make them "man or woman of the moment." They score the winning goal in the Grand Final, run or swim the race of their lives and win a gold medal, or perhaps they combine their talents with a great script and a creative film director and win an Oscar for their role in a blockbuster movie. Popular culture nominates these individuals as heroes, although all they have really done is utilize their skills, opportunities, and the archetypal Hero energy. This energy is universal and available to all of us.

There are many examples of individuals performing acts of courage or extraordinary feats. The soldier in the heat of battle, the fireman rescuing the elderly from a nursing home fire, and the mother protecting her child are just a few examples. Even though these people have drawn upon the Hero energy, they do not necessarily have the Hero archetype. Circumstances, survival mechanisms, and individual traits have combined to utilize the Hero energy.

People with a Hero archetype use it on a regular and consistent basis. They may be top sportspersons, film stars, rock icons, or national leaders, but just as likely they are a neighbour, cousin, or work mate. They are individuals who take risks. They are the first to volunteer for a difficult task. They enjoy challenges. They perform feats while others watch in awe and fascination. They are comfortable with being in the limelight. Heroes rarely doubt their own abilities.

**Negative Aspects:**
Afraid to move ahead ~ Fear of failure ~ Panic ~ Anxiety ~ Overprotective ~ Rejection ~ Having to prove yourself ~ Manipulative ~ Superior ~ Reckless ~ Playing to the audience ~ Lonely ~ Boastful ~ Arrogant ~ Vengeful

**Positive Aspects:**

Leadership ~ Solitary journey ~ Decisive conviction ~ Working for others ~ Perseverance ~ Determination ~ Courage ~ Humility ~ Leading by example ~ Inspiring ~ Confidence

**Archetypal Energy:**

The archetypal energy of the Hero is all about courage, leadership, and the will to succeed, no matter the cost. Courage is the element of determination that overrides fear. Fear can still be present in the most courageous of individuals, but that fear does not overcome the determination to succeed. Courage pushes an individual to the limits, where deeds, feats, and achievements are made into reality. Courage is a more powerful motivation than the fear of physical pain. Courage determines emotional strength and is a greater force than the fear of failure. Age is not a determining factor. The hero archetype is as present in Jessica Watson as it is in Aung San Suu Kyi or was in Nelson Mandela or Mother Teresa.

Heroes lead by example. Theirs may be a singular journey, such as the lone yachtsperson, the mountaineer, the astronaut, the balloonist, or the deep-sea diver. Though they seem to walk alone, their progress is keenly followed by many and admired by many. It raises the energy of a family, a community, a country, and the human race! Not all Heroes are famous or recognized, but they are the daredevils of a group and the people surrounded by friends, acquaintances, and admirers. They have a positive impact on those around them.

The Hero archetype can inspire others through leadership. It may be in the pursuit and achievement of individual or group goals. Tapping into that archetypal Hero energy can lift any group or organization. If the leadership is provided, then others follow.

A distinct aspect of the Hero archetypal energy is aloneness. Although the Hero may or may not be surrounded by companions, the Hero is always alone. The Hero has the responsibility. The Hero is the person who takes up the challenge when others walk away. The Hero is the person who makes the tough decisions and takes action. The Hero is the person who determines where the buck stops. In the end, the responsibility of any venture undertaken by Heroes rests on their shoulders and their shoulders alone.

The negative energy of Heroes is expressed in their recklessness and their manic need to succeed. As Heroes are not fearful of physical injury, they often indulge in acts of irresponsibility. They become a danger, not just to themselves but also to others. Heroes are often single-minded. They do not see the danger in a quest or a venture, just the thrill and the success.

They may also take a course of action that injuries, disregards or dispenses with others who stand in the way. Heroes can be ruthless and vengeful, and their single-mindedness dictates that the end justifies the means.

**Archetypal Combinations:**

The archetypal energy of the Hero combines well with the energy of:

Adventurer * King * Queen * Knight * Scientist * Warrior * Guide * Athlete * Servant * Peacemaker * Prophet * Witch * Wizard * Teacher * Shaman * Diva

**Effective Use of Hero Energy:**

- The productive power of Hero energy is in leadership. Use that leadership for the improvement and betterment of yourself and the group you influence.
- Show courage at appropriate opportunities.
- Be wary of recklessness.
- Be careful of the ego and of deeds used only to glorify.
- Be humble.
- Have respect and consideration for people who come from a different point of view.

# Joker

The Joker is one of the archetypes that depend on wit and humour. The others are the Court Jester, the Fool, The Clown, the Puck, and the Trickster. Jokers are very much like Court Jesters in the manner of their humour. Individuals with these archetypes are very good at making fun of their own looks, abilities, and personalities. They are the experts at self-deprecation. They do this to ease themselves into social settings and to allow everyone in their company to relax and feel comfortable. When the foundations of friendly relationships have been established, Jokers feel comfortable turning their humour onto others to test the strength of their relationships. If all the participants are comfortable with the wit and humour of the Joker, then the social protocols have been tested and agreed to.

The Joker uses wit and humour to establish a relationship and enliven a social setting. This differs from the Court Jester who uses a similar type of humour but does so to gauge people's reactions. The Court Jester is interested in testing the opinions of others, understanding their thoughts, and seeing how far they can be pushed. The Joker is more interested in finding suitable company in each social setting.

The Joker is also like the Trickster in that they both are involved with practical jokes and tricks. The difference is in rationale and intensity. The Trickster goes to a lot of trouble to put his deception into place. The Joker does things on the spur of the moment. Tricksters love an audience to witness their art, their cleverness, and their superiority over their victims. Jokers, however, are more content with furthering a relationship. Often their tricks and jokes are part of the bandy that goes back and forth within a relationship. No audience is needed. There is no need for a show of superiority. It is more of a gesture to balance the relationship.

**Negative Aspects:**

Over-the-top ~ Hurtful ~ Offensive ~ Low self-esteem ~ Foolish ~ Sarcastic ~ Put downs ~ Egotist ~ Mimic ~ Inane ~ Lacking confidence

**Positive Aspects:**
Funny ~ Clever ~ Insight ~ Witty ~ Placing people at ease ~ Light-hearted ~ Amusing ~ Life of the party ~ Understanding ~ Humorous

**Archetypal Energy:**

The archetypal energy of the Joker is all about adopting wit and humour to enliven a social setting or a relationship. Articulation, cleverness, and light-hearted entertainment are all used by the Joker to place people at ease. The Joker is articulate. Jokers use language with cleverness and purpose. They can tell a joke, make a funny comment, deliver an insight, and bring ease and relaxation to a relationship or social gathering.

Once you establish relationships with Jokers, they are fun to have around. They make good company. It is not just their wit and humour. Jokers also have a strong desire to enhance a relationship. In this regard, they are considerate of others and the dynamics of a relationship.

The negative energy of the Joker comes to the fore when the individual falls into a state of constant self-deprecation or even depression. It is important for the Joker to understand that to be funny and witty all of the time is an onerous task. When Jokers fail to live up to their expectations or the expectations of others, they can fall into a state of perceived failure.

Unlike the other archetypes that have wit and humour as their mainstay, the Joker does not rely on a performance. The Court Jester, the Puck, the Fool, and the Trickster all desire an audience to confirm their wit and cleverness. This allows them to turn off humour and divert their minds to other matters.

Jokers have the urge to be funny all of the time. Learning to switch off is important. A relationship does survive without constant humour. A social event can be a success without the need for jokes and amusement. The Joker has to be discerning. There is a time and place for their humour. It can be intermittent. It does not have to be constant. Understanding this takes the pressure off the Joker and removes the risk of self-deprecation and depression. It also keeps the Joker fresh with material that is suited to the occasion and to the gathering. There is no need to fill the void with inappropriate jibes or sarcastic put-downs.

**Archetypal Combinations:**

The archetypal energy of the Joker combines well with the energy of:

Court Jester * Trickster * Puck * Fool * Actor * Artist * Companion * Disciple * Adventurer * Peter Pan Child * Detective * Magician * Rebel * Father * Mother

**Effective Use of Joker Energy:**

- Use your wit and your humour to relax and entertain others.
- Understand your role is not that of a performer but more of a social advocate.
- Be aware of the appropriateness of your dialogue and your jokes.
- Timing is everything, so understand that there is a time and a place for wit and humour and a time and a place for serious discussion.

# Judge

The Judge archetype is found in people from various walks of life. It goes without saying that the individuals who sit as judges from the High Court down to the local court have this archetype. However, you also find the Judge archetype in teachers, business people, police, politicians, and diplomats. Many of these individuals have a strong Judge archetype and are required to use it strenuously at all times. We all remember the teachers at school who were sticklers for the rules and displayed strong arbitration skills. We understand that those in business rely on their judgments to make decisions that return a profit. The police are often placed in situations where their judgments and decisions have life-and-death consequences. Politics is a matter of judgments and priorities. Diplomats have skill and judgment to engage in effective conversations and decisive courses of action.

Rules! To individuals with the Judge archetype, rules are important. They are the very essence of how we live, and they are designed to create order and clarity out of discord and chaos. Society, institutions, and sporting games all depend on rules and adherence to strict codes of behaviour. Our society imposes rules for our own safety. How could we drive cars if there were no road rules? There are rules for social harmony. How would we know how to interact if there were no social rules of engagement?

People with the Judge archetype are usually found in positions of authority and power. This belief in social harmony and the implementation and adherence to regulation pushes these people to high rungs on the hierarchy of order and stability. If you believe in regulation and generally obey rules, you are likely to be trusted with a position to enforce those rules.

A sense of justice is another important aspect for those with the Judge archetype. As the famous quote from Lord Hewart goes, "Justice should not only be done, but should manifestly and undoubtedly be seen to be done." Therefore, the individual with the Judge archetype is keen to reward and punish. If you do the right thing and obey the rules, you are rewarded with praise and gifts. If you do the wrong thing, you are punished. Justice is done and is seen to be done. The positive aspect of this archetype is demonstrated in the individual who is prepared to balance that sense of justice and make it overtly universal.

**Negative Aspects:**

Rigid ~ Critical ~ Controlling ~ Perfectionism ~ Intolerant ~ Harsh ~ Biased ~ Self-critical ~ Judgmental ~ Lofty ~ Hypocritical ~ Prejudice ~ Open to bribery ~ Tainted ~ Corrupt

**Positive Aspects:**

Compassionate ~ Wisdom ~ Balance ~ Discernment ~ Mercy ~ Protocol ~ Detachment ~ Universal ~ Learned ~ Justice ~ Fair ~ Insightful ~ Good listener ~ Controlled ~ Independent

**Archetypal Energy:**

The archetypal energy of the Judge is about justice. Justice is the essence of this energy. There have always been laws, statutes, rules, regulations, protocols, and correct ways of doing things, but it is the implementation of this governance that gives the Judge his or her true worth. Justice is about balance, balance between the rights of an individual and the rights of the community. Discernment, independence, and wisdom are all used to maintain this balance. This is not just about the judge who sits in court. It is about politicians who make laws for the betterment of their countries and not just for their constituencies or individual grandeur. It is about the teacher who treats all students with respect and fairness. It concerns the mother who can love and devote herself to the needs of all her children. It is about the business that is ethical and genuinely interested in each and every customer. Justice is universal and independent of bias and prejudice.

Rules are important to those with the archetypal energy of the Judge. I have a Judge archetype. It is in my seventh astrological house, which concerns partnerships. My dear wife, Robyn, is the most non-judgemental person I know. She is accepting of everyone, finds competition overvalued and unnecessary, and is occasionally happy to bend the rules. We never play a game. Cards, scrabble, monopoly, and tennis have always ended abruptly. The Judge in me believes that if you are going to play sport or a game, then you stick to the rules; otherwise, there is no point in playing. The total absence of any Judge archetypal energy in

Robyn says that you play for fun, and you should change or ignore the rules as you see fit. Hence, our inability to cooperatively play games!

Discernment is another aspect of the Judge energy. If you have a Judge archetype, you are the individual who is a good problem solver. You are trusted in giving guidance. You are adept at solving disputes and getting to the truth of the matter. You are relied upon for your leadership skills and your sense of fairness. The positive energy of the Judge allows you the ability to step back from a situation, take an objective look, and give sound and fair advice.

**Archetypal Combinations:**

The archetypal energy of the Judge combines well with the energy of:

Peacemaker * Teacher * Servant * Advocate * Guide * Scientist * King * Queen * Mother * Father * Politician * Detective * Hero * Diplomat * Wise Woman

**Effective Use of Judge Energy:**

- Use your wisdom, discernment and compassion.
- Justice and fair judgments are all about balance.
- Independence is a gift and a virtue, so remember that you, personally, are never part of the solution. If you are, then you become part of the problem.
- Justice should be universal. Vested interests make it unbalanced.
- Are you able to place yourself in another's shoes and understand his or her decision-making process?

# King

The King is in charge. People who have the King archetype are leaders and decision makers. Watch them as they enter a room. They have a presence and a purpose. They instinctively understand what needs to be done and intuitively take control. Many people find the archetypal energy of the King to be overwhelming and, at times, abrasive. Both Kings and Queens can be bossy. This is not always deliberate. More often than not, it is the King's intent on putting plans into action and delivering a result. If others are not willing to be part of that plan, then to the King, they are a hindrance to be either ignored or removed. Kings are natural leaders. Using the positive archetypal energy, they can achieve great things and unite their whole kingdom with a common purpose.

Every King has a kingdom. It does not have to be a country, province, or territory as ruled by historical Kings. It may be a business, a classroom, an office, or a home. The size of the kingdom is not a concern so long as the King has his territory and a pathway to greatness. His achievement may be in the form of expansion. This is never a problem if the kingdom is a business that can be transformed, expanded, and developed. However, conflict does arise if the territory is too small or where there is more than the one King or Queen wanting control. Here is the perfect example. The husband with a King archetype and the wife or partner with a Queen archetype have a good understanding of what each should control and where their individual kingdoms lies. What if they both enjoyed cooking? From time to time, the kitchen becomes disputed territory and the cause of many a disagreement and verbal joust.

This is just a minor example of a territorial dispute. Unfortunately, history is full of examples of major territorial disputes. Some arise within a kingdom where the usurper takes action to gain control. Others arise where a stronger kingdom makes moves to overwhelm a weaker kingdom. It is important for Kings to understand and respect territorial boundaries. The kingdoms involved may be large entities like countries or states, or they may be small entities like offices, clubs, or homes.

Another lesson for the King to learn is to trust. Most Kings prefer to do the job themselves. This way they know it is done according to their wishes and standards. They also know, in the end, they are responsible for all aspects of governance and any errors come back to them for correction. This makes it a challenge for the King to trust others and delegate responsibilities. But as a kingdom expands, one individual always finds it difficult to control multiple aspects of that expansion. That is why it is important for the King to gather two or three devoted confidants, delegate authority, and communicate regularly and effectively. That is the secret for the King to achieve his goals and expand his kingdom.

**Negative Aspects:**

Rules the roost ~ Tyrant ~ Controlling ~ Self-centred ~ Arrogant ~ Manipulative ~ Power hungry ~ Self-serving ~ Disempowering ~ Dictator Intolerant ~ Class conscious ~ Condescending ~ Corrupt ~ Warmonger

**Positive Aspects:**

Divine right ~ Benevolent ~ Kind ~ Generous ~ Fertile ~ Empower ~ Protective ~ Pageantry ~ Rich ~ Wise ~ Power ~ Being looked after ~ Respected ~ Leadership ~ Visionary ~ Admired

**Archetypal Energy:**

The archetypal energy of the King is one of vision. The King defines his court and his kingdom and uses his strong energy to mould all within its boundaries. This, of course, means taking control. There is always that fine line that defines control. Control is the balance between achievement and encroachment, between punishment and compassion, and between dictatorship and benevolence. It is the balance in the decision to run roughshod over the courtiers or to empower them. The vision, trust, and individual ethics and values define that energy and how it is used.

The King is always aware of the kingdom. Money in the coffers is especially important. The King is very different from the spending whims and frenzies of the Prince or the Princess. The King waits until the money is there to be spent, or he spends his time and energy to enrich his budget. Only then does spending occur. Spending may be large in volume but only on items or projects that serve or expand the kingdom. Following a purchase, the savings process begins again.

Fall out of favour with the King, and it becomes a difficult task to regain that trust. Kings working in the same business, office, or school have to define their kingdoms and respect the boundaries of others. Other archetypal energies may often run afoul of the King. For example, the Rebel and the Fool are a source of frustration and intolerance to the King. They are not tolerated. The Rebel tests and defies the authority of the King, while the Fool makes fun of it. Never confuse the Fool with the Court Jester. They are very different archetypes. The Fool is never in favour with the King, while the Court Jester is. The Court Jester is the King's spy and confidant and a most useful ally.

The archetypal energy of the King is all about vision and leadership. Using that energy with wisdom and compassion ensures not only a peaceful kingdom but also one that flourishes and prospers. The King's vision, trust, and strength of character determine his success, but it is the King's individual ethics and values that determine his reputation.

**Archetypal Combinations:**

The archetypal energy of the King combines well with the energy of:

Warrior * Servant * Visionary * Athlete * Diplomat * Hero * Pioneer * Banker * Politician * Princess * Explorer * Peacemaker * Court Jester * Networker

**Effective Use of King Energy:**

- Determine your vision, but be adaptable, as circumstances may change.
- Gather two or three trusted confidants, give them responsibilities and trust their abilities and loyalties.
- Be aware of how you treat your subjects. Loyalty is given through respect not subjugation.
- Be aware of your territory and your kingdom. Encroachment into another kingdom always results in conflict.
- If you have the King archetype, remember that it is fine to pamper a daughter who has a Princess archetype, but she also has to be taught responsibility. This is your duty.

# Knight

The Knight is a man on a mission. He is the Adventurer, the Rescuer, and the person you can trust with your life. The Knight is always on the pathway of adventures. They may vary in duration, but the Knight is always determined to see each adventure to its final conclusion. It may be a marriage, building a home, completing a university degree, exploring the wilderness, creating a garden, or even something as simple as helping a friend through a crisis. Often these adventures are filled with challenges. The Knight's determination always rises to the occasion with an aspect of single-mindedness. Whatever is important is achieved while the other aspects of his life are placed on hold.

Many years ago, the Knight's greatest companion and assets were his horse and his weapons. Today the horse has been replaced by the car or motorbike and the weapons replaced by work tools. We all recognize a young man with the Knight archetype. His car is his prized possession. It is distinguishable from other vehicles because of the various additions or because of its exclusive make and model. His car is maintained impeccably and woe betide anyone who dares harm it. The young man with the Knight archetype has his own tools relevant to his position and needs. They are kept in perfect condition and well-organized, with a place for each in his tool box or shed.

The Knight maintains his physical fitness through participation in sport or a rigorous gym regime. Knights are also warriors, so many occupy themselves with team sports where physical contact is important. This is like going to war by testing oneself against rigorous opposition. Some Knights gravitate to martial arts where the contest is a one-on-one battle and the sport is seen to be more elite.

The Knight always defends his friends and often is all too ready for a fight. The negative energy of the Knight is expressed in the modern city in far-too-familiar street brawls or territorial battles. The positive archetypal Knight generally adheres to a code of conduct, hence the involvement in a sport where the rules and the battleground are defined, rather than a random fight where honour may not be so clear.

The Knight is a good companion and a great listener. If your partner has a Knight archetype, you soon become aware of how he is constantly in demand as a rescuer and confidant. Damsels, especially, have an instant recognition and attraction to the Knight. They may desire to fall in love, to be rescued, or to have a shoulder to cry on. In times of stress and weakness, the Damsel always seeks her Knight in shining armour.

Ladies, be tolerant and trusting of your Knight, especially if he is your partner. Understand that your Knight is always looking for adventure and a mission. To maintain the relationship, you may have to become a participant in that next adventure. The Knight often struggles with the mundane, nine-to-five suburban existence. Adventure is in his blood. Be prepared to take the journey together.

**Negative Aspects:**

Absence of honour ~ Lack of chivalry ~ Questions ruler or principle ~ Uncouth ~ Self-neglect ~ Misuse of power ~ Betrayal ~ Power hungry ~ Control ~ Rude Undisciplined ~ Fighting for an unjust cause ~ Lost on a mission ~ Corrupt

**Positive Aspects:**

Service ~ Loyalty ~ Protecting ~ Self-sacrifice ~ Battle for honourable causes ~ The will to see a project to a final conclusion ~ Chivalry ~ Endurance ~ Determination ~ Honour ~ Good listener ~ Trustworthy ~ Discreet ~ Good listener

**Archetypal Energy:**

The archetypal energy of the Knight is about stamina, resilience, and determination. Whatever projects, whatever adventures, whatever missions the Knight accepts, there is a remarkably strong determination to see them to their final conclusions. The tasks may be difficult, painstaking, or damaging to the Knight, and he will not surrender until the bitter end.

When one mission is complete, the Knight engages in a short recovery session and then begins the next task. It is important for the Knight to have this recovery period and his own sanctuary where this rest and regeneration can take place. One good friend of mine has a strong Knight archetype. He has the perfect sanctuary, a small, second-storey room in his house accessible only by a spiral staircase. The room even has small cathedral shaped windows that overlook the lay of his land. This is his sanctuary, his place of retreat, and his watchtower against the world.

The Knight also has the energy of the Rescuer. People are drawn to the Knight, as he always listens to their problems without criticism or emotion. A personal code of conduct and a chivalrous nature are strong within the Knight. Knights are reliable. When you need a hand that requires physical strength, the Knight is always be a willing participant. Loyalty is his other asset. The Knight is a faithful companion and is content to stick with you through both the joys and challenges of life.

The negative energy of the Knight is his misuse of power. The Knight is a warrior. He has physical prowess and mental toughness. These physical and mental attributes are sometimes used to intimidate and humiliate others. He may also indulge in temper tantrums, especially if frustrated or tired and battle weary. The combination of the Knight and the Avenger archetypes may fuel this misuse of power. The Knight may also indulge in philandering, always looking for the next conquest or adventure.

**Archetypal Combinations:**

The archetypal energy of the Knight combines well with the energy of:

Warrior * Athlete * Servant * Advocate * Avenger * Queen * King * Rescuer * Seeker * Prophet * Wanderer * Adventurer * Carer

**Effective Use of Knight Energy:**

- Remember to make your missions honourable.
- Keep to the Knight's code of chivalry and gallantry.
- Find your sanctuary and keep it sacred.
- Remember that rest and relaxation are important to your long-term well-being.
- Consider the broad picture, and do not get caught up in small details or singular considerations.

# Lover

Individuals with the Lover archetype have an enthusiastic zest for life. They have a need to participate in all aspects of this physical world. This reveals itself in the quest for sexual pleasures; enjoyment of good food and fine wine; a deep passion for creative expression; or immersion in occupations or hobbies that explore or challenge the world, such as cooking, landscape gardening, mountain climbing, deep sea diving, or surfing.

Don Juan is the fictional personification of the Lover archetype. Lovers are extremely proud of their sexual prowess and exploits. They revel in the thrill of the chase and throw themselves wholeheartedly into sexual satisfaction for themselves and their partners. As Doctor Frank-N-Furter from *The Rocky Horror Show* says, "I'm not much of a man by the light of day, but by night I'm one hell of a lover." The Lover's involvement in sexual activity may not be motivated by pure selfishness, as Lovers are also interested in the satisfaction of their partners. This motivation may be pure and positive in energetic form. However, it may also be negative and used to boost the ego of the Lover.

Some individuals with the Lover archetype are Leonardo da Vinci, Jacques Cousteau, John Kennedy, and Sir Edmund Hillary. These individuals had the drive and passion to reach the pinnacle of endeavour.

The wonders of the earth are deeply respected by individuals with the Lover archetype. The earth is their playground, and every little bit of it is there to explore, investigate, and use to its full capacity.

People do not need to be famous or well known to have the Lover archetype, although their exploits can lead to notoriety. We all know people who have the Lover archetype. They are likely to be the black sheep of their families, but they have enthusiasm for living and show deep enjoyment and satisfaction with all the physical wonders that surround them.

**Negative Aspects:**

Manipulative ~ Conditional ~ Promiscuous ~ Lack of self-love ~ Unfaithful ~ Selfish ~ Self-gratification ~ Exploitation ~ Seducer ~ Wayward ~ Promotion at the expense of others ~Power hungry ~ Ego driven

**Positive Aspects:**

Passion for life ~ Self-love ~ Comfortable with intimacy ~ Devotion ~ Drive ~ Unconditional ~ Achievement ~ Fascination ~ Motivation ~ Wholehearted ~ Enthusiasm ~ Excitement

**Archetypal Energy:**

The archetypal energy of the Lover is a very strong energy. It is full of passion, physicality, and enthusiasm. People with the Lover archetype make great lovers. They enjoy the sexual experience and have a desire to share that pleasure with their partners. They are comfortable with intimacy and develop and use techniques that seduce their partners into the same mindset. This enthusiasm to enjoy the sexual experience is one of the Lover's greatest assets, but it may also be one of the Lover's greatest weaknesses. This desire for sexual gratification may lead the Lover to a trail of short-term, meaningless relationships. Once the thrill of the chase has gone, the Lover may feel quite at liberty to move on to the next exploit. Often the Lover has several relationships at one time. Maintaining a long-term relationship or partnership with the Lover requires dedication and persistent hard work on the part of both individuals.

If you are a Lover, you can achieve great things. If you can harness that archetypal energy and direct it to a long-term goal, the result will be a product that is meaningful in achievement and accomplishment. It is a case of turning passion and determination into endurance.

Lovers rarely hesitate to act. They are decisive and tend to dive straight into a project, adventure, or conquest. They begin with optimism and enthusiasm and maintain a determination to succeed until satisfaction is gained or another opportunity is presented. Remember, they love all physical pleasures and environments. The emotion of the moment drives them, not considered opinion. Lovers make good company. They have contagious enthusiasm that drives adventure and a spirit of freedom that evokes joy and pleasure.

**Archetypal Combinations:**

The archetypal energy of the Lover combines well with the energy of:

Adventurer * Explorer * Martyr * Peacemaker * Teacher * Politician * Knight * Pioneer * Entrepreneur * Companion * Scientist * Advocate * Peter Pan Child * Hedonist * Athlete * Seeker * Addict * Servant

**Effective Use of Lover Energy:**

- Direct your passion and energy into building relationships and achievements that are meaningful and stand the test of time.
- Beware of your ego and where it may lead you.
- Maintain a balanced diet and a good level of physical fitness, for they are essential in supporting your passions.

# Magician

The Magician is the master of illusion. The individual with the Magician archetype is brilliant at making things appear in a different form or making things seem to be what they are not. Magicians do not change the substance of their subjects, only the appearance. The Wizard and the Alchemist have the archetypal energy to transform and manifest, but the Magician does not have this energy. When the Magician's archetypal energy is invoked, things appear to be different from what they really are. However, when the illusion dissipates, things appear as they always were.

Magicians perform magic tricks. They are performers and actors but usually of quality. As with any performer, they have a stage and an audience. This does not have to be an elaborate stage or a huge audience. The Magician is happy to come to the fore at the family dinner table or at a restaurant. Magicians are not likely to pull a rabbit out of a hat, but they seemingly solve a problem, pose a riddle, and temporarily make problems disappear, or get themselves off the hook for some indiscretion.

Magicians are good storytellers. They excel at make-believe, which is their stock-in-trade. Have you ever come across a salesperson that makes a product sound so idyllic that you must have it? It is the illusion being sold as well as the product. Remember the Magician can change the appearance of something but never the substance. Politicians, diplomats, and salespeople often use the energy of the Magician. Listen to politicians at election time. They are selling themselves or their policies. "Vote for us, and we will magically change your life." Watch a diplomat on television promise to solve this crisis or that conflict. Look behind the scenes of a fashion magazine, and take note of the effort put into advertising, photo shoots, and photo doctoring. All of this effort to create the illusion of a popular style of clothing, make-up, weight loss, beauty treatment, and the rest.

The key to the Magician energy is in the motivation. If it is to be popular, pork-barrelling, or to push an ideology, then the negative aspect of the Magician is invoked. If the motivation is to enlighten and educate society, then positive

Magician energy is invoked. Remember always to check the fine print and disregard the headlines. The Magician cannot deliver the magic fix, only the comfort of illusion.

**Negative Aspects:**

Black magic ~ Deceit ~ Devil worship ~ Illusion ~ False claims ~ Grandeur ~ Trickery ~ Subterfuge ~ Scams ~ Easy money ~ Get rich quick schemes ~ Pull the wool over your eyes

**Positive Aspects:**

White magic ~ Entertain ~ Creator ~ Management of time and space ~ Belief in achieving the impossible ~ Placebo ~ Storyteller ~ Aspiration ~ Inspiration ~ Self-belief ~ Trust

**Archetypal Energy:**

The archetypal energy of the Magician is based around illusion. The power of illusion can create positive outcomes. A Magician who instils the power of self-belief in an individual or those in a group may inspire them to achieve their ambitions. If people believe things have changed for the better or they have the ability to change aspects of their lives, they have taken the first step to actuate real change. This is where the Magician has the power to initiate change as a conduit of aspiration and inspiration.

Magicians who use their archetypal energy for self-promotion or to deceive cross a line into negativity. Magicians have great power. They excel at entertainment; and through mystique and grandeur, they encourage us to visualize the impossible as possible. Magicians grant us the power to imagine and wonder. Think for a moment on the impact of the fictional Harry Potter. Pure entertainment has inspired a whole generation to imagine, wonder, and believe that all things are possible! Now, that is a Magician's power in the most positive archetypal form.

There is much research about the placebo effect. The Magician has the ability to change our thinking, attitudes, and beliefs. This, in turn, gives us the freedom to change our behaviours and paths. The first step in the recovery from a state of ill health is belief in the possibility of changing to a state of good health. This is where the power of magic can be so important and powerful. It is the difference between the belief of the optimist and the belief of the pessimist. Yes! Magic is an illusion, but that illusion can become reality if the belief and action is sufficiently strong and positive.

**Archetypal Combinations:**

The archetypal energy of the Magician combines well with the energy of:

Healer * Actor * Storyteller * Peacemaker * Clown * Shaman * Court Jester * Entrepreneur * Detective * Fairy * Shape-Shifter * Servant

**Effective Use of Magician Energy:**

- Use your magic to inspire and stimulate self-belief in others.
- Remember that fraudulent magic is detrimental to the welfare of others.
- Be entertaining.
- Earn people's trust, and keep it sacred.
- Remember, the impossible becomes possible when positive energy is invoked.

# Martyr

We are all familiar with well-known individuals who have gained notoriety, influence, and fame using the Martyr archetypal energy. These include Jesus Christ, John the Baptist, Socrates, Joan of Arc, Mahatma Ghandi, and Martin Luther King. Many other Christian saints, victims of the holocaust, and various other persecutions suffered the same ultimate fate. Others with the Martyr archetype have managed to survive their trials, but they may have spent the vast majority of their lives fighting their causes. Nelson Mandela and Aung San Suu Kyi are the best modern examples who come to mind. William Wilberforce, who spent over two decades fighting for the abolition of slavery, is another who lived to tell his tale. However, he suffered severe ill health throughout the battle. These people were born with incredibly strong Martyr archetypal energy.

Others possess the Martyr archetype but manage to lead much simpler and well-balanced lives. These are people who just have to do the things that require attention. They are the family members who cook, serve the food, and clean up while the rest of the family sits back and enjoys the festivities. They mow a neighbour's lawn without being asked. They are a friend on your doorstep offering support the moment you fall into crisis. They are the volunteers at an op shop, Good Samaritans who stop to change flat tyres, or children who open their piggy banks and donate their savings to those less fortunate.

All Martyrs have a cause. It may be a simple need that requires attention or a deeply held social or religious belief. The amount of energy devoted to the cause depends on the strength of conviction; that is, how strong is the Martyr archetypal energy within the individual, and what other archetypes combine to enhance that conviction? Very few individuals with the Martyr archetype neglect a cause, and even fewer walk away once a battle has begun.

**Negative Aspects:**

Self-pity ~ Control ~ Manipulative ~ Conditional love ~ Fanatical ~ Obsessed ~ Indulgence ~ Self-harm ~ Low self-esteem ~ Harmful ~ Seeking sympathy ~ Attention seeking ~ Tunnel vision ~ Victim mentality

**Positive Aspects:**

Making sacrifices ~ Inspiring ~ Sacred cause ~ Fighting for just causes ~ Conviction ~ Courage ~ Suffers for the redemption of others ~ Advocate ~ Standing up for the rights of others ~ Unconditional love ~ Endurance ~ Commitment ~ Determination ~ Resilience

**Archetypal Energy:**

The archetypal energy of the Martyr revolves around commitment to a cause. The cause may be small in its effect on people, society, or the environment, but the Martyr generally has the determination and resilience to see that commitment through to an outcome.

Suffering is a common component within the archetypal energy of the Martyr. It may be simple suffering like being put out by something, or it may be major health issues that are physical, psychological, or emotional. In some cases, death is the final outcome. Martyrs are always prepared to suffer for their beliefs and actions. They understand that making sacrifices is part of the process, in the same way that athletes see training as part of their process or mothers see nurturing as part of their process. There is rarely a debate about the suffering, cost, or punishment likely to occur. The Martyr instinctively goes into battle.

The positive energy of the Martyr produces courage, determination, endurance, and resilience. Martyrs are determined to see through the process. They are courageous and determined to endure many a test and trial if that participation contributes to the cause. They are resilient and are prepared to overcome various setbacks and continue their courses of action until the desired results have been achieved. It takes all of these attributes to use the positive Martyr energy.

Negative Martyr energy is displayed when the cause or the means to achieve an end are unjustified. There is a distinction between the Martyr who is willing to die for a cause and the person who proposes that the death of innocent people is justified in achieving an end. Fanaticism does not encourage balance. Self-glorification does not encourage balance. Manipulation does not encourage balance. The Martyr, despite the self-sacrifice, should always remember that issues are not black and white; there are shades of grey in every struggle.

If you have a Martyr archetype, one important lesson to learn is preservation of self. It is important for Martyrs to understand they are an integral part of the cause. This is sometimes difficult to understand, because Martyrs are rarely willing to divert energy away from the just cause into their sense of well-being. However, Martyrs have to realize that without health, strength, and focus, their struggles are weakened. No matter what we take on in life, it is better to approach the task with fitness and health, physically, mentally, and emotionally.

**Archetypal Combinations:**

The archetypal energy of the Martyr combines well with the energy of:

Warrior * Servant * Advocate * Athlete * Teacher * Mother * Father * Nun * Monk * Priest * Priestess * Angel * Celibate * Healer * Politician * Mystic * Pioneer * Peacemaker

**Effective Use of Martyr Energy:**

- Make sure the cause is just.
- As the quote from Edmund Burke goes, "Evil prevails when good men do nothing."
- Be aware of the ego and the temptation of self-importance.
- Gather others of like mind around you to your cause. Many hands make light work.
- Remember you are a part of your cause, so take care of your health.

# Mentor

The Mentor is an old-fashioned archetype that is gradually transforming into the archetype of a Facilitator. The Mentor is the learned individual who shares knowledge with an apprentice. In days gone by, the Mentor would be the craftsman, the artist, the merchant, the mother, the nanny, the teacher, the witch, the shaman, the scribe, the priestess, or the wizard. These individuals possessed the knowledge, wisdom, and experience of their trades. They were special and highly regarded by their families, tribes, or societies. Mentors sometimes offer apprenticeships to the privileged few. They were often family members of the Mentors or sponsored by wealthy individuals. The relationship between the Mentor and the apprentice was often a one-on-one relationship. Sometimes the Mentor would be in charge of a small, selective group of apprentices. The learning was detailed, and often the apprenticeship lasted for several years.

In today's economic climate, we still have an apprenticeship scheme. Builders and trades people take on apprentices, although the mentoring is more general, and the apprentice quickly becomes part of the workforce. These days it is more a case of the sink-or-swim mentality. Teachers take on student teachers, and businesses take on younger employees, who have to work their way through the ranks. The one-on-one approach is not always economically viable, as the bottom line dictates the program of most businesses. So gradually, the Mentor is being replaced by the Facilitator.

Facilitators are organizers who oversee the newer, younger people coming into a business or enterprise. They may be responsible for some training, but often it is the delegation of duties and personnel that is of prime importance. This idea of passing on skills and knowledge to a larger audience has spread to all parts of modern society. There are universities, teachers' colleges, self-help seminars, sporting clubs, yoga clubs, and women and men's groups, to name a few, that all employ a similar routine. The Mentor archetype has become more of an organizer and facilitator than a personal, hands-on-approach tutor.

There are still individuals with the Mentor archetype. You can recognize Mentors if you watch them with young people. They show a special interest in the development and progress of their charges. They are prepared to share their time and knowledge. They are prepared to answers questions and experiment with various options put forward by a young and keen student. These are Mentors of the old-fashioned variety. On the other hand, Facilitators are great at networking and taking larger groups. Their organizational skills are second to none. They are the masters of adaptability and flexibility and, therefore, can arrange for someone else to fill a need if it is not in their power to do so.

**Negative Aspects:**

Leads astray ~ Controlling ~ Self-importance ~ Smothering ~ Manipulative ~ Secretive ~ Bully ~ Overprotective ~ Sarcastic ~ Impatient ~ Abusive

**Positive Aspects:**

Leading by example ~ Sharing ~ Altruistic ~ Protective ~ Idealistic ~ Caring ~ Responsible ~ Organizing ~ Considerate ~ Adaptable ~ Flexible ~ Networking ~ Patience

**Archetypal Energy:**

The archetypal energy of the Mentor is built around patience. We have all had to demonstrate a technique to someone younger or less skilled and experienced than we were. Frustration, impatience, and the desire to finish the job ourselves can hinder the process. It is important to remind ourselves that what is second nature to us is more likely be foreign, mysterious, and exciting to those we are mentoring. Patience is the key. Imagine how Leonardo da Vinci may have felt when confronted with a small group of beginners.

The Mentor has to allow the apprentice an opportunity to find his or her own path. I speak from my own experience as a teacher. For my student teachers, it was imperative I allowed them to discover their own style, find their strengths, work on their weaknesses, and establish their own methods to gain the children's attention. I could show them what worked for me, and I could instruct them on their responsibilities and school policies and methodology, but we needed to strike that balance and give them a chance to be themselves. Teaching is as much about relationships as anything else.

As the role of the Mentor changes into the role of the Facilitator so, too, does the archetypal energy. Organization, flexibility, and adaptability are the key components of the Facilitator's archetypal energy. This is dictated by the demands of the modern era where speed and mass circulation of information are measures of success. The aim today is to get your message out there in the shortest time possible to the greatest number of people. In the past, time was of less concern; student demand was lower in number; and the educative processes were allowed to be complex and intricate, without any great need to rush.

One of the most important energetic qualities that belong to both the Mentor and the Facilitator is the ability to communicate. To pass on knowledge in the most effective and desirable fashion requires the pathways of communication to be constantly open and accessible. That is why relationships are important. Relationships, built on trust and respect, keep those communication pathways open. A pupil-master relationship built upon trust and respect allows a bond to develop that can bridge any divide and endure the test of time.

**Archetypal Combinations:**

The archetypal energy of the Mentor combines well with the energy of:

Teacher * Artist * Craftsperson * Servant * Companion * Mother * Father * Shaman * Angel * Networker * Queen * King * Engineer * Witch * Wizard * Wise Woman * Priestess

**Effective Use of Mentor Energy:**

- Remember that patience is a virtue, and the role of a Mentor requires an abundance of patience.
- Your ability to communicate determines your success.
- Your knowledge is your gift to others, but remember and be open to the idea that others have the ability to educate you.
- Remember pride and pomposities are the pitfalls to failure.
- Even though flexibility and adaptability are necessary qualities, never allow your Prostitute archetype to deny your true essence.

# Monk

Those with the Monk archetype are now far more prevalent in eastern cultures than western cultures. People in North America and Europe have become accustomed to a lifestyle that shuns the simplicity of the Monk energy. The West encourages individual freedom, and capitalism encourages luxury, indulgence, and a must-have attitude. The pleasures of physical indulgence are an intricate part of western philosophy. Even religious zealots and mass-media preachers live a life of comfort. The archetype of the Monk is foreign to such razzamatazz and comfort. Positive Monk energy never engages in indulgence and excess. Most Eastern cultures have so far maintained a tradition of simplicity. Many also place social order above the rights of the individual.

Those with the Monk archetype have a devotion to the Divine. This devotion is expressed both covertly and overtly. Most Monks are identified by their dress. They are comfortable with their overt identification as a person connected spiritually with the Divine. They also participate in the many practices that require prayer with the Divine and focus on their spiritual selves. Spiritual focus for a Monk is a lifestyle. It is not an hour or two spent in prayer. It is a constant that governs every thought and action. For the Monk, every aspect of life is connected to the Divine, from breathing to eating to sleeping.

The archetype of the Monk dictates life is one of service to God or the Divine and service to humanity. This service has prerequisites. The ability to control individual expression is one, and the ability to curb individual freedom is another. This determines a simple lifestyle and focuses on individual introspection rather than espousing individual freedoms and flaunting physical and material acquisitions and successes. A simple lifestyle is the choice the Monk makes and accepts without question.

The tradition of the religious order, the monastery, the habit (monk's robes or clothing), and the shaved head are overt and obvious components of the Monk archetype, but like all other archetypes, the Monk archetype is not restricted to these individuals. The layperson can also possess the Monk archetype. Those of us with the archetype of Judge do not sit in a constituted court, wearing a wig and gown, deciding guilt or innocence. The layperson who has the Monk archetype may not join a monastery or religious order. However, he or she may possess the same archetypal energy and lead a similar, simpler lifestyle. Spiritual purpose and connection, simplicity, humility, and service will all be integral parts of the lifestyle of these individuals.

**Negative Aspects:**

Dogmatic ~ Escapism ~ Fundamentalist ~ Self-disempowerment ~ Self-absorbed ~ Overly pious ~ Self-indulged

**Positive Aspects:**

Connected to order ~ Commitment ~ Sacrifice ~ Sacramental ~ Ritualistic ~ Devotion ~ Dedication ~ Spiritual path ~ Intense focus ~ Service ~ Simplicity ~ Meditative ~ Control ~ Personal growth

**Archetypal Energy:**

The archetypal energy of the Monk is based on humility. To maintain a spiritual pathway and connection to the Divine, it is important for an individual to remain humble. Compare the humble Monk with the larger-than-life television preachers or spiritual gurus—personalities who are full of themselves and who boast of their devotion to God and their spiritual achievements. These zealots have a connection to ego but rarely to God or the Divine. They may fool others, they may even delude themselves, but God is another matter. Visit some of the most lavish and ornate cathedrals, and observe the statutes of gold, the marble altars, and the leadlight windows. As you stand there, you begin to understand that these are shrines to the men who built them. They are not shrines to God. As you stand silently, tune in to the energy. It is like a void, empty and hollow. Humility is a connection to God, peace, love, and contentment.

With humility comes simplicity. The archetype of the Monk requires a simple lifestyle. The purpose of a monastery is to provide a place of sanctuary and retreat away from the distractions and attractions of indulgence. The Monk with a positive energetic focus is strong enough to resist fripperies, even if living in the heart of temptation. With simplicity, humility, and focus, the Monk himself becomes the sanctuary. Through the connection with the Divine, with willpower of purpose, and with the disposition of service, meditation, prayer, and introspection, the Monk finds satisfaction in simplicity.

**Archetypal Combinations:**

The archetypal energy of the Monk combines well with the energy of:

Servant * Priest * Companion * Celibate * Hermit * Carer * Scribe * Craftsperson * Divine Child * Angel * Disciple * Prophet * Peacemaker * Scholar * Coward

**Effective Use of Monk Energy:**

- Focus on your connection with the Divine.
- Continue with a life of simplicity.
- Remain humble, and do not give in to the temptations that the ego craves and desires.
- Remember that none of us is perfect. If you fail in some way, forgive yourself and continue on the path of righteousness.

# Mother

The Mother and Father archetypes contain the most socially influential archetypal energy. It is the Mother energy that acts as a barometer to the nurturing aspect of any tribe or society. In its most positive form, the Mother is the expert at nurturing her children, partner, family, and self. The Father archetype, in its most positive form, is about example and modelling. The role that these two archetypes play in determining the family dynamic and social relationships is critical.

Having children is not a prerequisite for possessing the Mother archetype. Plenty of childless people have a strong Mother archetype, dominated by their nurturing personalities. They are always prepared to care for you; welcome you into their homes; offer food and drink; create engaging conversation; listen attentively; and give advice and physical comfort, such as a hug. It does not matter whether you are a baby, a child, a teenager, or an adult. Age is no barrier, because Mothers are mothers for life, and their caring roles are lifelong commitments they unhesitatingly make.

As there are people with Mother archetype who have never had children, the reverse is also true; that is, there are people who have children, but do not possess the Mother archetype. These people often have a strong Companion, Carer, or Rescuer archetype. The energy of these archetypes will bring out a caring, nurturing nature similar to the Mother archetype. However, the relationship is often more of a partnership. Here, from a younger age, the child takes on more of an adult role, while the parent treats the child, more or less, as an equal. This situation occurs especially between a single mother and her son. Extra responsibility is given to the child. More adult communication is the norm. This happens to fill the void left by the missing adult male.

The Mother archetype is recognizable from a very young age. Children who play with dolls, build or play in cubby houses, spend time helping their mothers around the home, have concern for their friends, and care for their younger siblings all have the Mother archetype. These individuals grow to love being around children and generally gravitate to careers with children. They are active at family gatherings, play groups, schools, sporting teams, and social groups. The instinct of the Mother archetype is to care in one form or another.

There is a fine line between nurturing and smothering. Those with the Mother archetype have to be aware of the distinction. Nurturing is caring and looking after those in your charge. It is also providing a safe environment, healthy food, reassurance, and security. It allows those in your care to be individuals, to learn with freedom, to make decisions, to explore their environments, and to learn about life. Smothering occurs when the Mother does everything for those in her charge, such as when she makes all the decisions, performs the actions the children should do, wraps them in cotton wool, stifles their independence, shows or verbalizes a lack of confidence in their abilities, and watches their every move and actions in a manner that is threatening in its attentiveness.

**Negative Aspects:**

Neglect ~ Abandonment ~ Conditional love ~ Abuse ~ Smother love ~ Control ~ Poor modelling ~ Choosing to live in a dangerous or unhealthy situation ~ Selfish ~ Stifle ~ Blackmail

**Positive Aspects:**

Provider ~ Protector ~ Nurtures ~ Caring ~ Mentors ~ Educate ~ Guide ~ Leadership ~ Selflessness ~ Allows individuality ~ Service ~ Acceptance ~ Encouragement ~ Provides a safe and secure environment ~ Praise

**Archetypal Energy:**

Let us first of all deal with the negative Mother archetypal energy. With the "smother mother" syndrome, mothers rarely understand the negative effect their behaviours have on their children. A son, in particular, is susceptible to becoming the product of a smother mother. This mother does everything for her son including to cook, clean, wash laundry, iron, act as chauffeur, care for his finances, indulge his spending, and give freedom without boundaries. She does this in a desire to be loved and needed, but she eventually discovers her son is a teenager, dependent and out of control. The relationship becomes that of servant and master. He has little ability or desire to care for himself. What does he do now? Live the life of luxury at home until he is well into his adult years? Some do. The alternative is to find a girlfriend or partner just like his mother. He may choose someone to look after him and care for his every need just as his mother did.

Children have to be taught responsibility and independence. They need the opportunity and encouragement to do things for themselves. They require teaching and modelling that allows them to take responsibility for their actions. It is important for Mothers to understand they are mentors and teachers. They are not servants and martyrs.

Second on the list is the neglectful or abusive mother. The neglectful and abusive Mother is bound to a mindset where her individual needs, desires, or challenges are overwhelmingly focused on herself rather than her children. She may abuse them physically, psychologically, and emotionally. Her children become a nuisance and a challenge, and this can lead to perfect conditions for the creation of the Wounded Child. It stands to reason that abusive mothers were also abused as children and unconsciously put into practice what they knew and was familiar to them. The challenge is to break the cycle. This is never easy, but at some point, the victim needs to have the courage to break this cycle of abuse and neglect and acknowledge how the behaviour affects her role as Mother.

"If it was good enough for me, then it's good enough for my children." How often do you hear this quoted by parents? This is such a lazy and misguided statement. Children are not their parents. They are themselves, and their archetypes can differ markedly from the major archetypes of their parents. For example, a mother who has the Mother, Servant, and Martyr archetypes has a different outlook on life from her daughter who may have the Queen, Adventurer, and Rebel archetypes. The Queen wants to be in charge, the Adventurer wants to go off and have adventures, while the Rebel opposes all forms of control and authority. That is what the daughter wants.

The mother sees her life very differently. Her archetypes value family, motherhood, duty, service, and sacrifice. How many mothers clash with their teenage daughters? I guarantee the daughter has the Rebel archetype. Rebels are misunderstood by their parents, unless the parents have a Rebel archetype themselves. Then it is usually a case of, "I know what I got up to when I was her age, and my daughter is not doing the same thing."

Here is some suggested advice for mothers with difficult daughters.

*Problem:* How to cope with daughters who have the Rebel archetype?

*Solution:* Walk a fine line between freedom and setting boundaries.

*Rule 1:* Never play the Rebel game. Rebels love to argue and disagree. They argue with passion, with emotion, and for long periods of time. Rebels have conviction and endurance. So, never argue with a Rebel! State your case, and finish the conversation.

***Rule 2:*** Finish the conversation on a positive note, a compliment or an expression of love. For example, "By the way your outfit looks great. That gothic look really suits you and I love your hair. I've got some leather boots you could borrow. They would really accentuate your long legs. Got stuff to do! Love ya!"

***Rule 3:*** Always praise and compliment Rebels. Make the praise meaningful but on irregular occasions.

***Rule 4:*** Where decisions are of minor importance, agree with the Rebel where possible.

***Rule 5:*** Where decisions are of major importance, state your position, the reasons for your decision, and the possible consequences of their likely behaviour. Then end the conversation with a compliment.

***Rule 6:*** If your Rebel child defies you, do not abandon that child. Be there to pick up the pieces, and never lecture. Do not bother with "I told you so." Just nurture and be there. We know when things go wrong and nobody wants that to be pointed out.

Every relationship is different. The rules are always flexible and open to change depending on the archetypal energy that two people bring to a relationship. Remember, we are all individuals, your daughter as much as anyone.

The positive archetypal energy of the Mother consists of nurturing, modelling, assistance, and support. All four of these energetic qualities can be used consistently and according to the age and maturity of the child. For a baby, nurturing is the overriding energy. For a toddler, modelling is of prime importance. For an older child, assistance and encouragement is the priority. As children grow into teenagers, the Mother archetype has to offer guidance and support to their growing independence. If Mothers keep these four energies at a consistent forefront, the relationships between mothers and children grow and flourish. Positive energy creates positive results. Negative energy creates negative results. Remember to nurture, model, assist, and support!

**Archetypal Combinations:**

The archetypal energy of the Mother combines well with the energy of:

Mentor * Teacher * Carer * Servant * Peacemaker * Angel * Companion * Sage * Diplomat * Fairy * Queen * Warrior * Judge * Advocate * Storyteller

**Effective Use of Mother Energy:**

- Nurture, model, assist and support.
- We are all individuals, as are children.
- Children are inexperienced, but it means they have more capacity to learn, not less.
- As a Mother, recognize your strengths and your weaknesses. If you have personal issues, take action. You are the only one who can break a cycle of negative treatment and behaviour.
- Raising children is a joy and a responsibility.
- For those with a Mother archetype but without children, do not feel guilty or unloved. Use your positive archetypal energy and you will be appreciated and possess the capacity to change lives.

# Mystic

The Mystic is an individual with a continual and direct connection to the Divine. This is maintained through a process of contemplation, meditation, and prayer. The image of a prophet sitting under the shade of a tree in deep meditation and espousing the occasional words of wisdom is one view of the Mystic. Another is the Monk or Nun locked away in solitude in the Monastery or Nunnery and deep in prayer for long periods of time. These individuals are less common as modern society, urban development, and a free-enterprise culture spread rapidly and as religious and spiritual practice decline in popularity and essence.

Mystics still exist, even traditional ones, but their roles have changed. They speak to a smaller audience but an enthusiastic audience that usually seeks their advice. This is because their presence and impact is now more out of tune with popular culture. Some mystics lead an almost hermit-type existence. They are rarely seen and almost never heard. Those few who gain popularity and status often achieve guru status. Once this guru status has been achieved, they are more often seen and their words are treasured by the faithful and exposed to popular opinion. A good example of one such individual is Maharishi Mahesh Yogi. He had a successful following and sphere of influence that exploded into notoriety when the Beatles sought his advice, spiritual techniques, and wisdom.

However, beware of the mystic who achieves guru status. To his credit, Maharishi Mahesh Yogi remained true to his nature and to his cause. There have been other notorious gurus who have not held their followers or their teachings in such good stead. Jim Jones is one such guru. Founder of the Peoples Temple, his sect ended at Jonestown with mass suicide and murder. Often the wisdom and company of a guru come at a price. The price may be engaging in psychological manipulation and emotional blackmail, demanding goods and money, expecting sexual favours, and enforcing a lack of freedom or the ability to leave the group.

Some individuals with the Mystic archetype lead fairly simple and mundane lives. They are true to the positive Mystic energy. They are humble. They have no need to advertise or display their Mystic energy. Instead, they use it to plot their personal pathway or to assist friends, when direction is sought. These people have the ability to tune into the Divine no matter their positions or circumstances. It is a quality they respect and use regularly as a part of their natural existence.

**Negative Aspects:**

Navel gazing ~ Self-centred ~ Self-importance ~ Spiritual expert ~ Delusional ~ Weekend expert ~ Boastful ~ Spirituality at a price ~ Isolate ~ Artificiality

**Positive Aspects:**

Illumination ~ Self-realization ~ Search of the spiritually symbolic ~ Evolve into transcendental ~ Inner knowledge ~ Inner peace ~ Harmony ~ Humility ~ Direct connection to the Divine

**Archetypal Energy:**

The archetypal energy of the Mystic is about inner peace and harmony. As Mystics have direct contact with the Divine, they have an ability to tune out the noise and turmoil of the physical world. Those individuals who have the focus, ability, and dedication to transcend into deep meditation know this energy well. It requires them to move past the power of the mind and the urges of the body. The energy of the Mystic is a connection of an individual spirit with the spiritual universe. It is like a drop of water falling from a plant and reconnecting with all the oceans of the universe. This connection embraces the love and joy of homecoming.

Humility is the key to Mystic energy. To embrace the positive archetypal energy of the Mystic, the individual has to block out all aspects of the physical world and dwell only on Spirit. Ego has no place in this process. Focus and humility are the tools. The negative energy of the Mystic takes hold of a person who sells spirituality and allows the ego to take control. These Mystics are the ones who set themselves up as gurus, experts, and controllers. Spirits are free. They are not for sale or open to bribery, control, and manipulation.

The other extreme use of Mystic energy is the traditional hermit. These are the navel gazers who isolate themselves from reality. We live in a physical world. We have a mind, body, and spirit, with a capacity for anything. It is just as limiting for the Warrior to live purely in the physical world and for the Scientist to live wholly in the intellectual plane as it is for the Mystic to live solely in the spiritual realm. Utilizing positive energy is all about the balance of the physical, the intellectual, and the spiritual.

**Archetypal Combinations:**

The archetypal energy of the Mystic combines well with the energy of:

Monk * Priest * Priestess * Nun * Wizard * Witch * Guide * Prophet * Teacher * Healer * Divine Child * Angel * Celibate * Pilgrim * Hermit * Seeker * Wise Woman * Shaman * Hero

**Effective Use of Mystic Energy:**

- Remember the balance between the physical, intellectual and spiritual.
- Do not allow your ego to overpower and control you.
- Do not neglect your spiritual connection. Use it on a regular basis to maintain stability and personal growth.
- Never neglect others. When asked, always assist those who ask for help in their spiritual quests. After all, we are but a small part of one enormous spiritual family.

# Narcissist

The Narcissist is a relatively new archetype. The term *narcissism* came from the ancient Greeks. It was advanced in psychology in the early twentieth century by Sigmund Freud. Narcissism is based on the story of a good-looking young man named Narcissus. He rejected the loving advances of the nymph, Echo, to spend his days gazing at his own reflection in a pool of water. Narcissus became so enraptured with his reflection and his inability to consummate his love that he changed into the flower bearing his name.

One can see the development of the Narcissist archetype with the advent of modern communications technology and the social and economic push for self-indulgence. The rise of social media allows for each and every individual to have a vehicle for self-exposure and opinion. The rapid development of phone technology allows each and every individual instant access to this exposure. Look at the plethora of selfies that find their way into so many forms of self-expression and personal and public communication outlets.

Since the 1980s there has been an expansion and a change of emphasis in the social and business structure. The whole economic argument has been about growth. To maintain economic growth, business and political leadership have encouraged policies of spend, spend, spend. The advertising for these policies has been all about the individual. The constant emphasis is that the customer is important. You deserve and are entitled to everything that a modern society has to offer. A bigger home, double garage, swimming pool, air conditioning, the very best family car plus a second vehicle, private schooling, private medical insurance, childcare, the latest conveniences for the home, the biggest and best home entertainment systems, the latest computer and phone technology, fashionable and labelled clothing and footwear, and the list goes on ad infinitum. Little wonder the majority of the population has become self-obsessed.

The Narcissist is all about the individual. The individual is important and takes priority over every other social and economic issue. The individuals are the centre of their world. They are entitled. They deserve. They have a story to tell and an opinion to express. The "fifteen minutes of fame" is alive and well in the world of the Narcissist.

**Negative Aspects:**

Self-obsessed ~ Self-absorbed ~ It's all about me ~ Selfish ~ Egotistical ~ Self-indulgent ~ Pretentious ~ False ~ Boastful ~ Obsessive ~ Irresponsible ~ Attention seeking ~ Poser ~ Social butterfly ~ Fifteen minutes of fame

**Positive Aspects:**

Proud ~ Concerned with self-improvement ~ Taking care of ~ Healthy ~ Responsible ~ Involved ~ Modern ~ Knowledgeable ~ Fashionable ~ Social

**Archetypal Energy:**

The archetypal energy of the Narcissist is all about balance. It is all a question of individual freedom and expression on the one hand and social responsibility and protocols on the other. The Narcissist has to recognize his or her place in society. We exist as both an economy and a society. We are a world of many individuals all attempting to find our place to live a contented and fulfilling life.

The pressure is on from many quarters for the individual to engage in self-obsession. The temptations are many and varied. Indulgence is encouraged, and self-control is discouraged. This is not only true at an individual level but also at a global level. The struggle for conservation and environmental protection is a challenging and an ongoing process. The struggle for the individual to be content without all the latest technologies and pampering is also a challenge. The Narcissist has to come to the understanding that contentment is an attitude and a personal feeling of well-being. Contentment is a fleeting moment when it is delivered through material gain or physical or psychological pleasures.

The Narcissist can easily fall back into the world of self-indulgence, selfishness, and impromptu fame. The television is full of stories and shows that recommends and encourages this type of lifestyle. The training begins at a young age, through children's television shows and advertising aimed at children. It then continues for a lifetime. Strength, discernment, and courage are all needed to withstand the pressure of self-indulgence and personal gratification. Questioning the necessity and effectiveness of what is being continually offered as the latest modern wonder is an ongoing and disciplined process. Remember, this is your life, and you are in control.

**Archetypal Combinations:**

The archetypal energy of the Narcissist combines well with the energy of:

Hedonist * Dilettante * Damsel * Diva * Princess * Prince * Lover * God * Goddess * Knight * Salesperson

**Effective Use of Narcissist Energy:**

- Strike that balance between pride and boasting, between control and indulgence, and between publicity and pretentiousness.
- At all times, consider the consequences of your actions.
- We all have social responsibilities as well as social privileges.
- Enjoy life, but be wary of false promises.

# Networker

The Networker is a modern archetype that has come into vogue with the development of city living and mass communication. The growth of cities has meant that a huge number of people are living in relatively small areas. This has created the desire and need for services and facilities that, by convenience, are located within those parameters.

Communication services, for example, have undergone rapid development and expansion. Every day this technology is changing, from the home telephone to the computer, from the computer to the mobile, and from the mobile to major broadband projects. With cities and the services come the people who develop, utilize, and take advantage of these changes. These people are represented by the Networker.

The Networker is the archetype of communication and service provision. Consider the rapid development of social networks. In such a short period of time, a vast amount of people has willingly and deliberately involved themselves in open communication schemes. Many of these avid communicators have the Networker archetype. Communication of every aspect of daily living, from general to personal, is on display. If you are hooked on Facebook, Instagram, Myspace, Twitter, and blogging to name a few, you have a Networker archetype. It may be to promote your business or it may be for social conversation, but the energy of the Networker is at play.

A Networker also knows people and services. Even before the explosion of computer and mobile technology, the Networker was prominent. They were the people you could always contact if you needed a service. They could tell you where the nearest doctor's surgery was, who had a trailer you could borrow, the name of a reliable tradesman, and the cheapest price of anything from bananas to beer. Those Networkers were a wealth of information. They were incredibly good at listening and storing information, just like the yellow pages and Google, before either was ever conceived. Those types of Networkers are still around today and have an amazing ability to collect and disseminate local information and are happy to share it willingly.

**Negative Aspects:**

Self-importance ~ Rigid ~ Manipulative ~ Power hungry ~ Embezzler ~ Gossip ~ Time waster ~ Tunnel vision ~ Spreading misinformation ~ Hacker

**Positive Aspects:**

Friendly ~ Good communication skills ~ People friendly ~ Organized ~ Concise ~ Adaptable ~ Good time management ~ Keeper of records ~ Knowledgeable ~ Develops social flexibility

**Archetypal Energy:**

The archetypal energy of the Networker is about communication. A number of energetic factors determine a Networker. The first is the desire, need, or want to open the lines of communication. It may be for social discourse, knowledge and information, employment, or fun and trivialities. Once the lines of communication are established, the Networker is in action.

The second factor is the storage of this knowledge. This is where computers are wonderful tools to the Networker. They have the capacity to store trillions of bytes of information that can be accessed at the click of a mouse. Organization is very important to the Networker. Information has to be found quickly and efficiently. If it involves business, then time is money, and you have to satisfy the customer in as short a time as possible. If it is social, the Networker finds it pointless talking about an event that happened a week ago, at times, even a day ago. The world has moved on, and social Networkers, in particular, do not like to be left behind. Therefore, organization is a must.

The crucial point for the positive Networker is that of discernment. Once the lines of communication are open and knowledge is stored and accessible, the Networker has to maintain discretion. Reputation is important. If Networkers are not discerning, they become just gossips. They may know everybody's business, whether it be fact or fiction, but spreading it around is not the way to win friends and influence people. We have all heard stories of Internet gossip that has ruined reputations and even lead to suicide. Credibility is a valuable asset to the Networker and discernment is the key to maintain that credibility.

Many Networkers love to talk and are extremely sociable, yet some Networkers could be considered rather antisocial. This does not interfere with their Networker energy or the way they go about their tasks. Rather the computer has given these individuals a wonderful way of participating in mainstream society whilst allowing them to remain on the fringe (as indicated with the Computer Nerd). Those individuals also have a strong Hermit archetype as well as a Networker archetype. All three archetypes, the Computer Nerd, the Hermit, and the Networker, complement each other quite well and allow the individual to be that strange mix of reclusive and mainstream.

**Archetypal Combinations:**

The archetypal energy of the Networker combines well with the energy of:

Computer Nerd * Pioneer * Detective * Engineer * Servant * Politician * Diplomat * Teacher * Seeker * Storyteller * Wanderer * Hermit * Entrepreneur * Advocate * Damsel * Knight * Scribe

**Effective Use of Networker Energy:**

- Remember that your reputation depends on how discerning you are.
- Your ability to network should be seen as a service to others.
- Do not be enticed into the "fifteen minutes of fame" syndrome.
- Remember that life should be lived, not just talked about.
- You are an individual. Always remember to be true to yourself. There is no need to live your life vicariously through others.

# Nun

The Nun and the Monk are the female and male aspects of the same archetype. Energetically they have many things in common, just as other archetypes with a similar duality. The Priest and Priestess, the Prince and Princess, the King and Queen, the Wizard and Witch, the God and Goddess, the Hero and Heroine, and the Knight and Damsel are the male and female equivalents of the one archetype. They can be separated into two archetypes when the male and female energy is distinctive enough to identify definitive traits.

The principles and characteristics that identify the Monk also identify the Nun. The Nun is found in greater numbers in poorer societies rather than affluent Western societies. Countries in Africa, Southeast Asia, and South America encourage the energy of the Nun. The Nun has a strong devotion to the Divine, and she devotes her life to service. Compared to the Monk, the Nun is more inclined to be active in serving the physical needs of humanity. You often find Nuns in a teaching capacity and in nursing and caring for the community. Brothers of Christian religious orders have also taken on teaching roles, so there are examples of Monks in the teaching arena, but the Nun archetypes are extremely active as nurses, carers, and rescuers. The sick, elderly, orphaned and abandoned children, homeless, persecuted, and marginalized minority groups all attract the Nun and her archetypal energy of service and caring.

Historically, Nuns have also been identified with their place of sanctuary and retreat, that is, the nunnery. Most people associate a Nun with her habit. These days, especially in Western societies, a Nun's dress is often similar to that of a layperson. Usually she wears a necklace with a cross as the identifying symbol of the religious order she represents and to emphasize her status as a devotee to God.

There are laypeople with the Nun archetypal energy. They follow the pathway of service for altruistic reasons that are often identified as following one's spiritual journey. These people have humility and gentleness that serve them well in their capacity as guides. As guides, they have endurance based on faith. This endurance assists not only their subjects, but themselves, especially through hardships and difficult times. Courage and determination are also integral aspects of the Nun energy.

Those with the Nun archetype may also be celibate. Although these people may be sexually active and have had sexual relationships, there is no great desire or enthusiasm for physical pleasure. Celibacy is a preferred state. Another aspect is the desire for simplicity. The person with the Nun archetype has no desire for big houses, luxury cars, shopping sprees, or pampering. They prefer a simple lifestyle and have a first-rate work ethic. They are excellent at making do and can adapt and recycle materials to make what is needed without tending towards excess. They tend to be frugal.

Although they understand the power of silence, those with the Nun archetype enjoy a good gossip when an occasion arises. The opportunity for a good chat about trivialities and the lives of celebrities, for instance, is worth the time and energy. This appears to be an energetic transfer from the time of the cloistered nunnery. It does provide a balance between the outside world of excess and the frugal life of the Nun.

**Negative Aspects:**

Dogmatic ~ Escapism ~ Fundamentalist ~ Self-absorbed ~ Gossip ~ Overly pious ~ Self-disempowerment ~ Self-indulged ~ Rigid

**Positive Aspects:**

Service ~ Commitment ~ Sacrifice ~ Spiritual path ~ Sacramental ~ Ritualistic ~ Control ~ Devotion ~ Dedication ~ Intense focus ~ Simplicity ~ Caring ~ Meditative ~ Personal growth ~ Endurance

**Archetypal Energy:**

The archetypal energy of the Nun is based around devotion, humility, simplicity, and service. Devotion to God is the driving force behind the positive traits of the Nun archetypal energy. It gives purpose and strength to the lifestyle of humility, simplicity, and service. The softness and gentleness of the female energy gives Nuns an advantage in humility over others of the faith. Most religious zealots tend to be male and have masculine energy of aggression and bravado of purpose. It is a constant challenge for the male to subdue his tendencies and utilize his feminine energy. The gentleness of the feminine energy is a greater friend to humility and simplicity.

Nuns also see their duty of service differently. The Nun feminine energy allows for a more subservient nature. This is not necessarily a negative trait that allows the female to be walked over, taken for granted, or abused. In the case of the Nun archetype, it allows the individual to place the needs of her students, patients, and wards above her own needs. This energy gives the Nun the power and ability to be caring, considerate, and loving to her full capacity.

Another component of the archetypal energy of the Nun is endurance. The individual who makes the decision to become a Nun is aware that her decision is for life. She devotes herself in the lifelong service to God. This is an admission that she is there for the long haul. You cannot commit to lifelong service without the capacity to endure. With this endurance comes dedication and determination. The Nun has an inner strength, the equivalent to any elite sports person or hero. Mother Teresa represents the perfect example of that strength and energy.

**Archetypal Combinations:**

The archetypal energy of the Nun combines well with the energy of:

Servant * Celibate * Disciple * Divine Child * Angel * Carer * Teacher * Rescuer * Companion * Coward * Peacemaker * Priestess * Healer * Warrior

**Effective Use of Nun Energy:**

- Service is to humanity as well as to God.
- Remember to take care of yourself, for you are only an asset when you can function at full health and capacity.
- Be wary of taking on too much.
- Being humble does not mean being taken for granted. You can be passive and assertive at the same time.
- Beware of gossip that undermines the good name of others and seduces you into the world of slander and envy.

# Peacemaker

Peacemakers are the voice of reason. They are willing to put their safety or reputation on the line to solve other people's disagreements. I clearly remember a schoolyard conversation with a group of eleven-year-old girls. We were discussing archetypes and what kind of archetypes some of these girls had. One girl, a most talented and considerate girl, waited patiently for her turn. When I told her that she was a peacemaker, she let out a huge sigh of relief. "That is so right," she said. "I always have to solve my friends' arguments and keep them happy." At that moment, she understood an aspect of her personality that had once puzzled her. She was a Peacemaker. Her friends knew she was the voice of reason, just as she knew that it was her obligation to resolve her friends' disagreements.

The Peacemaker is a skilled negotiator. Bob Hawke was a brilliant negotiator and peacemaker, especially in his role as head of the ACTU and later as Australian Prime Minister. Solving industrial disputes is never easy, especially in times of great social and economic change. Bob Hawke was the master. He was a specialist at bringing two parties together to work through problematic issues until a compromise and agreement was reached. That's what Peacemakers do. They engender good faith. Both sides of any dispute have to trust the Peacemaker before any worthwhile negotiation can take place. Both parties have to be confident their interests are considered by the Peacemaker and addressed in the course of negotiations.

Peacemakers have to be objective. They must be able to step back and understand where both parties stand and where they are likely to compromise. This requires Peacemakers to be good listeners and good communicators. They have to be persuasive in their discussions, as compromise is only the result of persuasive argument. When both parties are willing to compromise, then the Peacemaker has done his or her job. Each intervention and negotiated resolution adds to the Peacemaker's reputation. Success builds upon success, and reputation builds trust.

The Peacemaker and the Coward are very different archetypes. The Coward avoids conflict. The Peacemaker steps into conflict, never to take sides but to resolve difficulties. At times, the Peacemaker may take on the energy of the Warrior archetype and use this energy wisely. The Peacemaker may go into battle, but this battle is for a satisfactory resolution to a dispute. The Peacemaker is not interested in crushing an opponent. The Warrior is. The Peacemaker is interested in sharing the spoils of victory, with a win-win resolution. Strength, courage, and determination are the aspects of the Warrior energy that are also part of Peacemaker energy.

**Negative Aspects:**

Dictator ~ Confrontational ~ Conflict avoidance ~ Subjective ~ Ulterior motives ~ Hidden agenda ~ Self-importance ~ Bully ~ One-sided ~ Subterfuge ~ Power ~ Notoriety ~ Aggressive ~ Indifferent

**Positive Aspects:**

Mediator ~ Diplomat ~ Negotiator ~ Good listener ~ Objective ~ Patient ~ Determined ~ Courage ~ Trustful ~ Even-handed ~ The voice of reason ~ Good communicator ~ Persuasive ~ Understanding

**Archetypal Energy:**

The archetypal energy of the Peacemaker revolves around the skill of negotiation. The negotiator has to be trustworthy, for there is no settlement unless the parties in dispute have a regard for the third-party negotiator. This is the first step.

If possible, Peacemakers have to be knowledgeable about the dispute and the parties involved. However, there are occasions when the Peacemaker is thrust unprepared into the battlefield. There is no prior knowledge of the combatants. Assumptions have to be made and made quickly. In a violent confrontation, Peacemakers have courage, judgment, and intuition to guide them. Keep in mind that image of the Chinese Peacemaker standing in front of a tank in Tiananmen Square. That is the action of a Peacemaker.

Another aspect to the energy of the Peacemaker archetype is calmness. The ability to remain calm is paramount. Disagreements or disputes are often filled with emotion, and through all of this, the Peacemaker must remain calm. This calmness, though, retains strength and control. The disputing parties are almost forced to take notice. Through body language, tone of voice, and words, Peacemakers make it clear they are in control and possess the strength, determination, and confidence to resolve the disagreement.

If you are a Peacemaker, you are likely to be logical, practical and above all, persuasive. The peaceful resolution of any dispute occurs when the parties involved are persuaded to compromise their position. They have to be shown a way to move from their fixed positions. They have to be convinced the compromise does not totally disadvantage them. They have to be disarmed from the emotion of the situation. Your role is to achieve all of these things. This is no easy task, but the Peacemaker does not step away from a challenge. The archetypal energy of Peacemakers is strength and conviction. Their abilities and sense of duty stay with them for a lifetime.

**Archetypal Combinations:**

The archetypal energy of the Peacemaker combines well with the energy of:

Detective * Diplomat * Politician * Advocate * Judge * Warrior * Hero * Servant * Alchemist

**Effective Use of Peacemaker Energy:**

- Remember that it is your role to be the voice of reason.
- You are always part of the solution and never part of the problem. Leave your ego and personal beliefs out of your peacemaking.
- Utilize your strength, courage, determination and negotiating skills to advance your personal development and progress. Your journey is also important.
- Take the time for rest and relaxation. Your role as a Peacemaker requires focus and concentration in stressful situations. Give yourself time for recovery.

# Philosopher

The Philosopher is the archetype of thought. Philosophers are always thinking. There is just no escaping the saturation of activity in their minds. The Seeker is similar to the Philosopher, but the Seeker is full of questions, while the Philosopher is skilled at analysis. A question may come to the Philosopher, and he or she can become lost analysing that question. All aspects to the question must be considered, and that often leads to new thoughts that need analysis. There is a flow of thought with the Philosopher that never ends.

The Philosopher has lists. There are always things to be done, and each decision has its own list of pros and cons written on each side of the page. Philosophers are constant note takers. When attending a seminar, meeting, or workshop, Philosophers are the ones taking comprehensive notes. They may stop briefly to ask a question or clarify an issue, but then it is right back to writing.

Decision making is not easy for Philosophers. Lists help clarify what is in their minds, but there are always so many things to consider, and once decisions are made, Philosophers have the need to analyse their decisions and the possible consequences. They may even go right back to square one and start from scratch, for what if it is the wrong decision? What happens is that Philosophers spend eternity thinking about issues and delay action, negating any possible decision.

Philosophers have issues with trusting themselves. Those with the Philosopher archetype usually have a very active Saboteur archetype that is manipulated into operating with caution, mistrust, and suspicion. The Saboteur is the archetype of intuition and choice. Every time Saboteurs use their instincts, Philosophers come along and insist on discussion and argument. Positive Saboteurs make decisions in an instant with inner knowing. What is right? What is that gut feeling? The Philosopher makes decisions with the mind. It is analytical. What are the pros and cons? What needs deliberation? Philosophers occasionally listen to their gut feelings but find it a challenge to trust those instincts. Invariably, they fall back to the rationality of the mind and the whole analytical process.

**Negative Aspects:**

Cynic ~ Rationalist ~ Despair ~ Rigid ~ Single-minded ~ Tunnel vision ~ Dogmatic ~ Unable to make a decision ~ Lost ~ Confused ~ Time waster ~ Keeps on changing ~ Inconsistent ~ Frozen ~ Lacking self-belief ~ Distrusting

**Positive Aspects:**

Inquiring ~ Metaphysician ~ The journey is more important than the goal ~ Seeker ~ Teacher ~ Integration ~ Reflective ~ Lateral ~ Flexible ~ Logical ~ Knowledge ~ Romantic ~ Balanced

**Archetypal Energy:**

The archetypal energy of the Philosopher is about rational argument and consideration of the "big" questions. If the question does not seem big enough, then the Philosopher makes it so. Throughout history philosophers have devoted themselves to questions essential to our substance. The reason for existence, value systems, reasoning, ethics, power of thought and language, social values, systems of governance, relationship to the physical world, and spirituality have all posed questions and discussions for the great philosophers of our world. In turn, they have led the discussions and given each civilization and its people the opportunity to establish individual and tribal philosophy.

Philosophy has gone through several golden ages. As with all things, the cycles of change spin regularly, so who is to say that another golden era of philosophy isn't around the corner? The world, especially Western civilizations, has undergone a massive change in thought streams. As religions decline, the New Age is born. Individuals now have the freedom to question religious dogma and examine individual spirituality on a personal level.

Those people with a Philosopher archetype can find the archetypal energy overwhelming. It can paralyse an individual with indecision and procrastination. Philosophers love to talk, so take advantage of that strength. Join a book club or Toastmasters. Allow yourself the opportunity to verbalize your thoughts, which may enable you to prioritize other aspects of your life. Trust yourself, your intuition, and your gut feeling. Allow yourself the freedom to make mistakes; be aware that the journey is important and worth enjoying without the analysis. Take action with anticipation, excitement, and enthusiasm. This is your life; be prepared to live it to the full.

**Archetypal Combinations:**

The archetypal energy of the Philosopher combines well with the energy of:

Teacher * Prophet * Adventurer * Scholar * Guide * Pilgrim * Detective * Judge * Mystic * Storyteller * Wise Woman * Slave * Wanderer

**Effective Use of Philosopher Energy:**

- Actions speak louder than words.
- Balance your rational mind with your intuition. There is a time and place to listen to both.
- Write morning pages. First thing in the morning, before you do anything else, pick up a pen and write at least two pages. Do not think about what you are writing. Just write.
- Every five or six months review your priorities. Work out three or four areas of your life that are a priority and take action only in those areas.
- Remember that nothing lasts forever and that you are allowed to make mistakes.
- Be aware that molehills are not mountains.

# Pilgrim

The Pilgrim is the spiritual journeyman. Other travelling archetypes like the Pilgrim include the Adventurer, the Wanderer, the Explorer, the Seeker, and the Knight. The Adventurer travels to find adventure. The Wanderer meanders from place to place with little rhyme or reason. The Explorer seeks new territories and investigates the little-known aspects of our world. The Seeker is full of questions and sometimes travels to find the answers, although the Seeker is more likely to use books, the Internet, or people instead of excessive travel. The Knight does travel for adventure, but many of his quests are matters of the heart. The defining aspect of the Pilgrim archetype, as opposed to the other journeyman archetypes, is that the travel has a purpose. The Pilgrim's travels are generally spiritual in nature. The spiritual purpose may be connected to a religious belief or a highly personal ambition or desire close to the Pilgrim's faith.

Within various religions, pilgrimage is often an essential commitment. At some point in spiritual people's lifetimes, they are expected to make a pilgrimage to pay their respects at the home or birth place of their faith. Some pilgrimages may be within a short distance, while others could be halfway around the world. Mecca, Medina, Lhasa, Varanasi, Bodhgaya, Badrinath, Mathura, Angkor Wat, Jerusalem, Rome, the Vatican City, and Lourdes are just a few of the most well-known and popular destinations of the Pilgrim. Those with the Pilgrim archetype may not limit themselves to just one pilgrimage. They may be inclined to travel on many occasions, and one true faith experience may lead to another, in order to renew their spiritual energy.

Not all Pilgrims are necessarily motivated by their religious beliefs. Those with the Pilgrim archetype can be motivated to undertake journeys of personal value to connect with their ancestry. Within Australia, people are making the pilgrimage to Anzac Cove or to the Kokoda Trail to soak up the energy of places where their grandparents or relatives fought and died. This is a powerful personal journey. Pilgrims always have a purpose with their travelling, and the experience means everything to them.

**Negative Aspects:**

Personal glorification ~ Bound by duty not desire ~ Vagabond ~ Wanderer ~ Ulterior motive ~ Flippant ~ Disrespectful ~ Sanctimonious ~ Hypocrisy

**Positive Aspects:**

Spiritual connection ~ Bonding ~ Challenge ~ Conviction ~ Experience ~ Illumination ~ Healing ~ Motivation ~ Personal growth ~ Sacrifice ~ Religious ~ Harmony ~ Self-discovery ~ Heritage

**Archetypal Energy:**

The archetypal energy of the Pilgrim deals with the association of a spiritual belief with a historical, significant landmark, often the birthplace of that spiritual belief. History is important to Pilgrims, and they gravitate to places of historical significance where a fusion of energetic forces takes place. Pilgrims connect places of spiritual importance, which in turn, connect to God, Spirit, or the Divine. To Pilgrims it is an energetic return to their spiritual homes.

Motivation is important to the Pilgrim. The majority of people with religious, spiritual, or strong personal values are content to confine their practices to their local communities or spheres of influence. Pilgrims are motivated to take the next step. They are prepared to travel, sometimes vast distances and at great personal cost, to unite with a more significant component of their belief systems outside of what they can access locally. This is motivation. Once the first pilgrimage is taken and the spiritual connection made, the Pilgrim's motivation gains impetus, and the first journey often turns the pilgrimage into a lifelong experience of travel and spiritual connection.

Personal growth is a strong component of Pilgrims. They are searching for answers and the next step on the spiritual ladder of personal growth. They look forward to the continuation of their life experiences through the joy of pilgrimage. Personal growth is not learned through a book or service; it is an experience. It is the build-up of expectation, the enjoyment of travel, and the exhilaration of experiencing a physical location uniquely connected to shared, spiritual values.

**Archetypal Combinations:**

The archetypal energy of the Pilgrim combines well with the energy of:

Nun * Priest * Priestess * Seeker * Disciple * Angel * Philosopher * Peacemaker * Adventurer * Explorer * Wanderer * Pioneer * Shaman * Prophet * Scholar * Wise Woman * Monk

**Effective Use of Pilgrim Energy:**

- Stay true to your beliefs, and pursue your spiritual connection with enthusiasm.
- Pay respect to the beliefs of others and to their sacred places.
- Be modest and humble in your travels. They are not occasions or achievements to boast or brag about.

# Pioneer

Pioneers will push the boundaries of new frontiers. They might be traditional pioneers who carve a settlement out of the wilderness or explorers who find a passage through new and dangerous territories. Modern Pioneers may be scientists who discover a cure to a disease, environmentalists who discover a new species of plant or animal, entrepreneurs who invent a new product or service that transforms lives, or psychologists whose research gives us insight into our behaviours. Pioneers can be found in any area of human endeavour. They take up any challenge, no matter how difficult or impossible it appears to be.

Pioneers may be knowledgeable and possess the wisdom of learned scholars. They may also be raw and lacking in expertise. However, the one quality Pioneers definitely have is the tremendous belief in their abilities. Self-belief is the key to the Pioneer, as it breeds a fierce determination to succeed. The Pioneer must be prepared to endure setbacks, overcome obstacles, plough through the doubts of failure, and disregard the barbs of commentators. This requires determination and endurance of the highest quality. Marie Curie, Thomas Edison, Orville and Wilbur Wright, Vasco da Gama, and Leonardo da Vinci would not have succeeded without their self-belief and determination to finish their projects and introduce them to the world.

Many seemingly ordinary people also possess this archetype. Their successes, inventions, and exploits may not be earth-shattering on a grand scale, but every success and positive intention contributes to the well-being of all. Little ideas can also inspire big successes. A small event or idea sometimes motivate, stimulate, and manipulate a breakthrough. To the Pioneers, I can only say, "Keep the faith." Your efforts deserve to be recognized and rewarded.

**Negative Aspects:**

Isolate ~ Going around in circles~ Criticized ~ Introverted ~ Inflexible ~ Lost~ Abandon the present ~ Unsettled ~ Gung-ho ~ Rednecks ~ Defeated ~ Deflated ~ Reckless ~ Envious ~ Greedy ~ Self-importance

**Positive Aspects:**

Trail blazer ~ Risk taker ~ Brave ~ Intuitive ~ Strength of character ~ Flexible ~ Visionary ~ Faith in self ~ Hardened ~ New horizons ~ Determination ~ Endurance ~ Take up the challenge ~ Forward thinking

**Archetypal Energy:**

Inspiration is the key element of the positive archetypal Pioneer energy, inspiration borne of passion. Pioneers have a deep passion to improve, discover, settle, or invent for the betterment of humanity. This is demonstrated in their fields of expertise and natural love of human endeavour. They look beyond what is obvious or currently in fashion. They are visionaries and possess a clear idea of civilization and the direction worth travelling, but they may also be driven by the need for change. Inspiration and passion drives the action.

Timing is important. Famous people with the inspiration, intuition, and vision for new devices and understandings have been sidelined, ridiculed, or demonized by their society. Their understanding and progression has not correlated with that of their generation. Galileo and his pioneering abilities were not treated well by his contemporaries, but consider Bill Gates and how his successes correlated perfectly with the development of the computer age. The openness of social thought and the imperative needs of that society play a large part in the success of the Pioneer.

Resilience is another key aspect of the Pioneer. If timing is a challenge, then the Pioneer has to have an abundance of resilience because there are plenty of pitfalls in the life of the Pioneer. The progress of Pioneers can be compared to working on a giant jigsaw puzzle. Pioneers may or may not have a clear picture of the finished product, but they understand some pieces fit easily, and others are much more mysterious and may not seem to have any purpose at all. As with jigsaw puzzles, there are times of momentum and times of stagnation. Stagnation draws upon the resilience of the Pioneer, and this is when self-belief is drawn into action to re-enforce the Pioneer's resilience.

The Pioneer must also be adaptable and flexible. Stubbornness may seem contrary to the previous two traits, but it is just as necessary. Pioneers must have the determination to persist no matter what the challenge, but there comes a point when they need to take a fresh look at their problems or digress down a tangent to find fresh perspective.

This requires flexibility and the ability to think laterally. The Pioneer has to have the strength of character to undertake the required self-assessment without denial. Added to this task may be the critical voice of his compatriots and peers. The Pioneer has to be flexible and listen to constructive criticism to improve his or her work. Taking advantage of all the Pioneer's positive qualities may mean the difference between success and failure, progress or regression.

Negative Pioneer archetypal energy is expressed when stubbornness becomes so strong that it blocks rational thought and dismisses alternative scenarios. The Pioneer becomes trapped in a never-ending circle. Pioneers also have to be aware of their motives. There are occasions when research and pioneering discoveries have wide-ranging and deadly consequences. The development of the Atomic bomb is one such example. Even today one has to wonder about the philosophy behind the development of weapons that are designed to inflict death and destruction upon fellow humans. The Pioneer has to answer the difficult questions. What are my motives? Does my research benefit others, or am I involved in a process where monetary gain and self-glorification are the driving forces?

**Archetypal Combinations:**

The archetypal energy of the Pioneer combines well with the energy of:

Adventurer * Scientist * Explorer * Nature Child * Healer * Servant * Seeker * Wizard * Witch * Hero/Heroine * Networker * Warrior * Gambler * Engineer *Athlete * Rebel * Peter Pan Child * Entrepreneur * Addict

**Effective Use of Pioneer Energy:**

- Understand the task in front of you, set your vision and attack it with enthusiasm and determination.
- Remember that "it is always darkest before the dawn."
- Be prepared to listen to others.
- Assess your strengths, and work with them.
- Remember your achievements and failures can be the inspiration for the success of others.
- Always question your motives, and consider where your research may lead.

# Politician

The Politician is the Jekyll and Hyde archetype. In its purest form, the Politician archetype is the servant of the people. This is the case with some individuals. They see themselves as servants of the people and remain accurate to that cause. These Politicians tend to find their places in civil realms or in lower-ranking ministerial positions. They are likely to be junior politicians, local government councillors, presidents of junior football clubs, or secretaries of local school parent associations. These are the Politicians whose duties and roles are defined by higher authorities or set in concrete by society or associations and their members. For example, presidents of local football clubs have fairly defined roles. They are the leaders of the clubs, they chair the meetings, they have roles in coach selection and player recruitment, they attend the games, and they socialize with the players and club supporters.

Presidents are also the face for publicity. They support fundraising. They are the voices of explanation in both good and difficult times. They present awards and make speeches. Their roles are defined, their power is limited, and their commitments are of service. The focus of service is very much aligned with their personal values and loyalties. They remain true Politicians.

The higher up the political ladder the Politician archetype climbs, the more difficult it is to maintain independence and integrity. Every senior or junior Politician I have listened to has said that he or she entered politics to make a difference and serve the people. Somewhere in the process, Dr Jekyll turns into Mr Hyde. The Politician changes from the servant of the people to the servant of the political party and its backers, as well as the controller of the people. As the new Politician enters the political party system, compromises are demanded and given.

The party executive generally reflects the personal views of the country's leader who expects loyalty and agreement. There is no pre-selection, no endorsement, no rise up the ranks, no promotions, no influence, and no opportunity to make a difference if this demand is not met. Often, strongly held personal values of the new Politician are rapidly compromised. Toe the party line is the first principle of survival. Then, there is the short election cycle. In some cases, the local member has three years before facing an election. Any hint of radical expression or controversy means the end to that political career. The narrower a political party's spectrum, the less compromise and room there is for the individual politician's personal views.

Politicians have enormous power. They make the laws. They decide how much tax you pay. They decide where this money (your money) is spent. They decide who comes to your country, and who stays. They decide if you go to war. They decide what medicines you are allowed. They decide what kind of residence you can build and where you can build it. They decide your human rights. They decide what offences deserve jail and for how long the offender stays there. A huge responsibility is given to those with the Politician archetype. The challenge for each individual with the Politician archetype is ongoing. Stop Doctor Jekyll becoming Mr Hyde.

**Negative Aspects:**

Autocrat ~ Power hungry ~ Self-glorification ~ Control ~ Self-importance ~ Parochial ~ Serving vested interests ~ Unapproachable ~ Condescending ~ Insular ~ Patriarch ~ Hypocritical ~ Corrupt ~ Prejudice ~ Yes Minister

**Positive Aspects:**

Servant of the people ~ Inclusive ~ Principled ~ Considerate ~ Approachable ~ Communicator ~ Leader ~ Statesman ~ Caring ~ Genuine ~ Empathetic ~ A representative of the people ~ Energetic ~ Altruistic ~ Humility

**Archetypal Energy:**

The greatest challenge for the Politician is to maintain the balance between positive and negative energy. For the Politician, it becomes too easy and convenient to move to the side of negative energy. This process is so beguiling. The ideals of genuine empathy and a willingness to assist people are so easily lost in party loyalty—personal achievement and bureaucratic double speak. As the politician is thrust into the combative nature of politics, attitudes harden, principles are attacked and challenged, the pressure to conform to the values of the leader becomes an issue, identity is lost, and opinions of difference and diversity are lost in the strengthening and hierarchy of the tribe. It is us against them. As Lenin, Mussolini, and Bush have more or less stated, "You are either with us or against us." You cannot get any more black or white than that. Where is the room to manoeuvre for the Politician placed in that situation? There is none. Where is the service to the people? It is given only in terms of bribery. Agree with me and I serve you. Disagree with me, and you are excluded. Is it any wonder why so many citizens become cynical of the political process? This is the expression of negative energy at its worst.

The positive energy of the Politician is best expressed in humility. The duty of service is a humble profession. The duty of service loses its meaning if expressed in arrogance and misplaced loyalty. It is easy to understand how the lay Politician, the president of Little Athletics, the local councillor, the principal of a school, and others can maintain the energetic balance. Their roles are more defined, and their loyalties are less divided. Duty and humility are more acceptable partners. As the duties increase and the loyalties divide, humility can lose its significance and importance.

Throughout history there have been Politicians who have served many with humility and inclusiveness. These are the genuine leaders, the great statesmen and women. They have been the stimulus for hope, achievement, and the advancement of society—physically, emotionally, and spiritually. The energetic forces of humility, passion, empathy, and righteousness dominate their lives and their values. Unfortunately, there are many more who have ruled with dictatorial control and division. They are the war mongers, the tyrants, the control freaks. They are the Politicians responsible for death and destruction, responsible for the suppression of populations, ideas and human rights, and enveloped in the delusion of self-glorification. The energetic forces of arrogance, power, corruption, and self-importance dominate their lives and their values. Ask yourself which Politician best serves your society's interests, not necessarily their interests or your interests. After that, ask your local Politicians how they are serving your community and your society.

**Archetypal Combinations:**

The archetypal energy of the Politician combines well with the energy of:

Servant * Statesman * Diplomat * Martyr * King * Queen * Advocate * Networker * Banker * Detective * Hero/Heroine * Mother * Father * Slave * Peacemaker * Wise Woman * Warrior * Wizard

**Effective Use of Politician Energy:**

- Always keep in mind that Politicians are there to serve the people.
- Beware of vested interests, party-political ambitions, self-importance, paternalism, and self-justification.
- Humility and service is the key in maintaining your values and principles.
- Flexibility is important but it may lead to compromise and betrayal.
- Actions speak louder than words. Be judged on your actions and achievements, not on your ramblings and boastings.

# Priest

The Priest and the Monk are the male archetypes of spiritual connection. The fundamental aspects of these two archetypes are similar in nature: a lifetime of devotion to God (the terminology of the Priest) or the Divine. The Priest is a more traditional Western identity associated with religion. The expectation of lifetime service is reinforced by both personal belief and religious dogma. Hand in hand with devotion to God is service to God. Priests are there to do God's work, and service is an important energetic aspect of the Priest archetype. Priests also have a duty to serve humanity. To that end, they are not locked away in purpose-built edifices, but are found active in communities and teaching the Word of God to their communities. They provide both spiritual and emotional support to their parishioners.

The Priest is the active connection between God and the people. Monks generally do not play such active roles in their communities, but Priests do. They are seen as God's representatives on Earth, the physical link to the spiritual God. Community members wishing to be part of a religious gathering seek the blessing and acceptance of the Priest and, in return, receive all the spiritual services on offer. These services are made available and are generally administered by the Priest. The Priest is often a partner in the spiritual celebrations of the individual.

Priests are the conduits of sacred rituals and rites. Their task is to explain the significance of each sacred ritual and rite to the members of their religious or spiritual communities. This may require the teaching or explanation of religious dogma to the general public who are not associated with their religious or spiritual groups. They also conduct all ceremonies and rituals that are sacred and special to their congregations and belief systems. Priests are the keepers of sacred truths and the celebrators of their faith.

The Priest is a specialized archetype. If laypeople have this archetype, they generally follow the path to priesthood. It is not an easy vocation. The Priest archetype has to have a consistently strong positive energy to commit to such a vocation. Insistence of celibacy in some religions and the denial of intimate relationships are commitments that test the strength of this energy. Those who leave the priesthood or those with the Priest archetype who cannot commit to a religious order generally devote their spiritual connection in a much more private fashion. They may involve themselves with small fringe groups that align their spirituality or a religious connection to the main church. The layperson with the Priest archetype may be found with youth groups or programs that involve the passage to manhood or spiritual rituals.

**Negative Aspects:**

Power hungry ~ Rigid ~ Manipulative ~Controlling ~ Abuse of power ~ Hypocrite ~ Lapse of personal morality ~ Self-importance ~ Exclusive ~ Threatening ~ False teachings

**Positive Aspects:**

Traditional ~ Leader ~ Ceremonial ~ Powerful ~ Pastoral care ~ Wisdom ~ Orator ~ Channel of Divine energy ~ Keeper of sacred rites and rituals ~ Blessed ~ Disciplined ~ Spiritual connection ~ Service ~ Humility

**Archetypal Energy:**

The archetypal energy of the Priest concerns itself with three essential elements. The first is the spiritual connection to God or the Divine. The Priest generally maintains a constant practice of prayer, meditation, or ritual for this connection to remain strong and to keep the Divine channel flowing. This is the energy of commitment and discipline, commitment to the Divine, and the discipline of regular sacred connection.

The second essential element is to act as God's representative for the congregation. This requires the energy of service. Priests are there to serve the people. Their spiritual needs and beliefs must be tended, reinforced, and celebrated. Service is spiritual in nature, but it may also involve emotional support, especially in times of hardship or grief. The Priest has to have understanding and empathy for these occasions. He also has to be approachable as a person and as a giver of pastoral care. Discretion and trust are other essential energetic components to this role. Service is a hard taskmaster, and there is no easy option when you enter in the service industry. Duty comes before everything else.

The third essential element is leadership—a key element. The Priest is the figurehead for his congregation and community. He is the celebrator and keeper of the community's spiritual history. Within this context is the energy of leadership, performance, and oration. Sacred rites and rituals are not only saturated in spirituality but also in performance. The Priest, as the orator, has the task of conveying the spiritual message and ritual significance with reverence and dignity.

Overseeing all of these essential elements is the discipline of self-sacrifice. As well as the demands of service, the Priest enters into an agreement to forego many of the physical pleasures available to others. There are many examples where this trust and agreement has been broken. Many lives have been severely damaged and even cut short by the unholy sexual misdemeanours of individual priests. This has been compounded by the various cover-ups that have occurred. This misuse of position and power is made worse given the spiritual and leadership reverence and authority given to these priests by their congregations.

Self-sacrifice requires constant dedication and devotion. Priests are a demanding and unique archetype, and their roles in modern society are becoming more difficult to carry out.

**Archetypal Combinations:**

The archetypal energy of the Priest combines well with the energy of:

Disciple * Servant * Mystic * Advocate * Carer * Warrior * Martyr * Pilgrim * Divine Child * Angel * Celibate * Monk * Prophet

**Effective Use of Priest Energy:**
- Remember you are a servant of God and a servant of God's people.
- Honour your traditions and spiritual practices.
- The connection with God and the Divine is a constant dialogue.
- Maintain your strength and dedication to your vows of sacrifice and service.
- Be inclusive, never selective or exclusive; for we are all God's creatures and connected by Spirit.

# Priestess

The Priestess is the feminine equivalent to the masculine Priest archetype. She has a similar spiritual connection to the Divine; service to a congregation, tribe, or community; knowledge and leadership of spiritual rites and rituals; and dedication and self-sacrifice. The things that are relevant to the Priest are also relevant to the Priestess.

The differences mostly lie within the different gender energies and historical practice. Historically, male energy has dominated religions, leaving the Priest in control. The Priestess has a strong history in Celtic traditions and tribal communities that maintain an energetic balance between male and female importance. As the role of Priest was the dominion of men, the Priestess was moved to the social fringes to operate in smaller communities. Only now are some Christian churches recognizing the roles of Priestesses and acknowledging their right to leadership, celebratory and service roles. Unfortunately, many religions have not. They have maintained their traditions and kept exclusivity for the male Priest alone.

The expression of feminine energy allows the Priestess to stand separate from the Priest. The Priestess has a greater role in the physical and emotional well-being of her community, while the Priest will generally concern himself with more worldly spiritual matters. The Priestess is often a sage or wise woman, and her community often seeks her advice on health issues, medicines, foods, births, deaths, children, rites of passage (especially for young women), education, and relationships. The nurturing aspect of the Priestess pays respect to all these aspects of community living. She is often the linchpin of her community.

In today's world, the person with the Priestess archetype is often on a singular spiritual path. She has a spiritual connection and devotion to the Divine, a practice in prayer and meditation, and her own private altar or ceremonial retreat. She devotes time and attention to her special place. She is consulted by her friends and family for advice and may lead spiritual, emotional, or physical development courses for small groups. She is devoted to her personal spirituality. She involves herself with the connection of spirit and her community by becoming a spiritual servant for herself and others. She is the bridge to the feminine aspect of the spiritual world.

**Negative Aspects:**

Abuse of power ~ Self-importance ~ Rigid ~ Overbearing ~ Power hungry ~ Manipulative ~ Controlling ~ Delusions of grandeur ~ Irreverent ~ Exclusive

**Positive Aspects:**

Wise woman ~ Leader ~ Channel of Divine energy ~ Ceremonial ~ Empathetic ~ Traditional ~ Powerful ~ Orator ~ Service ~ Intuitive ~ Visionary ~ Blessed ~ Keeper of sacred rites and rituals ~ Disciplined ~ Pastoral care ~ Inclusive

**Archetypal Energy:**

The archetypal energy of the Priestess revolves around her ability to use her spiritual connection with the Divine to assist all in her sphere of influence. The Priestess needs, and often has, powerful energy. For her to fulfil her duty, she has to maintain that strong connection to the Divine. Consistency with prayer, meditation, and ritual is imperative.

Her duty of service may be for her own personal growth and spiritual awareness, but the growth in her energetically attracts others who seek her company, influence, and advice. If the Priestess is true to her positive energetic nature, she recognizes and understands her calling. She has the confidence and inner knowledge to lead her group in a responsible manner through the practicing of rituals. This may be a challenge, but a challenge such as this is what the Priestess thrives on.

Another challenge for the Priestess is staying grounded. Her spiritual connection with the Divine allows her the privilege to experience, with relative ease, the love and gentleness of spiritual energy. It is easy to become self-obsessed within that energetic dimension. Humility and selflessness are positive energetic traits of the Priestess, and she is required to call upon these aspects to assist with her earthly duties. It is important for the Priestess to remember that, like the Priest, she is a servant of her people.

Another challenge for the Priestess is to control the ego. The Priestess has great power. The Priestess may foster or be trusted with singular leadership within her group. In positions of leadership, where trust and power is freely given, it is imperative to honour that trust and power. The ego loves power and self-importance. When the ego takes control of the individual, there is the opening for abuse, manipulation, and delusions of grandeur.

**Archetypal Combinations:**

The archetypal energy of the Priestess combines well with the energy of:

Wise Woman * Servant * Warrior * Martyr * Mystic * Carer * Advocate * Divine Child * Healer * Goddess * Teacher * Peacemaker * Visionary

**Effective Use of Priestess Energy:**

- Take up the challenge and become a servant of the people.
- Maintain your connection with the Divine through constant prayer, meditation, and ritual.
- Remain grounded, and be wary of losing your way in the spiritual energy of the Divine.
- Honour your sacred shrine.
- Stay strong but remain humble.
- Be aware of the temptation of self-importance.

# Prince

As we are led to believe, the Prince lives in a castle. He dresses with great refinement. He speaks eloquently. He marries well. He has servants to assist him. He has a King or Queen to finance his spending. The Queen adores and protects the Prince. The King has a different attitude. The King barely tolerates the Prince, as the Prince is content to spend as little energy as possible on his duties but much more time and energy on his recreation. The Prince is well educated, is often trained in the arts, and is encouraged to be creative. He collects articles of beauty or value. Deep down the Prince has no desire to be King, as that position is dangerous, filled with responsibilities, and at times, rather tedious.

The Prince just described is the mould of a medieval Prince, but the modern-day Prince is no different. We have all come across the individual who has the Prince archetype. He is the indulged child who is protected by his mother, loves playing in and around the family home, enjoys model-making and building with Lego blocks, and attends a private school. As he gets older, he may become a businessman who takes over the family business. If he develops his own venture, it is likely to be supported by finances given to him, inherited by him, or lent to him by his family. The Prince's business or venture is likely to be creative or connected to the arts.

The Prince may be your best friend. He is usually charming and sophisticated. He enjoys the finest that life has to offer. After he has spent his money, he is happy to spend his friends' money. He is good company but every so often is inclined to throw a tantrum or to sulk.

Do not take what you have read so far to be demeaning. The Prince and the Princess archetypes constantly combine both positive and negative energy. They are charming and adorable, even when they are sulking or spending your money. They have a sensitivity and enchantment about them that make them so beguiling, and they hypnotize you with their positive energy while at the same time indulging themselves with their negative energy. When you recognize an individual with the Prince archetype, step back a little and observe your interaction with him. Do you see how wonderful the Prince is with those who surround him? Notice how he gently manipulates the agenda to achieve his ambitions.

**Negative Aspects:**

Above everyone else ~ Self-centred ~ Arrogant ~ Manipulative ~ Self-serving ~ Intolerant ~ Conscious of class ~ Condescending ~ Irresponsible ~ Frivolous ~ Tantrums ~ Airs and graces ~ Spendthrift

**Positive Aspects:**

Divine right ~ Protected ~ Pageantry ~ Rich ~ Looked after ~ Control ~ Heroic ~ Get what you want ~ Indulged ~ Creative ~ Educated ~ Charming ~ Elegant ~ Classy ~ Entertaining ~ Righteousness ~ Articulate

**Archetypal Energy:**

The archetypal energy of the Prince is fluid, and he is a master of manipulating energies to achieve his wants and desires. He understands his station in life and is prepared to use both positive and negative energy to maintain the comfort and security of that position. Prince Charles is the perfect example. He was able to charm the elegant and beautiful Diana Spencer into a royal marriage. This was achieved by using positive archetypal energy, but it wasn't long before the negative energy came to the fore, and the games began. When Princess Diana was contained under his control, cocooned in her role, the Prince turned his attention to Camilla. Having a wife and a lover is a challenge, but the Prince was up to the task. After the death of Diana, Charles then had to woo Camilla, convince his mother of their eligibility to wed, charm the media, and gain the sympathy of the general public. We all know the ending.

It is important to understand that those with the Prince archetype usually have no ambition to become King. Prince Edward, who briefly became King Edward, abdicated to marry Mrs Wallis Simpson. He relinquished the throne to return to his Bohemian princely lifestyle. This was cleverly portrayed in the film *The King's Speech*. Consider two movie stars, Kevin Costner and Sean Connery. In real life, Costner possesses the Prince archetype, while Connery possesses the King archetype. Look at their movie roles. Kevin Costner is always suitably cast as a

Prince, such as Robin Hood. However, Sean Connery could not be cast as anything but a king. Look at his persona as his on-screen roles of James Bond, King Arthur, Richard the Lionhearted or as the father of Indiana Jones.

Looking back through history, some princes have taken a throne by force. However, these men, who usurped the throne of a relative, never had a Prince archetype. They would have the King, the Avenger, or the Warrior archetype. These archetypes acknowledge the use of violence to achieve the position of power. The Prince does not want the responsibility of running a kingdom with all the assorted demands of duty. The Prince is happy with the benefits of courtly life, and he has the archetypal energy that blends perfectly with that situation.

The Prince has charm. When the occasion demands his attention, the Prince, in full regalia, has the persona to stand tall and proud. He has a command of language that entices his listeners into his conversation. He is fine company within the confines of his circle of friends, as this is his court and courtiers. Prince Charming was well named, but the negative archetypal energy comes to the fore when the Prince is denied that to which he feels entitled. Then the sulking and the tantrums begin, and he is capable of emotional blackmail and manipulation. The Prince learns quickly that if the charm doesn't work, the sulking usually does. Hence, we see a blend of negative and positive archetypal energy.

**Archetypal Combinations:**

The archetypal energy of the Prince combines well with the energy of:

Scholar * Indulged Child * Queen * Artist * Entrepreneur * Scribe * Companion * Disciple * Networker * Seeker * Pilgrim * Dilettante * Craftsperson * Engineer * Philosopher

**Effective Use of Prince Energy:**

- Recognize and accept your responsibilities.
- Treat all people with respect and dignity.
- You are in a privileged position so use your charm, manners and influence to assist those less fortunate than you.
- Keep control of your emotions.
- Pursue your artistic endeavours with wisdom and passion.

# Princess

Now we come to my favourite archetype, the Princess. Children who have the Princess archetype know from a very young age exactly who they are. They are very careful in choosing their parents, and more often than not, the Princess determines that her father has the King archetype. How often have you heard fathers call their daughters Princess? How many times do you notice the little pink Princess T-shirt? Princesses seek protection, and they are so clever at finding a father with the King archetype and later a partner with the King archetype. The Princess is extremely efficient at getting all her needs and desires met.

Children with the Princess archetype have a most identifiable appearance. They are like fragile little dolls. They are immaculately dressed and groomed and can have a faraway look in their eyes. If they are safe in their home environments (it used to be a castle), they are talkative and sometimes rather precocious, but if they are out and about in the big, wide world, they often feel insecure and cling to their mothers or fathers.

As they grow into adulthood, very little changes. They like to be noticed (just watch Paris Hilton). They like to dress in pretty, fashionable clothes. They are beautifully groomed. They are compulsive shoppers. They spend their money, their partners' money, their friends' money, and in fact, they spend anyone's money. My Princess wife has always said, "What's mine is mine, and what's yours is also mine."

As castles are rare these days, most Princesses live in large houses. Many have mansions that resemble castles, but most reside in a residence that is a castle sanctuary to them. It is their safe haven and a place of relaxation. Watch how the Princess sits on the couch. She does not sit; she lounges, often clinging to a pillow or cushion or curled up in a blanket. When she is at home, the Princess doesn't concern herself with protocols or decorum. Her home is a place of relaxation. She is content. A Princess's home is hers to design and decorate with beautiful things. The outside world is scary and a challenge, but home is security.

The Princess is a collector. Whether she has collections of shoes, clothes, china statues, dolls, books, paintings, or works of art, they are all treasured by the Princess and adored by her friends. Princesses excel at art, craft, and dramatic performance, but work, however, does not come easily to the Princess. It demands responsibility and for the Princess to take charge of her life. She actually prefers to be looked after. She is happy to leave the duties and responsibilities to the King, Queen, or Servants. When the Princess does have a career, if it is not in the creative or performing arts, it is likely to involve young children. Childcare and teaching are suitable careers for the Princess. She can establish her own court, and her charges are the courtiers.

As in the story, *"The Princess and the Pea"*, Princesses demand comfort and satisfaction. They love to be tantalized. Have I mentioned chocolate? Do I need to say more? My wife, while munching chocolate, tells me that you cannot get too much of a good thing. Fine food and drink are demanded but not to be overdone, as the Princess likes to keep her figure and health. Like the Prince, the Princess generally gets what she wants and is happy to use her charm, femininity, vulnerability and, as a last resort, a tantrum to achieve her desired result. Should you indulge a Princess? Of course you should. How could you resist? If you would like to know how to resist indulging a princess, just ask a Queen. She'll tell you in no uncertain terms.

**Negative Aspects:**

Irresponsible ~ Self-centred ~ Spendthrift ~ Flippant ~ Frivolous ~ Arrogant ~ Above everyone else ~ Manipulative ~ Condescending ~ Conscious of class ~ Temper tantrums ~ Intolerant ~ Lazy ~ Dependent ~ Fragile ~ Spoilt

**Positive Aspects:**

Adored ~ Being looked after ~ Composed ~ Elegance ~ Charming ~ Indulged ~ Divine right ~ Get what you want ~ Pageantry ~ Artistic ~ Rich ~ Cultured ~ Heroic ~ Beguiling ~ Empathetic ~ Protected ~ Popular ~ Desirable

**Archetypal Energy:**

The archetypal energy of the Princess centres on her attraction and vulnerability. Princesses have characteristics that attract attention. They have a soft beauty and charm about them that commands attention. They compel observers to drop their defences and tune into the energy of purity and vulnerability. Princess Diana and

Princess Grace were the perfect examples of that attractive energy and vulnerability. They exuded grace and composure that would melt the harshest critics.

The Princess uses her attraction and vulnerability to find safety and security. The King has the perfect archetypal energy to protect and defend the Princess. In Diana's case, she was bemused by the royal energy of a Prince who would never be King, and the relationship deteriorated. In most cases, the Princess does live happily ever after, not with her Prince but with her King. Once the safety and security of the Princess is established with a relationship with a King, she then seeks the equivalent of a courtly life. She looks to a home she can decorate. She seeks the finances that support her spending. She seeks company who entertains her. She expresses her creativity in artistic endeavours. Finally, where possible, she has servants to perform the menial chores.

The key archetypal energy that challenges the Princess is responsibility. It is important she understands the limitations of the world around her and to be responsible and content within those boundaries. She has to organize and budget, not only her finances but also her time and energy. The Princess may be required to work, and usually she calls upon other archetypal energy to assist her in her duties. There are work opportunities that suit the Princess archetypal energy, but more than that, the Princess generally has little difficulty in finding a suitable position. Her attractive energy guarantees popularity.

It is important for the Princess to be aware that her seeming naivety and the lure of public exposure can produce unedifying consequences. The media delights in the exposé of young females behaving badly. More often than not, these young ladies have Damsel archetypes, but occasionally there is a Princess thrown into that mix. If you are looking for a Princess role model, Princess Diana was a wonderful example. She showed how a Princess can use her beauty, charm, and eloquence to engage the public and the media. She did this not for her own edification but to highlight the plight of others less fortunate than she was. Diana was content to use her privileged role to contribute to the betterment of society. This was positive Princess energy at its most effective.

**Archetypal Combinations:**

The archetypal energy of the Princess combines well with the energy of:

King * Artist * Scholar * Advocate * Actor * Mother *Networker * Indulged

Child * Craftsperson * Diplomat * Dilettante * Angel * Servant * Engineer * Peacemaker *Rescuer * Teacher * Philosopher

**Effective Use of Princess Energy:**

- Take responsibility for your actions, desires, and behaviour.
- Maintain your strength of character, even in times of need.
- Enjoy and appreciate the beautiful things that surround you.
- Indulgence may be a right, but it is also a treat or a special gift.
- Use the positive energy of the Princess to motivate others. Leadership is disguised in many forms, and the power of persuasion is one such form.

# Prophet

The Prophet is often associated with the Visionary. People who possess the archetype of the Prophet may also possess the archetype of the Visionary, but this is not always the case. There are many ways of accessing information. Vision is only one of them. Others tune in by listening, knowing, interpreting, dreaming, and transcending. We all have moments of déjà vu. Some we recognize and wonder at their occurrence. For most of us, it is a power beyond our comprehension. This is understandable, as most of us do not have the Prophet or Visionary archetype. The Prophet experiences these situations as normal. However, some with the Prophet archetype may not recognize this as normal, as they are surrounded by doubters and disbelievers. Imagine how difficult this archetypal energy is for a child. Children have an understanding and a knowing that the adults around them do not possess and are possibly chastising them for daydreaming or making up stories. For the prophet, it is a case of best keep the information a secret and stay in denial than be ridiculed or punished.

Prophets may be spiritual in nature. Jesus Christ was one such Prophet. Other Prophets may explore a more physical existence. Their prophecies are usually about natural phenomena, disasters, and human invention. Prophets often live before their time. Nostradamus was a Prophet of this type, who spoke about the Great Fire of London that occurred in 1666 and destroyed all of medieval London ("the ancient lady") within the old Roman walls.

> "The blood of the just will commit a fault at London, Burnt though lighting of twenty threes the six: The ancient lady will fall from her high place. Several of the same sect will be killed."

Our five senses limit us. They allow us to view the physical, and this is important, as we are physical beings in a physical world. Our intellects give us the freedom or restriction to go beyond or stay grounded to that physical world. Our spirits or souls give us the knowing or faith to move beyond the physical and view worlds and energies differently from the physical plane. It is understandable that many of us limit our knowledge and opinions to the world of sensory experience. It is also understandable that our intellects give us reason to limit our thinking. The reverse is also true, as our intellects give us the power to reason worlds beyond sensory capacity. This is the unknown and, to the majority of humanity, represents danger. The known is safe territory, while the unknown is scary and full of potential dangers.

Our spirits or souls live more in the realm of the unknown. There is nothing to see, hear, smell, touch, or taste. Our five senses, which govern a major part of our existence, are redundant. Our intellect gives us choice to explore beyond our senses but no proof of what we cannot see, hear, smell, taste, or touch. It is only our knowing or faith that gives power to the spirit or soul. So imagine our disbelief when the Prophet comes along with the ability to move beyond the present sensory and intellectual world and presents a clear picture of our spiritual selves, or a clear picture of ourselves (individually or as humanity), in a different time frame within a physical world vastly different from the one we currently reside in. For this ability, the Prophet may endure a tough time.

There have always been individuals who have the Prophet archetype. This is still the case in the modern world. However, there are also shysters determined to make a living from people's gullibility. They are found in all walks of life, including within religions, sects, and the New Age industry. It is not always easy to discern a genuine Prophet.

The positive energy of the Prophet does not endorse self-glorification or the accumulation of a fortune. They accept what is reasonable, if they choose to accept anything at all, and move on with life. The ethical Prophet is humble. Some individuals with the Prophet archetype prefer to stay silent or confide in a few close friends. Life is to be enjoyed, and we are thrown enough challenges without going out of our way to incur the barbs of cynics and doubters.

**Negative Aspects:**

I-told-you-so personality ~ Conditional ~ Pessimist ~ Cynic ~ Fear of rejection ~ Rigid ~ Doom and gloom ~ Limited ~ Self-seeking ~ Self-importance ~ Glorified ~ Profit driven ~ Exaggeration ~ Ego driven

**Positive Aspects:**

Predictions ~ Bringing the message then letting go ~ Catalyst of change ~ Confronting ~ Validated ~ Self-conviction ~ Universal ~ Bravado ~ Intuitive ~ Bold ~ Visionary ~ Interpretation ~ In tune ~ Psychic

**Archetypal Energy:**

The Prophet is a conduit who receives and sends information from one dimension to another. This information may be spiritual in nature or it may be about physical change, restructure, or developmental. The energy that allows the Prophet to be this conduit is psychic energy. As with all archetypal energy, we have the capability of utilizing minute or copious amounts. It depends on our personal archetypes. Even if you do not have the Prophet archetype, you are still capable of harnessing psychic energy. If you are blessed with the Prophet archetype, you are blessed with incredible psychic energy. Psychic energy is like potential. We never lose our potential, and when we practice, we turn our psychic energy into psychic ability. When Prophets tune in and open the line of communication to the greater universe, they are rewarded with a constant stream of information. Much of this information may be confusing or frightening to Prophets. It may be difficult to read and comprehend. It is easy to understand the challenges that confront Prophets.

The other challenge for Prophets is the doubters who surround them and the social beliefs of the time. Jesus knew his fate and his betrayal, yet his disciples, his friends, and those he had mentored did not believe him. Peter, especially chosen by Jesus to follow in his footsteps, scoffed at the suggestion that he would ever defy Jesus. Jesus knew better. Although his heart must have been filled with sadness and disappointment, Jesus had the strength to remain true to his Prophet archetype. There is much debate about Nostradamus. Many of his famous quatrains are difficult to read and open to interpretation, but we have to be aware that his time was dominated by the Inquisitions. This was not the age that encouraged truth, prophecy, or expression contrary to religious dogma. The consequences were obvious. It is to the credit of Nostradamus that he was prepared to put pen to paper in any form whatsoever.

The archetypal energy of the Prophet is the essence of letting go. The Prophet's task is to be a channel and relay information to the people. There must be no personal involvement in this process. As soon as the Prophet becomes involved as an individual, then the material presented to his listeners is tainted. There is to be no subjective censorship. The information—good, bad, or indifferent—has to be presented intact. If the Prophet's channelling is not understood, so be it. Most importantly, Prophets have to understand their role. There should be no withholding of information for profit. If the Prophet has a service to offer, then it is fine to be recompensed. Taking advantage of the very people you are pretending to advise is delving deeply into the negative archetypal energy. The

Prophet's vocation is to pass on information and then let it go. The Prophet does not own that information. The Prophet is not dependent on that information or the resulting conclusions that come from it. The pathway travelled by Prophets is a lonely one, but Prophets have to remain independent, and in their hearts, they know that to be the case.

**Archetypal Combinations:**

The archetypal energy of the Prophet combines well with the energy of:

Mystic * Visionary * Wise Woman * Shaman * Wizard * Witch * Hermit * Hero * Servant * Seeker * God * Goddess * Philosopher * Wanderer * Adventurer * Divine Child * Pilgrim * Rebel * Monk

**Effective Use of Prophet Energy:**

- Keep your pathways of communication open.
- Have enough strength in your convictions to tell the truth. Remain independent from the information. Do not fall into the web of subjective censorship.
- Be wary of dark entities. Do not dwell on their energy.
- Say the word, and let it go.
- Do not be taken in by the rewards and self-importance of your work.

# Prostitute

We all have a Prostitute archetype. It is the archetype that tells us what we are worth. How are we valued? What is the value we place upon ourselves? What is the value accepted by us given from others? There is more to the Prostitute archetype than the literal meaning and use of the word. The value the Prostitute archetype determines is not just for our physical selves. It is the value placed on our emotional selves. It is the worth of our intellectual selves. It is the value of our psychological selves. It is the worth of our artistic selves. In other words, whenever we participate in social interaction, there is a process, for each of us, that determines our individual worth. That process is deeply ingrained in the archetypal energy of the Prostitute.

The Victim archetype works hand in glove with the Prostitute. The Victim is the archetype that determines our self-esteem. It stands to reason that if our self-esteem is high, we place a high value on our worth. Alternatively, if our self-esteem is low, then we are inclined to place a low value on our worth.

The Victim and the Prostitute archetypes work together. Both are strong archetypes, so if you are feeling bad about yourself, you are likely to be undervalued or taken for granted. It requires some positive thinking and determination to move from the negative to the positive. The good news is that if you strengthen your self-esteem, you increase your worth. Alternatively, if you increase your worth, you strengthen your self-esteem. Most people understand the emotions felt when promoted, given a raise in pay or better conditions, acquiring a new job or winning an award. They feel elated, satisfied, proud, and valued. Their self-esteem is enhanced and strengthened. The Victim and the Prostitute work well together. Look after one, and the other looks after itself.

**Negative Aspects:**

Selling yourself out ~ Compromising your integrity ~ Up for sale ~ Exploiting ~ Taken advantage of ~ Immoral ~ Lacking in value ~ Cheap ~ Weak ~ Used ~ Taken for granted ~ Blackmail ~ Abused

**Positive Aspects:**

Maintain your personal boundaries ~ Be true to yourself ~ Principled ~ Courage ~ Sticking to convictions ~ Strong-willed ~ Worth your weight in gold ~ Valued ~ Take a stand

**Archetypal Energy:**

In its basic form, the archetypal energy of the Prostitute is about survival. Our Prostitute archetype assesses the surroundings we find ourselves in and determines the best strategies to survive or to change the environment. In most cases, the basic instinct to survive is a powerful energy. Humans have been able to withstand horrendous situations and circumstances. War, prison camps, torture, psychological threats, natural disasters, accidents, ill health, the death or disappearance of family or friends, and poverty are some of the dire circumstances that occur every day. Our Prostitute archetype determines how we approach and survive each situation and every challenge.

The first step in the battle to survive is psychological. We determine our circumstances and ascertain if we have the necessary strength to survive. We have the ability to entertain the mind with games and activities to alleviate stress and the pain of the real world. We think of ways and make plans to improve or change the stressful circumstances. Our Prostitute is hard at work. What are we worth? Is it worth enduring these circumstances to survive, or should we just give up? In most cases, our Prostitute works determinedly to ensure our survival for as long as possible.

The second step in the battle is physical survival. Have we sufficient food and drink? What do we need to maintain our health? Can we alleviate physical pain? What are we willing to do to ensure our physical survival? This question is answered by the strength and will of our Prostitute archetype. History has shown that in life-threatening situations, humans are capable of any deed, be it heroic or degenerate. Heroic deeds such as rescuing a stranger from a car accident, a house fire, or a shark attack are common. So, too, are degenerate deeds of rape, robbery, torture, and murder.

The third step in the battle is emotional survival. Emotions are often kept under control when physical survival is at stake. There is no time to feel pity for ourselves or anyone else. All energy diverts into the action of survival. It is when imminent danger has passed and there is some time and space for assessment that emotions become involved. Is there an emotional attachment to another that can assist with my survival? Is a change of emotion needed? Does survival depend on hardening the emotions or softening the emotions? Does one need anger to survive this situation? Perhaps calmness or detachment is needed. It is the job of the Prostitute archetype to determine what emotion or mix of emotions allows one to overcome the various challenges.

Fortunately for many of us, our survival issues are under control. The archetype of the Prostitute is able to devote energy to satisfaction. Again psychological, physical, and emotional factors are all considered. Unlike survival energy, there is a freedom associated with satisfaction energy. We are free to choose how we think. We are entitled to opinions. In many cases, we are even entitled to express our opinions. We are able to express satisfaction or dissatisfaction with ourselves, our families, our friends, our social structures, and our social norms. We have psychological choices. We also have physical choices. There is an array of food and drink available to us. We can exercise. We are able to seek medical advice. We can titillate our physical selves with all kinds of pleasures. We also have choices about how we feel. We have the freedom to feel the full range of human emotion. We have the freedom to change how we feel about a person, an idea, or an event. We have the artistic freedom to express our emotions. Our Prostitute has the freedom to expand energetically.

In many societies, especially those that are free and open, the freedom to satisfaction is tempered by social structures and personal relationships. Another challenge for the energy of the Prostitute is to determine an individual's worth in various social settings and in comparison with others. Therefore, if you have tertiary qualifications and experience, you may be worthy to apply for certain employment positions. If your passion is for an artistic endeavour, your worth may be determined by the quality and uniqueness of your expression. This worth is determined by you and others. When you begin a relationship, your emotion and the emotion of your partner determines satisfaction, success, and longevity. The energy of the Prostitute has the job of assessing and valuing our worth in a variety of situations. Little wonder that the energy of the Prostitute has the strength of courage, discernment, and resilience.

**Archetypal Combinations:**

The archetypal energy of the Prostitute combines well with the energy of:

* Victim * Saboteur * Child
* All other archetypes depending on the circumstances.

**Effective Use of Prostitute Energy:**

- In all circumstances ask yourself the basic question, "What am I worth?"
- Evaluate your self-esteem, and be aware of the part your Victim plays in determining your self-worth.
- Change your self-esteem, and you change your worth. Change your worth, and you change your self-esteem.
- Maintain your optimism when you value yourself, for there are plenty who maintain realism when they determine your value. Compromise always strikes a balance.

# Puck

Puck is the archetype of making mischief. Making mischief may be a deliberate act, or it may be accidental. Whatever the situation, the individual with the Puck archetype derives satisfaction from the deed. There may be a mix of other emotions ranging from happiness to remorse, but no matter the result, the Puck is satisfied.

The person with the Puck archetype sees his or her role as a conduit for others to self-assess. In other words, it is the duty of the Puck to make people take a good, hard look at who they are. If someone does not have a sense of humour, the Puck is inclined to play a practical joke on that person to point out that lack of humour. If someone is a stickler for punctuality, the Puck deliberately arrives late to demonstrate there are more important things in life. If someone falsely claims to have a certain skill, the Puck delights in exposing the falsehood. The Puck is capable of spreading the truth through gossip. If this does not work, the Puck is happy to spread falsehoods through gossip. The act of vengeance is a necessary weapon in the Puck armoury.

Social networks are a wonderful invention in which the Puck can operate. Before the Internet, the sphere of influence of the Puck was limited to an individual or a small group of associates. With the advent of social networks, the Puck can make mischief on an unprecedented scale.

Individuals with the Puck archetype may not have a Joker archetype, but they can tell jokes, usually at the expense of others. Pucks may not have a Trickster archetype, but they can, and do, play tricks on others. Pucks may not have a Fool archetype, but they can be foolish, mainly to point out the absurdity of a situation or the stupidity of others around them. Pucks may not be Court Jesters, although they are capable of making fun of themselves and others with impunity. The Puck may use the skills, tools, and energy of the Joker, the Trickster, the Fool, and the Court Jester, but the Puck is a different archetype in design and purpose. The objective of the Puck is to hold a mirror to society. It is to challenge an individual, an organization, or a society to examine opinions, priorities, and behaviours. When chicanery is needed to illustrate a point, the Puck feels no qualms in its use.

People with the Puck archetype are articulate and quick-witted. They have to react to personalities and situations quickly and with authority. This articulation and quick-wittedness allows them to maintain composure and a position of strength. Those with the Puck archetype make excellent stand-up comedians. The greatest skill of the stand-up comedian is to engage the audience but keep the upper hand at all times throughout the performance. There is nothing worse for the stand-up comedian than to be outshone or outwitted by a member of the audience. The same is the case for those with the Puck archetype. Their desire is to remain in control. The greatest challenges for Pucks are to maintain their composure and control their emotions. As soon as Pucks become emotionally involved in a situation, their authority, influence, and power diminish.

**Negative Aspects:**

Meddler ~ Spell caster ~ Con man ~ Fraud ~ Cruel ~ Hypocrite ~ Teasing ~ Humiliate ~ Critical ~ Sarcastic ~ Cynical ~ Bad taste ~ Hurtful ~ Tantrums ~ Inconsiderate ~ Interfering ~ Blatant ~ Vindictive

**Positive Aspects:**

Playful ~ Fun-loving ~ Mischievous ~ Absurdity in life ~ Quick-witted ~ Don't take yourself too seriously ~ Easy going ~Articulate ~ Controlled ~ Entertaining ~ Holds a mirror to society

**Archetypal Energy:**

The archetypal energy of the Puck revolves around communication with a message. The method of those with the Puck energy is to shock people in a good-natured, fun-loving, but sometimes, mischievous way. The Puck energy wants people to have a good look at their own lives. Self-examination is the message. Shakespeare provides the perfect example of this energy in *A Midsummer Night's Dream*. Titania, proud and beautiful, is cast in a magic spell by Puck to fall in love with Nick Bottom, a man who has been given the head of an ass. Imagine Titania's horror when the spell breaks and she realizes how foolish she has been made to look! Does the Puck's mischief-making change the behaviour of his victim? Perhaps not! Yet the message has been delivered, and the Puck has been true to his nature.

The communication used by a Puck requires a quick wit, the clever use of language, and performance within a social context or situation. Pucks must always remain in control and at a distance from their quarry. As soon as Pucks becomes personally involved in the process or outcome, they draw in negative energy. The process becomes a personal vendetta. The energy becomes more like that of the negative Avenger. Pucks lose their strength of character, their purpose, and their integrity.

The energy of Puck requires discernment. Mischief-making is an art form that can easily deteriorate into cynicism and sarcasm. Discerning Pucks retain their integrity. They retain the positive energy of that fun-loving spirit. The wit, the charm, and the joviality of the Puck energies are able to retain their purity. Once Puck becomes emotionally involved in the result, discernment disappears. The battle of personalities begins. The message and manner deteriorate into nastiness and vilification. The positive energy of Pucks allow for individuals with that archetype to stand tall and alone. They remain untouchable as fun-loving, playful, quick-witted, mischievous characters.

**Archetypal Combinations:**

The archetypal energy of the Puck combines well with the energy of:

Trickster * Court Jester * Joker * Judge * Actor * Artist * Storyteller * Detective * Scribe * Fool * Networker * Clown * Peter Pan Child * Rebel * Hero/Heroine

**Effective Use of Puck Energy:**

- Discernment is the cornerstone of Puck energy. Emotion is the undoing of this energy.
- Remember your purpose is to communicate a message that gives people the choice to examine their lifestyles and make changes or remain just as they are.
- Do not become personally involved in either the process or the outcome.
- Remain true to your fun-loving nature, but be aware of the dark, negative energy.

# Queen

The Queen is a powerful archetype of command, strength, duty, and achievement. We are immediately aware when those with the Queen archetype enter a room. The energy totally changes. The Queen demands to be noticed. Her clothing is regal. She chooses to sit at the head of the table. She chooses a special chair, maybe even the highest chair in the room, or she sits on the arm of a couch just to be above everyone else. The Queen is always in command. She demands to be heard, and when she speaks, others listen and dare not interrupt. The Queen speaks with authority and is rarely challenged.

The Queen is in command of her realm, whether it be a household, office, classroom, school, business, government department, state, territory, or country. Whatever her situation, the Queen claims a territory and rules it as her own. This can happen at a very young age. A fine example of this was a student named Sasha. When she was only five years of age and in her first year of school, she clashed constantly with her teacher. They were warring over the territorial rights of the classroom. The young Queen gathered three other students as her allies. They were all Princesses. If the young Queen couldn't win the battle over the classroom territory, she certainly made sure she ruled over her court and her courtiers. Her realm included her corner of the classroom and the playground.

There is always a clash of archetypal energy when two strong archetypes interact in the same space. This is also the case when two individuals with the same strong archetype are forced to interact in shared territory. Two individuals with the Queen archetype are likely to be at loggerheads if they are forced to share the same space. The Queen enjoys the ability to define her realm. There is peace as long as she is not challenged in her own territory. Business managers, personnel officers, school principals, and parents have to be aware of those with the Queen archetype. The Queen is a valuable colleague, an efficient organizer, an effective leader, and an industrious worker. However, she needs to own territory, be in command, and have the right to perform her duties.

One of the greatest challenges for the person with the Queen archetype is to trust and allocate responsibility to others. The Queen has an innate need to manage all affairs, and she finds it extremely difficult to let go of any task, no matter how simple. She understands that if you are going to do something, you do it well. If something goes wrong, the Queen must be made aware of the problem so it can be dealt with immediately. The Queen has a strong personal attachment and duty of care to her people and her tasks. It is akin to the attitude between landlord and tenant. What does the Queen do to maintain control? She learns to delegate effectively. She gathers two or three trusted advisers and administrators. If she can confidently pass over some of her responsibilities and maintain good communication, then her realm flourishes and she maintains her stamina and health.

Unlike the Princess who spends money just for the sake of spending, the Queen always has a purpose to her purchases. She is happy to splurge occasionally, but the Queen spends to enhance her realm. Spending is usually on practical items, although every so often, items are purchased to beautify the Queen and her realm. The Queen then finalizes her expenditures, and the savings begins again. The Queen manages money very well.

Everyone is aware of the drama Queen. This behaviour is negative Queen archetypal energy. The drama queen is in constant emotional turmoil over petty issues, behaviour that often occurs when the Queen is denied territory and responsibility. Parents, in particular, have to be aware that a child with the Queen archetype desires a place to rule. She wants responsibilities and duties and the trust to carry out those duties. Restriction and boredom of the Queen creates emotional overkill, so allowing the Queen a realm resolves some of the negative drama-queen behaviour. Another cause of this dramatic Queen behaviour is her low tolerance of others, particularly with individuals with certain archetypal characteristics. The Queen is not fond of Princess archetypal behaviour. She is less tolerant of the Damsel and totally abhors Fools. Drama-queen behaviour is often caused by the Queen reacting to the perceived stupidity and weaknesses of those who surround her. The responsibility of being Queen is stressful. It is all work and all responsibility. The slightest infraction against her personal rule generally sets off an emotional response. Place a drama queen in a drama school to challenge the Queen archetype's energy and give purpose to dramatic performance.

**Negative Aspects:**

Rules the roost ~ Condescending ~ Tyrant ~ Class conscious ~ Self-serving ~ Intolerant ~ Manipulative ~ Arrogant ~ Self-centred ~ Drama queen ~ Disempowerment ~ Suspicious ~ Harsh

**Positive Aspects:**

Wise ~ Benevolent ~ Rich ~ Divine right ~ Pageantry ~ Kind ~ Generous ~ Fertility ~ Empower ~ Protective ~ In charge ~ Organized ~ Regal ~ Powerful ~ Inspiring ~ Loyalty

**Archetypal Energy:**

The archetypal energy of the Queen revolves around her power and how she uses it. The energy of the Queen can be overwhelming. Some Queens are a little scary. Remember, the Queen likes to be in charge, and because her work ethic is so strong, she expects everyone else, especially those in her realm, to be as committed as she is. She is also a stickler for rank and duty. Everyone in the realm has his or her position, and she insists upon order and stability, which in turn, allows all her subjects to carry out duties with clarity and certainty.

If you are aware of these expectations, you become a valuable asset and friend to the Queen. The Queen rewards hard work and duty. She also rewards loyalty with loyalty. As a friend, the person with the Queen archetype is happy to take you places and provide opportunities that might ordinarily be out of your reach. Treat the Queen with respect and dignity, and she returns that treatment with honour and high favour.

If you have a Queen archetype, remember to find good advisors. Allow them responsibilities, and trust their loyalty. You are there to lead responsibly, not to carry out all tasks personally. The archetypal energy of the Queen is laced with endurance. She also has the courage and fortitude to withstand all kinds of pressures and challenges. Remember that delegation is the key! The Queen is there for the long haul. Consider Queen Elizabeth. She has ruled since 1954 and shows no sign of retiring. Strength and endurance, with the ability to delegate, are trademarks of the archetypal energy of the Queen.

Service is another important aspect of this energy. As much as the Queen loves to be in control, she also serves her subjects in her position as ruler. She gives them leadership, opportunities, protection, organization, ethics, and loyalty. It doesn't matter if the individual with the Queen archetype is a family's mother or the leader of government. Service and duty run deep in the archetypal energy of the Queen. The Queen's energy relies on give and take, pageantry and flow. She carries colour and tradition and is the feminine half of leadership. Long live the Queen!

**Archetypal Combinations:**

The archetypal energy of the Queen combines well with the energy of:

Heroine * Statesman * Warrior * Wise Woman * Judge * Peacemaker * Athlete * Teacher * Servant * Martyr * Indulged Child * Advocate * Politician * Networker

**Effective Use of Queen Energy:**

- Remember to delegate duties to your trusted advisors.
- Maintain your territorial boundaries. Disputes are costly - physically, psychologically and emotionally.
- Be loyal and trust your subjects and, in return, they will be loyal and give trust to you.
- You are both a leader and a servant.
- Maintain your personal integrity. The morality and worth of a community reflects the morality and worth of its leader.

# Rebel

The Rebel defies authority and social norms. An individual with the Rebel archetype tend to argue just for the sake of argument. Some deliberately choose behavioural attitudes and lifestyles vastly different from the majority. Those with the Rebel archetype can be terrifying to other members of society who thrive on order and compliance. Rebels dress differently. They deliberately lack social protocol. They regularly challenge or defy authority. They often create anxiety in others. They may seek trouble, and sometimes just rebel because they can, anywhere, anytime, and for no obvious reason. The extreme Rebels may be members of motorcycle gangs, criminal gangs (especially those involved in the drug trade), environmental warriors, computer hackers, and corporate whistle blowers.

Not all Rebels live an extreme lifestyle; some have seemingly regular lifestyles. However, you find that they do many things differently. Rebels are particularly strong in their personal beliefs. If they believe that something should be done or that some things need changing, their rebellious, independent streaks ensure they act no matter what the consequences or odds of success. Their nature is to challenge, and to Rebels, this is not only the right thing to do, but the only thing to do.

Let me give you further examples so you can define yourself (although most Rebels know if they have a Rebel archetype) or recognize the Rebel archetype in those around you. You might notice that Rebels drive above the speed limit, pirate music and movies, jump a fence to attend a festival or concert, drink to excess, or use illegal drugs. They argue about the price of a meal or the quality of service and refuse to pay. They are defiant children, rebellious teenagers, aching for independence and suffocating under the restrictions placed upon them by family and social norms. They may be the school dropouts, the troublemakers, or the tricksters.

Many Rebels find their positions on the social fringe. Working in an office, teaching in a school, and being part of a business are far too restrictive and authoritarian for Rebels. They may manage to work part-time in an organization or on a part-time business, but full-time employment under the command of other people is a compromise that most Rebels are not prepared to make. Rebels happily run their own businesses. They enjoy being their own boss and often contract their own services or goods. They may also volunteer or be part of non-government organizations, such as Sea Shepherd, AusAid, and Medecins Sans Frontieres. Rebels lead lifestyles and fill positions in society that define their values. They do not like to be told how to live their lives or how to manage their own affairs. Rebels define their individual personalities without input, and that is that. So, go suck a lemon!

**Negative Aspects:**

Stubborn ~ Wilful ~ Disrespectful ~ Misplaced anger ~ Violent ~ Fanatical ~ Hot-headed ~ Insensitive ~ Bully ~ Tunnel-vision ~ Peer pressure ~ Intolerant ~ Misuse of power ~ Open to abuse ~ Criminal ~ Self-obsessed ~ Irresponsible ~ Not owning the consequences of their behaviour ~ Reactionary

**Positive Aspects:**

Bringer of change ~ Strong-willed ~ Determined ~ The emperor has no clothes ~ Challenge ~ Nonconformist ~ Whistle-blower ~ True to self ~ Independence ~ Honesty ~ Innovator ~ Holds a mirror to life

**Archetypal Energy:**

The archetypal energy of Rebels revolves around independence. They do not like to be told what to do. This independence is noticeable from an early age, with young Rebel toddlers who get into everything. These children use their toys in ways that defy expectation and instruction. Rebels are the students always in trouble, for challenging school rules or teacher authority. These are the teenagers who dress differently, sneak out at night, revel in excess, argue with parents, and quite possibly, are thrown out of home more than once.

As they move into adulthood, Rebels rarely compromise their independence. If they cannot find a legal way to survive and make an income, then they find an illegal way. They might be part of a socially respected organization, but Rebels still cherish their independence. In this situation they tend to find their own niche in a business. Alternatively, Rebels start their enterprises or businesses. The chances are these businesses are alternative, bordering on illegality but with a sharp insight into fringe culture. Julian Assange is the obvious example of an individual with a Rebel archetype.

Rebel energy is defiance, a natural response to any challenge to their independence. If the value systems of Rebels are under attack, they tend to act defiantly to win back their autonomy. If the social norm, law or authority figure is incongruous, weak, superfluous, inconsistent, and hypocritical, does not make sense, or is just plain silly, then the Rebel is happy to respond with defiance. If Rebels are angered, they act with more than defiance. They possibly take on the energy of the Avenger and retaliate with whatever means available to them.

As the energy of Rebels challenges the social norms and authority, they essentially hold a reflective mirror to society. This energy is like ripples from a pebble thrown in a pond. This can be challenging, especially if others join with the Rebel. The pebble becomes a boulder, and the ripples become waves. For example, John Lennon and Yoko Ono conducted a press conference from their bed. Their aim was to challenge the western world as to the real meaning of peace. This was part of the opposition to the war in Vietnam. This opposition began with small amounts of Rebel energy and ended with vociferous popular demands. This is positive Rebel energy directed at causing social change. The conservative forces of society prefer no change or limited change in an ordered fashion. This conservative energy constantly attempts to limit the influence of the Rebel.

For Rebels to challenge authority and force social or political change, they need conviction. The impact of Rebel energy is determined by the strength of the individual Rebel and his or her knowledge and ability to communicate that strength. If the conviction is strong, the impact is strong. A "flash in the pan" challenge to authority or social normality may be brief and ineffectual. Strong, enduring Rebels have the capability of bringing change that is effective and memorable. Rebels must draw upon their personal strength of character and come to the understanding that their rebellion should not just be for personal gain or pleasure. It should also have a social or cultural impact that enhances the lives of others. This is when Rebels use their archetypal energy to its full strength and capacity.

**Archetypal Combinations:**

The archetypal energy of the Rebel combines well with the energy of:

Warrior * Peacemaker * Advocate * Adventurer * Pioneer * Entrepreneur * Prophet * Wanderer * Avenger * Servant * Hero/Heroine * Networker * Shaman * Statesman * Peter Pan Child * Hermit * Puck * Martyr * Athlete * Shape-Shifter

**Effective Use of Rebel Energy:**

- Be discerning in your use of Rebel energy.
- Stay strong to your convictions, and do not be swayed by peer pressure or personal glorification.
- Be aware of your actions, and be responsible for the consequences.
- Personal safety may not be a personal priority, but understand you are less effective if your judgment is overruled by emotion.

# Rescuer

The Rescuer's task in life is to rescue whoever and whatever he or she can. Mechanics, engineers, and handymen rescue old cars and restore them to their shining best. Antiquities specialists restore paintings and furnishings with elaborate and painstaking care and precision. Pieces are cleaned and invigorated with love and passion and then displayed with pride or sold for profit. I remember one client who took pride in rescuing old boats. Many others rescue animals. When I talk to these animal Rescuers, I always ask what pets they had as children. They not only tell me about the numerous pets they had but also the numerous pets they were not allowed to have. Then, they tell me about every animal, wild and tame, they have ever saved and rescued. As adults, these individuals still have many pets. Some devote their lives to animals as veterinary scientists, environmental warriors, conversationalists, zoo or wildlife keepers, or carers in animal shelters or refuges.

Even though many Rescuers save things, the most common Rescuer is a young female who rescues people. Any one in need, but especially challenging males, tends to be the target for this kind of Rescuer. Many of these women are inclined to begin a relationship and become emotionally involved with their subjects. They believe they can not only rescue their partners from patterns of self-destruction but also change their personalities and behaviours. The Rescuer rarely realizes this is usually a futile exercise.

A force within Rescuers causes reason and discernment to be abandoned. They can make the same mistake on a rotational basis, working through yet another failed relationship. After figuratively banging their heads against brick walls for the umpteenth time, the penny finally drops. Rescuers eventually realize the act of rescuing is a noble act, but the act of them changing somebody else is a futile exercise. People can only bring about change in themselves. It is an internal decision to enact self-transformation. It may be assisted by external forces, but the external forces do not control the change in energy, will, or behaviour. When Rescuers understand this truth, they are acting with positive Rescuer archetypal energy. The Martyr aspect of the Rescuer disappears, and the Carer aspect takes over. As a Rescuer, care for people when they need assistance. Give them the opportunities and the ability to pick up the pieces. Firmly remind them the rest is up to them. Nobody else can do it for them. It is important for the Rescuer to understand this and to put it into practice.

On a related topic, Rescuer must remember to take care of their mental, physical, and emotional health. Rescuers are amazing and giving personalities. They give fresh energy to others, but Rescuers tend to neglect their health, career, personal desires, and dreams in subjugation to another. Rescuers have to remember that they must be the first ones to be rescued. When the Rescuer is healthy and balanced, there is more energy to devote to others. Rescuing should be a win-win situation. Restore the balance, and the Rescuer restores a positive energy flow.

**Negative Aspects:**

Co-dependent ~ Compulsive ~ Neediness ~ Self-serving ~ Control freak ~ Self-destructive ~ Undermine ~ Smothering ~ Eternal optimist ~ Self-sacrifice ~ Uncontrolled emotion

**Positive Aspects:**

Assistance ~ Humility ~ Empathetic ~ Letting others grow and move on ~ Strength and support ~ Caring ~ Loving ~ Encouragement ~ Belief in others ~ Sacrifice ~ Good causes ~ Determination

**Archetypal Energy:**

The archetypal energy of the Rescuer suggests that all things deserve rescuing and can be transformed by the Rescuer into a healthy entity. This idea of reality is often a fantasy, confined to the imagination of the Rescuer. This energetic transformation may be possible for inanimate objects, but the Rescuer confronts a greater challenge when rescuing people.

People can be helped physically, psychologically, and emotionally. However, changing patterns of behaviour must come from within. By becoming emotionally involved in their subjects' every drama, Rescuers can move totally unaware and rather rapidly from employing positive archetypal energy to employing negative archetypal energy. They sacrifice their own development and lifestyles to the people they want to save. They become dependent on the result of changing someone else. They begin to lose their own identities. They begin to employ negative Rescuer archetypal energies, such as blackmail, tantrums, servitude, and the like.

The positive energy of the Rescuer allows assistance to a person. This energy allows that person to grow and move on. Relationships are about growth together, with shared values and activities but also about granting your partner the freedom to pursue his or her own interests and move at his or her own pace. Rescuers must maintain that balance between objectivity and subjectivity, between growth and smothering.

Rescuers generally have beautiful, soft energy. There is empathy, love, care, and nurturing within their intentions. Rescuers must remain true to these qualities. They should also maintain their own personal balance. There are times when Rescuers can easily be taken advantage of. They have to call upon inner strength to counteract any imbalances. It takes courage for the Rescuer to walk away from a harmful relationship. However, in the long run, it is more beneficial than to remain within it.

**Archetypal Combinations:**

The archetypal energy of the Rescuer combines well with the energy of:

Carer * Warrior * Mentor * Advocate * Mother * Father * Knight * Hero/Heroine * Priest * Priestess * Wise Woman * Networker * Wounded Child * Judge * Companion * Healer * Peacemaker

**Effective Use of Rescuer Energy:**
- Remember that the first person to be rescued is you.
- Your task is to assist others and to let them grow.
- Rescuing is caring for others, not continual martyrdom for you. Learn your lesson the first time, not the twentieth time.
- Control and force is in direct contrast to rescue and assist.
- Not everything and everyone can be rescued. The cycle requires death and the transformation of energy.

# Saboteur

The Saboteur is our archetype of intuition and choice. Each one of us has a Saboteur archetype, just as each one of us has the gift of choice. Whether we use this gift to make positive or negative choices is up to us. We have the power. We make the decisions.

Please understand that I am not indicating that everything that happens in our lives is our choice. Some disagree with that statement. That is their prerogative. The idea that we control each and every aspect of our lives is a thought of the New Age. It is a reaction to the imprisonment of choice and personal freedom that, for so long, was bound up in religious dogma and practice. For many years, religions had control, not only over spiritual matters but also over physical and psychological affairs. Our fate, our destiny, and our ways of living were dictated to us through religious teachings. It was as if individuals had no choice. It seemed the only way to live our lives, as well as gain eternal salvation, was through religion. Fate and God was one and the same thing, and religious practice was the only pathway. As spiritual awareness took hold and religions lost relevance, humanity, for the first time, became aware that each individual had control of his or her destination. Some New Age teachings preach total control. I believe this is an overreaction, but within a certain framework—a framework that is somewhat controlled by our society and our place within that society—we all have choices, and we all make decisions that impact our lives and our destinies.

Our Saboteur archetype works well with our other archetypes. They may be partners in crime, or they may be partners in success. The Saboteur works on two levels. The first level is intuition. The second level is reason and intellect.

We all recognize intuition. For a variety of reasons, we do not always follow our intuitive choices. Our intuition is our gut feelings. It is our instant reaction to a posed question. We know instantly if an action we take is right for us or likely to cause challenges. We know instantly if a decision is for our positive well-being or it is a decision likely to send us on a detour. We make positive, intuitive decisions every day. Some are major decisions like buying a home, changing jobs, eating healthy food, beginning a relationship, or sending children to a particular school. Others are minor decisions like purchasing a suitable outfit, seeing a thought-provoking movie, or joining a local choir. We generally spend less time dwelling on the minor decisions, but in all cases, we instantly know if these actions are for the best. As we walk into a house, the combination of our Saboteur energy with the energy of the house tells us instantly if it is for us. To use the characters from *Star Wars*: as Obi-Wan Kenobi says to Luke Skywalker, "Use the force, Luke," and "The Force will be with you, always."

Believe it or not, many people operate at this instant, intuitive level all the time. However, most people take more time and make considered choices, especially with major decisions. This does not mean their intuition has gone on holiday. What it does mean is that they have logical, intellectual, or emotional factors that have worked with their intuition or overruled their intuition. If individuals have a Philosopher or Seeker archetype, the chances are their intuition is ignored and discounted. Philosophers and Seekers have a great challenge trusting their intuition and are constantly drawn to logic and consideration. They are bound to conduct a survey or debate about each side of every argument or decision. Often they are paralysed into never making a decision. In most cases, our choice is a combination of intellect and intuition.

We have all had occasions when we sabotage ourselves. This is our Saboteur in operation. If we have ignored our intuitive selves and made decisions with intellect, or more likely emotions, and if these decisions have not been satisfactory, edifying, or positive, we can always make other decisions to change our circumstances. Within our social framework, we always have choice. If we have sabotaged ourselves, our Saboteur is capable of guiding us back to a positive path. Listen to your intuition. Trust your gut feeling. Ask yourself, is this right for me? The answer is either yes or no. If you can frame your questions to a yes or no answer, your intuition works effectively. When you have the answer, act upon it. Keep your intellect and emotions out of the choice. There should be no thinking about the answer, no discussion, and no evaluation. Your intuition is instantaneous. Trust yourself, and go with the flow.

**Negative Aspects:**

Lack of discipline ~ Set you up for failure ~ What will other people think? ~ Incomplete ~ Inconsistent ~ Fear-based decisions ~ Unfocused ~ Scared ~ Lacking confidence ~ Non-trusting ~ Staying with the familiar

**Positive Aspects:**

Intuitive-based decisions ~ What you need to do ~ Feels like yes ~ Consistent ~ Disciplined ~ Focused ~ Goal-orientated ~ Gut feeling ~ Taking chances ~ Trusting ~ Know what you want ~ Compelling

**Archetypal Energy:**

The archetypal energy of the Saboteur is about trust. Decision making is all about trust. Trust ourselves, other people, and the process. Above all this, the most important person to trust is our self. In the end, the directions we take and the choices we make, our values, and our attitudes are up to us. There is little comfort and no point in making excuses. They may satisfy our emotional needs and delude our intellect, but excuses never change our situation. Excuses indicate a lack of trust in our decision-making. We can always blame our parents, our children, our bosses, our neighbours, the bank, or the government for our situations. They do not change our situations, only we can. Trust yourself, and move on with your decision making. Change your attitude, and be more positive. Trust your gut feeling, and follow your intuition.

Many people blame their parents for their own lives and the situations they find themselves in. Many people are justified in feeling hurt, angry, and neglected. They may have been the victims of neglect and abuse. My advice is never easy to adopt, but it is rather simple. Wounded people need healing, but they also need to take control. The blame game is not going to change their circumstances. My advice to them is take control, trust yourself, make intuitive decisions, change your attitude, and change your life. Attitude change is the key. A change of attitude allows people to place trust in their own abilities. It gives them the freedom to change their circumstances and not stay stuck in a rut.

It is no different for those in an unsatisfactory relationship. There are only two possible answers to the question, is this relationship right for me? If the answer is in the positive, then stay committed, work hard, and contribute to the relationship. If the answer is in the negative, then it is time to move on. Intellect and emotion does not change the course of an unsatisfactory relationship. The same situation exists with your job. Trust your Saboteur. If your job is not meeting your needs, then begin to look for something else.

The Law of Attraction works effectively when we kick-start our strong archetypes into action. Our Victim, which regulates our self-esteem, has to be strong. If we feel that we do not deserve a reward or a change, then nothing changes. Our Prostitute, which regulates our worth, must lift the bar with our self-evaluation. Our Saboteur, which regulates our intuition and our choice, must be put into overdrive to bring to us opportunities that we desire. However, we must always trust ourselves and be in control to choose change. Otherwise, we remain where we are, or others decide on change, and we relinquish any control.

**Archetypal Combinations:**

The archetypal energy of the Saboteur combines well with the energy of:

\* Victim \* Prostitute \* Child
\* All other archetypes depending on the circumstances.

**Effective Use of Saboteur Energy:**

- Trust yourself.
- Listen to your gut feeling, and move forward with your decisions.
- Attitude change is the key that ignites all other change.
- Do not be deceived by your intellect and your emotions. They should be used to support your intuition and not to overrule it.
- If you have sabotaged yourself, then change your circumstances to a more positive situation.
- Learn from your mistakes. We all make mistakes, but the key is never to make the same mistake twice.
- Your Saboteur is your friend. Treat this archetype with honour and respect, and it shall treat you with wisdom.

# Salesperson

The Salesperson is an interesting archetype. This archetype is closely linked to the Servant archetype, as the Salesperson is in the service industry. Generally speaking, though, Servants have a direct relationship with the authority they serve. It is often a servant and master relationship. The Salesperson is generally the middle man. Like the Servant, Salespeople have a direct relationship with the authority they work for but, at the same time, serve the interests of customers or clients. They are in the middle of their employers and their customers and are there to satisfy the demands of both. This situation can present Salespersons with a challenge, as it is often difficult to please both parties. Politicians have a similar dilemma. Their direct employer is their political party, yet they are there to serve the people.

Many Salespeople are shop assistants. Goods ranging from food, clothing, accessories, entertainment, technology, communications, and the like may be the products they sell. Services such as repairs, education, maintenance, security, health, and travel all rely on the Salesperson. Door-to-door salespeople have declined in recent years with the exception of a few businesses that still maintain this form of marketing. Avon is still the most well-known of these companies.

Other companies rely on a similar personal approach but have a marketing plan with a networking and reward mechanism built into the business structure. Amway is the typical example. Business franchises work on a similar basis, as they provide the structure and the marketing, while the individual franchisee buys the store or geographical area and works within this structure. More likely in a modern economy, you find Salespeople on the end of your phone, wanting to sell you the latest deal offered by the companies they represent. This business structure, like many others, is based on commission. Some businesses are owned and operated by the individual Salesperson. These may be expanded to involve family, friends, other partners, and employees.

An individual may have both the Salesperson and the Servant archetype. It is possible that both of these archetypes work together on different occasions. However, many people have the Servant archetype but do not have the

Salesperson archetype. My dear wife, Robyn, offered herself as the perfect example. At interval at our drama productions, we offer hot drinks and food. For these events, Robyn is perfectly happy to bake and provide the cakes and slices, the action of a Servant. However, there is no way she would be in the canteen to sell them, the work of the Salesperson. There are plenty of other examples showing the difference between Servant and Salesperson. A visit to your local mall or shopping centre provides numerous examples. The waitress serving tables and cleaning up after the patrons is performing the duties of a Servant. The gentleman or lady standing at the front of the shop spruiking their specials via an amplifier is performing the duties of a Salesperson.

Salespeople are active in the pursuit of customers and sales. There may be something of the Entrepreneur combined with the Salesperson. The Entrepreneur is selling a product, a service, or an idea. So, too, is the Salesperson. It is the largeness of scale and the high degree of risk that separates the Entrepreneur from most of the individuals with the Salesperson archetype.

**Negative Aspects:**

Deceptive ~ Take advantage of ~ False promises ~ Fly by night ~ Pushy ~ All show and no substance ~ Insincere ~ Unethical ~ False claims

**Positive Aspects:**

Offering a service ~ Customer care ~ Ethical ~ Responsible ~ Genuine ~ Stand by your product or service ~ Quality control ~ Reliable ~ Good listener ~ Respect

**Archetypal Energy:**

The energy of Salespeople is all about honesty. They constantly strive for the correct balance to satisfy the interests of two parties. Of course, Salespeople wish to make a sale. Their jobs, careers, and sometimes their very livelihoods depend on these transactions. However, they are also there to satisfy the needs of their customers. This is where the balancing act comes into play. The Salesperson is looking for the win-win situation. Make the sale and keep the customer satisfied. All of this requires the Salespeople to be honest about their knowledge and abilities, about following the procedures of their employers, and about respecting and satisfying the customers.

The positive energy of the Salesperson involves good listening skills. Listen and understand what the customer wants. We have all come across the pushy Salesperson who talks a lot and doesn't really listen. Even when you are talked into buying, you often feel bullied and resentful. Future sales are off your agenda. This is the Salesperson using negative archetypal energy. In a similar situation there is nothing worse than liking a product and wanting to purchase it but having to endure the annoying behaviour of the sales representative.

Reputation is another important aspect of the archetypal energy of the Salesperson. Good products, reliable service, fair prices, attention to detail, quality control, and dealing with any problems are all areas that either enhance a person or company's reputation or drag it down. We can all relate to experiences where we, as customers, have been treated with respect and dignity. This is the Salesperson using the positive energy of humility and empathy to really understand customers and to make them feel good about the shopping experience. This enhances reputation. We, as customers, are happy to return and recommend this person or business to our friends.

No doubt we have also experienced the shopping venture from hell. Little or no service, sales people too busy or preoccupied to care or acknowledge your presence, the sales attendant complaining about his job or other aspects of his life, the know-it-all sales attendant who treats you with condescension (this seems rather prevalent in the technology area), the aggressive salesperson who hassles you into a product that is not suitable to you but who is instructed to move an oversupply of product or the store brand, the service or tradesperson who makes an appointment and fails to arrive or even ring you to explain his absence. All of these things denigrate reputation.

Timing is important for the Salesperson. Products come and go. Customers need change. Efficient Salespeople are knowledgeable. They know about the products available in their businesses and their industries and can pass that information on to their customers. They know about the quality, price, and longevity of the products. They also have to be adaptable and to understand the trends and the changes that are taking place.

**Archetypal Combinations:**

The archetypal energy of the Salesperson combines well with the energy of:

Servant * Entrepreneur * Pioneer * Advocate * Lover * Networker * Judge * Knight * Damsel * Queen * King * Carer

**Effective Use of Salesperson Energy:**

- Be honest in your dealings with your ability, your business, your employer, and your customers.
- Understand your products and service and the needs of your customers.
- Look for opportunities to improve your skills and enhance your reputation.
- Be wary of the easy fix.
- Remember the customer is always right.
- If you are involved in entrepreneurial development, consider the options, the risks, and the expansion details.

# Scholar

The Scholar or Student archetype defines the person who is always studying and participating in various educational courses. Do not confuse study with learning. Every one of us is learning. Only a few of us are studying. The Scholar is the perennial student, who has a thirst for knowledge that takes precedence over all other activity. The Scholar is an educated and knowledgeable person. This is an archetype that determines a lifelong quest for the adventure of study, learning, and knowledge.

The Scholar has a natural love, not only for learning but also for structure and setting for learning. School is important to the Scholar. It is a place of interest and intrigue, security, and comfort. Once the challenges of primary and secondary school have been met, Scholars continue their treks into university and tertiary education. There are, of course, many ways to continue study once the initial university degree has been achieved. There are plenty of postgraduate courses that can enthral the Scholar and meet this lifelong need. The beauty of university courses these days is the flexibility that allows the Scholar to earn an income from part-time work and to study part-time. This extends the study period, which, for the Scholar, is often an ideal situation. There is a process by which a Scholar can complete one degree and perhaps work for several years until the time is right to begin another degree. This process can be repeated well into the Scholar's mature years.

Not all Scholars possess the financial support to have a lifelong university career. However, Scholars are never denied. They find many other opportunities for study and learning. There are myriad community learning centres, private educational institutions, and Internet courses that offer all kinds of learning opportunities. You name your topic, and the Scholar finds a course about it.

Scholars are on a quest for knowledge. They learn from a young age that the ability to read is a vital component to their quests. Scholars generally love to read. It is a process vital to academic success. The other quality that Scholars possess is focus. They are able to concentrate for long periods of time and to set long-term goals. Scholars love the process of learning. Nothing gives them greater pleasure than the joy of finding new information that they can absorb and transfer to a different scenario. Scholars look forward to the next challenge or a new challenge.

**Negative Aspects:**

Hide behind theory ~ Impractical ~ Irrelevant ~ Intellectualizes ~ Elitism ~ Jack of all trades and a master of none ~ Withdrawal from the real world

**Positive Aspects:**

Love of learning ~ Seeking mastery ~ Thirst for knowledge ~ Understanding ~ Industrious ~ Knowledge into action ~ Learned ~ Focused ~ Literate ~ Pride ~ Setting goals ~ Educated ~ Recognition ~ Rewarded ~ Achievement

**Archetypal Energy:**

The archetypal energy of the Scholar is defined by two aspects: the sense of achievement and a love of learning. In most cases, they both play a significant role motivating the Scholar to academic success and moving the Scholar to new areas of study.

Success is like building a stairway to achievement. Each and every success for the Scholar is a stepping stone to the next level. Every examination passed with success, every assignment that is commended, every year of study completed, and every course mastered becomes a building block in the mansion of achievement. Success builds upon success. Achievement determines the continuation of the journey. The Scholar has pride associated with achievements and rightly so.

There is a special ability associated with learning. The love of learning is important, but there is a mastering of the system that is also important. We have all been to school. We have all been confronted with exams and assignments. Our successes were not just determined by knowledge but also understanding of the process of reproducing information that was relevant, coherent, and justified. This is the mastering of the "exam technique." Reading and understanding the question, presenting relevant information concisely and coherently to answer the question, presenting a logical and relevant argument, having the ability to précis and draw out relevant facts and exclude trivialities, and presenting material in a logical and ordered sequence are some of the skills involved in mastering the exam technique. The Scholar understands this process from a very young age.

Many of us have a love of learning. For the Scholar, this love becomes a passion. Most of us are passionate about some aspect of our lives. The Scholar's passion is learning. When there is passion involved, challenges are overcome. Nothing is insurmountable. So, for the Scholar, learning becomes a passion, study becomes a joy, and success turns into achievement.

**Archetypal Combinations:**

The archetypal energy of the Scholar combines well with the energy of:

Seeker * Philosopher * Hermit * Teacher * Prince * Princess * Pioneer * Scientist * Wise Woman * Monk * Nun * Addict * Computer Nerd * Scribe

**Effective Use of Scholar Energy:**

- Celebrate and enjoy your academic achievements.
- Remember to put your knowledge and learning to a practical purpose.
- There are other aspects of your life that need consideration. Beware of becoming insular and aloof.

# Scientist

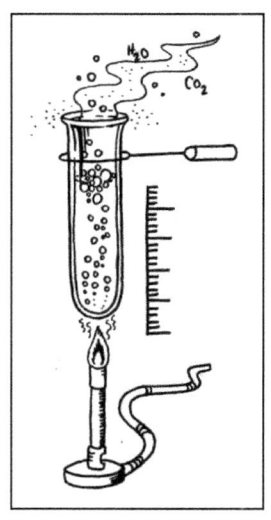

The Scientist and the Inventor are archetypes similar in practice and energy. For the sake of convenience, I deal with them under the title of Scientist. The Scientist deals with a range of investigations, methods, hypotheses, and conclusions. The general aim of the Scientist is to establish a theory and prove the theory to be fact. This, of course, is not always possible. Even established facts are challenged, as scientific methods and equipment improve and allow for more detailed analysis. However, the aim is always worth pursuing, and the advantages that science has given us are worth the effort.

The Inventor may follow a similar path, although the Inventor is often driven by need. The Inventor is always aiming for a finished product. The finished product may solve a problem or improve a process. The Scientist may also be an Inventor looking to produce a finished product, but many Scientists do not involve themselves with products or inventions. They turn hypotheses into reality, research into knowledge, investigation into fact, discovery into awareness, and proposal into consensus.

Individuals with the Scientist archetype are generally well educated. They certainly have a passion for learning and a deep sense of intrigue. The Scientist archetype is evident at a very young age. These are the children who collect things, usually animals. Frogs, tadpoles, lizards, ants, crickets, and all kinds of mini-beasts are fascinating to the young Scientist. In the plant kingdom, carnivorous plants seem to be the stimulus for investigation. Dinosaurs are the perennial favourite on the extinct-animals list. Sea animals are also high in the popularity stakes, with whales and dolphins topping that list.

Then there are the children who love nature. Walking through the bush, climbing over hills and rocky outcrops, wading through creeks, investigating wombat diggings, and sighting snakes and lizards are all fascinating adventures and stimuli to the young Scientist. We should also mention volcanoes, for they are an amazing source of wonder for a Scientist. As young Scientists move through school systems, their ranges of interest broaden. With the right encouragement, a stimulating curriculum, and a dynamic teacher, the seeds of scientific passion are sown. Chemistry, physics, anatomy, botany, and biology are a few of the possibilities that can stimulate a scientific mind. Success in these branches of science requires study and successful educational advances into tertiary education and private and government research.

The questions that science poses may be broad or extremely specific. In every question, the Scientist must begin with an open mind. Objectivity is paramount. The Scientist who begins a project to prove a point for an institution or business that provides the funding is automatically compromised. The Scientist walks that fine line between independence and compromise. Certainly Scientists need a working hypothesis, but at all times, they must be prepared to be surprised.

Scientists initially prove their knowledge and abilities through education and academic success. Inventors often prove their capabilities through experience. Remember, the Inventor is looking for a product. Past experience often suggests to the Inventor that a process can be improved, that some article makes life easier, or that time and money can be saved if certain steps are taken or some machine is redesigned. The majority of people with the Scientist and Inventor archetypes work within business and industry. Medicine, mining, agriculture, and communications are boom industries for Scientists and Inventors, but some excel at backyard inventions. They may make their living in a non-scientific industry, but their tinkering and inventiveness indicate the archetype of Scientist or Inventor.

**Negative Aspects:**

Tunnel-vision ~ Lack of common sense ~ Unintuitive ~ Unethical ~ Plagiarist ~ Selling out to the highest bidder ~ Subjective ~ Impractical

**Positive Aspects:**

Challenging ~ Practical ~ Truth-seeking ~ Realist ~ Adventuresome ~ Ethical ~ Enquiring ~ Inventive ~ Objective ~ Learned ~ Experienced ~ Follow a process ~ Recognizing a need

**Archetypal Energy:**

There are many aspects to the energy of the Scientist. The first is passion. The enquiring mind develops a passion to find out how things work. The passion elicits questions. Observation takes place. Experiments begin to happen.

Imagination is set free. Natural wonders are there for the exploration. Puzzles and blocks are there for fitting together and finalizing a product. Scientific method is already in use, and the process is explored.

The essential energy of imagination mixes with the practical energy of learning and education. The tools of discovery become involved in the Scientist's life. Books, magazines, computers, science lessons, and discussions begin to educate the Scientist who develops that love of learning and understanding. Education has a purpose. In time, education turns into experience. As Scientists become more familiar with the scientific process and their chosen fields, they gain experience.

Education and experience lead to opportunities. This is when objectivity is put to the test. The Scientist has to be strong enough to resist temptation. There have been many glaring examples where Scientists have lost their independence and objectivity to fame, fortune, or personal belief. Scientists who supported the tobacco industry come readily to mind. Medicine, agriculture, the fossil fuel industry, and climate change are all subjects where debate rages and the ethics and objectivity of various individuals and expert committees are called into question. Unfortunately, in many of these cases, only time and further research is likely to elicit the truth. The Scientist has to have the strength to resist pressure, not only from within but also from external sources. Galileo and Darwin are perfect examples of Scientists who maintained integrity in the face of external pressure.

Another aspect of scientific energy is the ability to follow the process. Methodology and order are core components of scientific research. The Scientist has to have the ability to maintain order out of chaos. This energy is prevalent in the Engineer and the Servant. Engineers are often Scientists and Inventors, and Inventors and Scientists are often Engineers. Another challenge for the Scientist is to remain flexible and adaptable amidst an ordered structure. This is a special challenge to the Inventor. If something is not working, then it needs changing. If a piece of the jigsaw puzzle does not fit, then a new piece needs consideration. All this requires adaptability, but the overriding process must be maintained or the results are tainted and open to question. Finally, the Scientist must be practical. Theory is necessary but theory needs to be understood and turned into practical application. There is much discussion about scientific jargon. Usefulness is definitive. Impracticality is luxury.

**Archetypal Combinations:**

The archetypal energy of the Scientist combines well with the energy of:

Scholar * Engineer * Nature Child * Servant * Seeker * Entrepreneur * Pioneer * Witch * Wizard * Computer Nerd * Detective * Visionary * Wise Woman

**Effective Use of Scientist Energy:**

- Maintain your strength and objectivity on all occasions. An ethical reputation is priceless.
- Imagination, intuition, and passion are strengths. Never let others discourage or deny you.
- Remember science deals with theory and practice.
- Scientific method is a process that must be honoured.
- Proof, fact, and conclusiveness are the goals of science but may not always be achieved in any one lifetime.
- Encourage others in your field and seek their opinions. Exclusiveness may be good business practice, but service to humanity is a more ethical practice.

# Scribe

The image of the Scribe is one of a literate scholar or Monk carefully copying a valued text onto a manuscript. In the days when the majority of the population was illiterate and books were handmade, the Scribe was a valuable resource. The Scribe's ability to read and write was an absolute asset, especially to the religions of the day. Church hierarchies were keen to preserve their manuscripts and keep records of religious texts, the Bible being the most valuable. The monk, whose existence was often confined to a monastery, was the ideal Scribe. There was relative safety in the monastery, and the monk had ample time to perfect his craft.

Several centuries later the archetype of the Scribe is more abundantly found in the offices of a news corporation. With the invention of the printing press, books were easier to make and newspapers emerged as a reliable source of information. As technology changed, Scribes were more commonly named Reporters or Journalists. They still perform the same function. Although with the trend of the modern era, the Journalist often becomes a Storyteller relying on embellishment to sell copy or write opinion pieces. However, the main function of the Reporter or Journalist is to retell an event or story with objectivity and accuracy. This is the modern Scribe at work.

Another modern Scribe is the Biographer. These individuals are often Journalists as well. The Biographer performs an almost identical function as the old-fashioned Scribe. The Biographer writes about the life and times of a particular individual or set of events. The Scribe sitting daily in the monastery, fastidiously copying the Bible, was writing about the life and times of Jesus and the people of the Jewish faith. The person who is inspired enough to write an autobiography calls upon the energy of the Scribe. The key to the Scribe archetype is that the process is about retelling not creating.

**Negative Aspects:**

Distorting ~ Plagiarizing ~ Piracy ~ Gossip ~ Subjective ~ Offering opinions ~ Glamorizing ~ Stretching the truth ~ Tunnel-vision

**Positive Aspects:**

Copier ~ Accuracy ~ Keeper of facts ~ Link between generations ~ Objective ~ Authentic ~ Knowledgeable ~ Literate

**Archetypal Energy:**

The archetypal energy of the Scribe revolves around accuracy, authenticity, objectivity, and knowledge. Scribes needs knowledge and understanding of the process and their subjects. Without this knowledge, Scribes lack credibility. The journalist whose background and expertise is sport is not a likely candidate to write the financial column. The Monk transcribing the pages of the Bible would need a thorough knowledge of the language. The biographer is not likely to breeze into sessions with a well-known public figure without conducting some background research. Watching elite television interviewers at work, such as Michael Parkinson or Andrew Denton, is watching professionals who have truly done their research. Much to the surprise of their subjects, these professionals often remind them about incidents or conversations that were turning points or key moments. Research and subject knowledge is a must, and the Scribe must be qualified in learning and experience.

The Scribe must be accurate. Our senses are not a reliable tool. Various people watching the same incident report different versions. Technology is marginally better, although covering the totality of an event is a real challenge, and editing can corrupt the most accurate of interviews or occurrences. To use the positive energy of the Scribe, there must be dedication to accuracy. Authenticity and objectivity are the key ingredients to accuracy. Opinions, statements, or photographs the Scribe uses must be authentic. Inserting something that is false or misleading corrupts the energy of the Scribe. On many occasions, news reporters flirt with the truth. They use file footage that has no relationship to the current story, they stage audio and vision sequences that purport to show an incident, they plagiarize articles and claim them as their own, they run opinion pieces or advertisements as news items, they deliberately change the context of conversations or event, and so on. This is cheating. All these tricks are used to improve their popularity and ratings. They are no longer using the energy of the

Scribe. They are using the energy of the Magician and the Thief.

Objectivity is always a challenge. We all have opinions, and there is always the temptation to add our opinion to a story, even when this opinion is unnecessary and has no relevance. If you are a Scribe, your opinion should never be heard. Your aim is to be a channel. There should be no filtering of what flows through this channel. The channel should be clear; what enters at one end flows out unadulterated at the other end. Unfortunately, in today's world where money is king, the role and energy of the Scribe has been tainted. Objectivity has been corrupted in the desire to make money and control social opinion. Switch on many television stations throughout the world, even in the free democratic countries, and instantly you detect bias. Objectivity has been cast aside and replaced with distortion and tunnel vision. The energy of Scribes must remain pure if their true roles in the modern world are to be honoured.

**Archetypal Combinations:**

The archetypal energy of the Scribe combines well with the energy of:

Seeker * Detective * Craftsperson * Servant * Networker * Hermit * Monk * Engineer * Scholar

**Effective Use of Scribe Energy:**

- Be aware of the four key components of the Scribe; knowledge, accuracy, authenticity, and objectivity.
- How thorough has your research been?
- When you are using your Scribe archetype, your opinion is not important. Keep it to yourself.
- Be aware of the temptation of money, pride, and self-glorification.
- Maintain your personal strength, ethics, and dignity. Keep your work away from the influence of executive or peer pressure.

# Seeker

Are you the kind of person who is always asking questions? If so, you have the Seeker archetype. The Philosopher and the Seeker are similar in that they constantly ask questions. The difference is the Philosopher asks a question and then spends time contemplating the answer and all the possibilities that the answer raises. Analysis is part of the Philosopher energy. The Philosopher also favours asking the "big" questions, such as, "What are the origins of our species?" and "What is my purpose in life?" On the other hand, Seekers have a constant flow of questions about every single thing that warrants their attention. When one question is answered, the Seeker is asking another within seconds.

As a consequence, the mind of the Seeker is always full of thoughts. Relaxing the mind is a difficult task. Most of us are capable of relaxing our minds. We have quiet moments when our thinking is subdued or involved in trivialities that require little of our attention. Most of us are capable of meditating. Not so for Seekers. Their heads are always full of thoughts or questions. Many of these thoughts may be trivial or they may be important, but they all have relevance for Seekers and make peace of mind almost impossible to acquire.

The Seeker is also fastidious with lists. Taking notes, writing down answers, and analysing the pros and cons of an idea are all Seeker behaviours. Books and the Internet are tools that the Seeker enjoys, as they offer the answers to so many questions. As with the Philosopher, the Seeker is often paralysed with inaction. Minor decisions are likely to become major issues. They may require hours of analysis or set off myriad questions. Alternatively, when Seekers are burdened with questions and ideas, they behave like the proverbial "chook with its head cut off" and run around doing unwarranted and inconsequential things in search of answers.

A technique I employ with individuals who have the Seeker archetype is to get them to write a list of three or four priorities. On this list may be their children, their jobs, their homes, their health, their fitness, a holiday, more income, a new car, and so on. When they have made their lists, then any questions or thoughts they have are only to be acknowledged and acted upon if they pertain to the subjects on the priority list. There is to be no discussion. If this question concerns a subject on my priority list, then I act upon it. If a question does not relate to a subject on my priority list, then I move on. There is no alternative. Act or move on. This process immediately eliminates many thoughts. It allows the Seeker to be discerning. It gives the Seeker focus and the ability to act on important matters. In time it allows the Seeker to use intuition as well as intellect.

**Negative Aspects:**

Cynic ~ Rationalist ~ Despair ~ Rigid ~ Single-minded ~ Tunnel vision ~ Dogmatic ~ Making molehills into mountains ~ Unfocused ~ Undisciplined ~ Gossip

**Positive Aspects:**

Inquiring ~ Seeker ~ Integration ~ Reflective ~ Lateral ~ Knowledge ~ Logical ~ Balanced ~ Intuitive ~ Consideration ~ Inquisitive ~Precise

**Archetypal Energy:**

The energy of the Seeker is devoted to finding the answers to myriad questions that flow continuously into the Seeker's mind. Those questions may be mundane. They may be of a personal or general nature. They may be important and life-changing. No matter the scale of their importance, the Seeker is not content to let a question go until a satisfactory answer is forthcoming.

The Seeker may be an intellectual who prefers the comfort of home-based learning. This is where the Internet, books, and magazines are the Seeker's best friend. The mystery of human behaviour is a source of great fascination to the Seeker. There's nothing like good gossip or the supposition as to why somebody has acted in a particular way. These Seekers are social butterflies. Other Seekers explore, travel, and investigate all corners of the world. They are prepared to go to great lengths to acquire first-hand knowledge and honour conclusively the quest of their enquiry. The most obvious example of these Seekers is the travel show host and the show's participants. Think of the television show *The Amazing Race* and you have Seeker participation. However, some Seekers lead a simple and typically common lifestyle. They are employed in all sorts of jobs. They raise children, go on holidays, play sport, go to movies, and they watch videos and television. They are still Seekers, and questions fill their everyday lives with everyday issues.

Consideration is another aspect of the archetypal energy of the Seeker. Seekers are fantastic at considering all of the positive and negative elements involved in decision making. If you ever need advice on the best car, mobile phone, or television to purchase, then take along friends who have the Seeker archetype. If they do not know all the ins and outs of a product, they are bound to ask the pertinent questions of the sales rep. You then have all the information laid out before you, and you can make your decision based on that information and your personal choice. Unfortunately for the Seeker, decision making does not come as easily for them. Once all the facts are known, the Seeker is likely to begin an investigation of the consequences of a decision. This creates uncertainty, and often the process begins again. Decisions! Decisions! Decisions!

**Archetypal Combinations:**

The archetypal energy of the Seeker combines well with the energy of:

Adventurer * Explorer * Detective * Scholar * Scientist * Mystic * Pioneer * Networker * Gambler * Pilgrim * Actor * Entrepreneur * Wizard * Witch * Storyteller * Shape-Shifter

**Effective Use of Seeker Energy:**

- Use your Seeker energy to find answers to relevant questions.
- Find some quiet time to relax your body and your mind.
- Indecision is not a state of mental or emotional satisfaction.
- Allow yourself the luxury of making mistakes. They can always be corrected.
- Use your knowledge, logic, and intuition for your development and for the progression of those within your family and social sphere.

# Servant

The Servant is a very common archetype but one of our most valuable. Gone are the days when every basic act of survival depended on the individual. Humankind has developed into a complex social network. We have become dependent on each other for our quality of life and, in some cases, our very survival. The Servant archetype is evolving and maturing as our societies become more civil.

For eons, our civilizations relied upon the Warrior archetype. Empires, kingdoms, and tribes were ruled by a wealthy or powerful family or minority group. They offered protection to their citizens by the employment of Warriors. These Warriors protected the society from outside threats and predators. They also maintained internal order, which perpetuated the line of heritage. Many countries today still operate under the energy of the Warrior. Most Middle Eastern countries are ruled by individuals or families who utilize the Warrior energy to maintain their power and control. In time, the winds of change sweep through such countries. Popular revolution is railing against the Warrior energy and pushing for individual choice and freedom. As the hold of the Warrior is swept away, the social energy moves away from the Slave energy to the Servant energy.

Many occupations call upon the Servant to play an active role in service. Politicians, healers, lawyers, engineers, reporters, priests, monks, nuns, mothers, fathers, teachers, kings, and queens are all specific and individual archetypes in their own right. What they have in common is an element of the Servant archetype. To utilize the positive energy of these archetypes, one needs to add the positive energy of the Servant.

Individuals who have the Servant archetype and the dominate Servant energy, place themselves in service industries. These are the nurses, the waiters and waitresses, the sales personnel, the shop assistants, the maids, the cleaners, the chauffeurs, the taxi drivers, the porters, the receptionists, the secretaries, the gardeners, and the nannies. All of these people have the Servant archetype. They often move from one occupation to another in search of change or better opportunities, but they are always to be found in the service industry.

Servants are invaluable, and their roles should never be underestimated. Ask barristers or solicitors how important their legal secretaries are. Ask hotel managers how much their businesses depend on the friendliness and efficiency of their staff. Ask business people how their growth relies upon the performance of their sales representatives. Servants should always value their roles and their attributes. All members of a civilized society are becoming increasingly dependent on the Servant. If, like Henry Higgins from *My Fair Lady*, we take these individuals for granted, there comes a time when we regret our lack of understanding and courtesy.

**Negative Aspects:**

Accepting your lot ~ Fated ~ Unworthy ~ Lack of self-determination ~ Trapped ~ Mediocrity ~ Lack of power ~ Lack of focus ~ Lack of ambition ~ Servile ~ Taken for granted ~ Abused ~ Class conscious

**Positive Aspects:**

Self-directed ~ Organized ~ Carer ~ Service ~ Humility ~ Trust ~ Simplicity ~ Master of your own life ~ Dependable ~ Reliable ~ Giver ~ Duty ~ Accepting ~ Consideration ~ Efficiency ~ Patience

**Archetypal Energy:**

There are many positive energetic aspects to the Servant. This is why those with the Servant archetype are so valuable to our social structure. They often do not receive the recognition they deserve, as many are required to work in lowly and poorly paid positions. Yet their function is often vital to the foundation of a progressive and civilized society. One of the reasons the United States has not forced its illegal migrants out of the country is because the majority of them are in service-based industries. The removal of these workers would require a painful and large-scale overhaul of the social and economic framework of the country. If you have a Servant archetype, give yourself credit and recognize your individual worth to your family, friends, employer, and country.

The first positive energetic aspect of Servants is their organizational skills. Servants are organized. They have to be. To fulfil the demand for their services, they must be as organized as possible. There is forethought for every situation. Servants use their insight and are often prepared for circumstances well before they occur. Servants stand ready and prepared for any number of eventualities.

Servants are logical in their organizational skills. They understand that service is an ordered sequence of steps. Each step is vital to the whole process, and each step must be taken in the correct order. Imagine if the nurse, assisting in an operation, failed to check the patient's details, forgot to lay out the proper instruments, or decided to have a tea break halfway through a procedure. Those with the Servant archetype are also flexible. If events suddenly change and things do not go according to plan, the Servant has the flexibility to go with the flow and bring the whole episode back to order.

Servants are reliable and dependable. Many of us excuse ourselves if we occasionally have a forgetful moment or a period of lazy self-indulgence. That leeway for the Servant rarely exists. Others depend on the Servant. Reliability and dependability are necessary elements for the whole service industry. Even in the very finest of restaurants, you know what your response is likely to be if you have to wait two hours for your meal. How many times have you been frustrated when you stay home all day waiting for the tradesman who never appears? What is your reaction when you arrive for an appointment to be told the receptionist made a mistake and double-booked? There is very little slack given to the Servant who is not reliable and dependable.

Servants are the backbone of duty. They have an inbuilt sense of responsibility. They are willing to endure many challenges to oblige and honour that sense of duty. Servants are humble. It is difficult to have an ego when you are serving. Many times Servants have to be humble to endure their customers, their customers' moods, inappropriate jokes, lack of respect, and complaints. As we all know, the customer is always right. One needs a deep sense of humility to continually obey that service slogan.

Simplicity is another aspect of Servant energy. Servants are extremely good at keeping matters simple. They are ordered in their priorities. Many of us, with other dominant archetypes, love to complicate matters, be they family, work, relationships, or purchases. The Servant keeps it simple. The Servant sees a need or a deficiency and solves the situation with a logical change or the acquirement of equipment. Many servants lead simple lives. For some it is due to social circumstances, such as poor wages and lowly status. For others it is a matter of personal choice.

**Archetypal Combinations:**

The archetypal energy of the Servant combines well with the energy of:

Healer * Carer * Rescuer * King * Queen * Priest * Priestess * Teacher * Advocate * Knight * Martyr * Wise Woman * Diplomat * Politician * Companion * Nun * Craftsperson * Disciple * Detective * Judge

**Effective Use of Servant Energy:**

- Do not be dismissive of your importance and the quality of service you provide.
- Constantly affirm your power and dependability.
- Never allow others to denigrate your integrity and self-esteem.
- Your ability and reputation determines your worth, so seek employment that recognizes that worth.
- When loyalty and reward are given to you, remember your commitment and loyalty to your station and duty.

# Shaman

The Shaman is the archetype that works with nature, the seasons, plants and animals and their energy. In days gone by, the Shaman was a most treasured member of the tribe. When the very survival of the tribe depended on food gathering and hunting, the Shaman played the pivotal role. He tuned into the animal energy He understood animal habits and their behavioural patterns. He read the signs of nature and understood the cycles of the seasons. He guided the tribe to reliable food and water sources and safe havens. He was the master guide and intuitive leader.

He was also the traditional tribal healer. His knowledge of plants and animals allowed him to make medicines and herbal remedies. The Shaman may have indulged in some magic, but usually this was unnecessary. The Shaman's ability to heal and guide the tribe to food and safe havens gave him the air of a magician. The Shaman may have used magic if his position was threatened or in times of natural disasters. This would consolidate his status and give hope and respectability to his tribe.

The role of the traditional Shaman was reserved for a male. In most tribes, the males were dominant because of their superior physical strength and their dual roles as hunters and warriors. Warrior energy does not like to be dominated by any other archetypal energy; hence, the males dominated tribal society. However, there were female Shamans. They played a more covert role in tribal society. Their knowledge and understanding of plant and animal energy was comprehensive but confined to domestic matters like female health issues, childbirth, and child rearing. Many of these female Shamans were given the title of Sage or Wise Woman.

With the urbanization of modern society, the recognition and status of the Shaman has declined. City and suburban dwellers do not need a Shaman to tell them where the food sources may be found. These days we do not have difficulty in finding the local shops or supermarkets, although we may have difficulty getting parking spots. Despite this, the Shaman still has an important role to play. As the human population has exploded, we are taking over more of the earth's resources. Plant and animal species cannot compete, and extinction is very nearly a daily occurrence. To many people, especially those with the Shaman energy, a change in attitude and habit is required. Is seems humanity is coming to the realization the earth is a finite planet with finite resources. Conservation is essential not only for plant and animal species but also for the human species. The role of the conservationist is natural for the Shaman. It is important for the Shaman to step up and challenge the values of our modern urban society. If not, his extinction as an archetype is just as likely as the extinction of many of our plants and animals.

**Negative Aspects:**

Manipulated ~ Control ~ Charlatan ~ Power abuse ~ Substance abuse ~ Fake ~ Pretence ~ Pointing the bone ~ Old wives' tales ~ Superstition ~ Self-importance ~ Magician ~ Plagiarist ~ Arrogant

**Positive Aspects:**

Ritual ~ Healing ~ Totems ~ Symbols ~ Guide ~ Mystical ~ Visionary ~ Knowledge ~ Conservation ~ Tribal leader ~ Wisdom ~ Keeper of tradition

**Archetypal Energy:**

The archetypal energy of the Shaman revolves around healing and guidance. The Shaman is a leader. He may not always be the tribal chief, but if not, his role is equally important. The health and fortune of the tribe depended on the knowledge, leadership, and integrity of its Shaman. The Shaman's position was to use his spiritual and physical connection to nature to assist those who required his guidance and assistance.

It is important for the Shaman to practice his trade. This is no easy task in an urban society. This may be done by involvement in conservation movements; visits to zoos and wildlife parks; treks through national parks and wildernesses; personal conservation of threatened plant and animal species; meditation; and symbolic rituals involving plants, animals, and Shamanic medicine. It is important for the Shaman to have both a physical involvement and a spiritual involvement in his life. Rituals provide both physical and spiritual opportunities. The Shaman has to balance both sides of this equation.

The Shaman has a duty to take on the responsibility of leadership. If he is on the path of both physical and spiritual growth, his channels to access knowledge remain open and active. This information can be passed down to the tribe. The Shaman does have a tribe. If you have the Shaman archetype, people actively seek you out. They need guidance, teaching, and active participation in ritual and leadership. This is the core of Shamanic energy. It is important for the Shaman to be both available and responsible. Be ready for those who seek your assistance and guidance. Be responsible for your teachings and leadership.

The other aspect of Shamanic energy is that of healing. This may be a physical healing. However, with government regulations and accompanying legal obligations, delving into physical healing becomes a delicate situation for the Shaman. More likely the Shaman is on safer ground with healing that involves emotional and psychological repairs. This is a welcome situation as our modern societies, and medical systems are quite efficient in physical healing. They are much weaker at emotional and psychological healing, and the stresses of modern living create more challenges in these areas. Here, the Shaman can step up and take up the slack. This is especially true in a world where the dominant species, the human, has lost touch with nature. The minority who still have a connection with the earth need care and attention. Those who treat the earth with apathy and distain need reminding that we are not the only species on this finite planet. The Shaman, who can involve himself in tribal guidance and conservation, is playing the dual role that caters for all people.

One other energetic quality of the Shaman may be that of the Visionary. Most Shamans have visions. For youngsters, these may be frightening, and this ability may have a rather alienating effect. Most people are not Visionaries. Most people probably do not believe that others can see things, so the general response is to tell children that this is their imagination, the visions are not real, and to stop making things up. Imagine how this affects a young person.

I remember talking to a year-six class full of eleven-year-old children. We were discussing death. One girl told of her ability to see some family members who had passed on. I knew she was being truthful. I told her I believed her and explained to the other children that some people are Visionaries and have the ability to see things. Most of us do not. This young girl breathed the biggest sigh of relief. I suppose for the first time in her life, somebody believed and understood her situation. To all of you who do not possess the ability of the Visionary be gentle. Never judge the ability of others on the comparison of your own abilities. We all have different archetypes with their individual energetic qualities. Accept who you are. Accept who others are.

**Archetypal Combinations:**

The archetypal energy of the Shaman combines well with the energy of:

Guide * Healer * Teacher * Visionary * Advocate * Wizard * Networker * Nature Child * Witch * Priestess * Wise Woman * Rebel * Mystic * Warrior * Disciple * Carer * Rescuer * Mentor

**Effective Use of Shaman Energy:**

- Continue your practice of ritual, and keep the channels of information open and flowing
- Maintain your connection to nature, to the wonder and preservation of the plant and animal kingdom and to the sacred medicine they contain, and to the bridge you must build between them and others of the human race.
- Use your knowledge and leadership to guide all those seeking your assistance.
- Leave delusion and tricks to the Magician. Shamanic energy is pure and without pretence.
- Be discreet and discerning with your visions. Develop your talent but leave the dark arts in their place.

# Shape-Shifter

Shape-shifters are fascinating. There are very few people with the Shape-shifter archetype. Because of their very nature, they are difficult to identify. The individual with the Shape-shifter archetype has the ability to blend into different cultures and societies. This is not just a social blending but also a physical transformation. Shape-shifters have physical features that allow them to look like indigenous members of various communities.

Along with the ability to blend in physically, Shape-shifters also have the ability to blend in culturally. Shape-shifters often speak several languages. This is common in Europe where language structures are similar and exposure to other languages is normal. However, it is not unusual for Shape-shifters to master languages that have little in common and are spoken in countries well apart. It is not just language that is mastered by Shape-shifters. They also have a deep knowledge and understanding of distinct and separate cultures.

Shape-shifters feel comfortable in a variety of situations. They are like Actors in that regard. The difference is Actors have the ability to take on roles that give them authenticity and comfort in different social settings. With the Shape-shifter, there is no acting involved. They have an uncanny ability to integrate in all situations physically, culturally, socially, and emotionally.

**Negative Aspects:**

Pretence ~ Illusion ~ Take advantage of ~ Fraudulent ~ Impostor ~ Deception ~ Trickery ~ Forgery ~ A jack of all trades and a master of none ~ Spying ~ Cloak and dagger

**Positive Aspects:**

Integrate ~ Multilingual ~ Multicultural ~ Sensitive ~ Respectful ~ Bipartisan ~ Blending in

**Archetypal Energy:**

The archetypal energy of the Shape-shifter is about transformation. Individuals with the Shape-shifter archetype have the ability to transform themselves. Their physical appearance takes on subtle changes by playing with light and shadow. Skin tones may appear to darken or lighten. Facial features appear larger or smaller or seem to change shape. Smiles become frowns, and frowns become smiles. Identifying a Shape-shifter with a particular nationality confuses the senses. Is this person that I am speaking to an Aboriginal Australian, a Polynesian islander, or a Maori? Perhaps he is French. He speaks English with various accents, yet he speaks fluent French. This is the art of the Shape-shifter. Transformation!

The Shape-shifter has the ability to feel comfortable in many situations. Some of us experience a sense of anxiety when we are thrown into foreign situations. It may be a social event, an experience at work, or going overseas on holiday. Shape-shifters, however, take in all of these situations with ease. They have the ability to relax and integrate peacefully and gracefully.

Tuning in to a variety of cultural structures is an energetic gift given to the Shape-shifter. There is an awareness of how to act, speak, and behave with cultural sensitivity. There is knowledge of protocols. There is a mastery of language. There is the appearance of likenesses. The Shape-shifter has an intuitive knowledge in how to live in a variety of cultures and societies. This is not acting. This is living with complexity and wholeness.

**Archetypal Combinations:**

The archetypal energy of the Shape-Shifter combines well with the energy of:

Detective * Diplomat * Adventurer * Explorer * God * Goddess * Magician * Actor * Scribe * Alchemist

**Effective Use of Shape-Shifter Energy:**
- Use your abilities for your personal growth and adventure.
- Be wary of deception for self-glorification, impropriety, or theft
- Be aware that you have the ability to be a peacemaker and a bridge that links cultures and alleviates misunderstanding.

# Slave

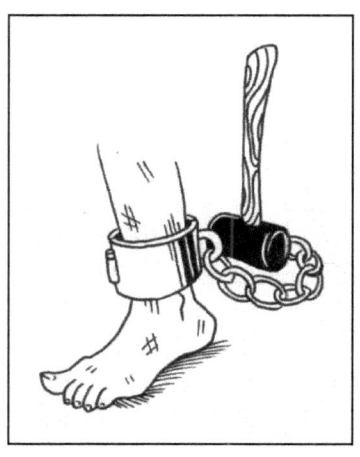

The Slave is the archetype where an individual is held captive by another individual, a group, a government, or a society. Slaves have various individual rights denied to them. Freedom of movement is a basic human right denied to the Slave. This is usually accompanied by the Slave forced into labour without recompense and provided with only the basic elements of food and shelter. History has shown us the typical lifestyles of incarcerated Slaves. Empires were built on the exploitation and free labour given to them by slavery. From the Egyptians, Romans, and more recently, the United States, these societies prospered through the use of slavery.

Slavery is still prevalent today, and although the scale is smaller, the human tragedy is no less compelling. Parts of Africa, Asia, and the Middle East still condone human trafficking and slavery. The importance of free labour is still a driving force in the continued use of slavery. However, the unwilling incarceration of people as soldiers, drug traffickers, and sex and marital slaves, appears to be more common today than in previous eras.

The physical plight of the Slave is obvious. There is generally no subtlety surrounding this type of slavery. The boundaries are clear, the duties are the will and whim of the master, and the punishment for breaking the rules is harsh. Slavery can be at an individual level, or it can involve a mass of individuals. En masse slavery is usually enforced by the state to maintain power, control, and order. Some authoritarian governments do not allow their citizens a whole raft of freedoms. We have experienced popular uprisings throughout the world; people who have been denied their freedom rebelling en masse.

The fight against enslavement has been repeated throughout history. In the modern world, the spread of improved communications, such as the Internet and social networks, has given millions of people a glimpse of freedom and a hope of a less rigid and restrictive society.

However, individuals with the Slave archetype often fall into some form of bondage. It is part of their personalities. This energy is recognized by individuals with other archetypes who often take advantage of the Slave energy and personality. The Bully, the Vampire, the Destroyer, the Entrepreneur, the Avenger, the Thief, the Magician, the Warrior, and the Politician are just some of the archetypes that identify the Slave energy. They can, and occasionally do, make use of the Slave energy to advance their own personal wealth and desires.

Physical incarceration is not the only form of slavery. Often with physical imprisonment comes psychological imprisonment. Various sects, religions, and states all utilize some form of psychological imprisonment. The need to belong and for acceptance are important human desires. Sects are extremely effective at meeting these needs. The desire to have a spiritual connection to a divine power and the acceptance of a lifestyle with the promise of a better afterlife are satisfied by religion. The state draws on nationalistic slogans and the fear of outsiders. All of this is psychological imprisonment. It is brainwashing either overtly or covertly. It denies the individual the right to psychological freedom. It preys on personality weaknesses. Slaves fall into this kind of slavery under the delusion of free choice and their acceptance of dependence, caused by negative Slave energy.

Lastly, there are the emotional slaves. These are the individuals with the Slave archetype who fall into a relationship and become totally involved and dependent. For these individuals, there is no escape unless it is at the wish of dominant partners or outside forces, such as death or illness. These Slaves lose the ability of independent thought. Their emotional states dominate their lives, and other aspects of daily life are neglected or determined by the commands of these relationships. Emotional Slaves can become truly trapped.

**Negative Aspects:**

Enslaved ~ Accepting your lot ~ Trapped ~ Fated ~ Imprisoned ~ Dependent ~ Lack of self-determination ~ Lack of power ~ Out of balance ~ Frustrated ~ Put down ~ Unworthy ~ Exploited ~ Fearful

**Positive Aspects:**

Master of your life ~ Self-directed ~ Simplicity ~ Humility ~ Mental toughness ~ Patience ~ Courage ~ Determination ~ Endurance ~ Resilience

**Archetypal Energy:**

The archetypal energy of the Slave is about acceptance. It is the acceptance of boundaries. It is the acceptance of fate. It is the acceptance that others control your life and your destiny. It is how the Slave works within the confines of a situation determined by others. Having a choice is still important to the Slave, but there is a realization that the choices open to the Slave are within the boundaries of a pre-existing situation or a situation controlled by others. By this understanding, we can see that you do not have to be in actual slavery to feel like a Slave. If you believe the decisions that impact your life are made by others or by a greater force than yourself, then you've become a slave to those forces. You accept that somebody or something else controls your life.

The positive energy of the Slave is about freedom. It is the energy of freedom that determines how an individual thinks and his or her attitude. The individual heads down the path of self-determination when that individual focuses on freedom rather than restriction. We all have the ability to change our attitudes. A change in attitude brings a change in action. A change in action brings a change in circumstances.

Mental toughness is important to the Slave. Without this toughness the Slave is lost and withers away. There are many films and stories about the mental toughness of the Slave archetype. My favourite is *Rabbit-Proof Fence*. It is a story about Aboriginal children taken from their families and sent hundreds of kilometres away to live on a church mission. They escape the confines and cruelty of the mission and walk the long, exhausting trek homeward via a fence constructed to keep rabbits from the pastoral lands. This is the ultimate story of courage, determination, endurance, and resilience. These are the positive energetic attributes of the Slave.

Other positive energetic attributes are patience, humility, and simplicity. Slaves lead simple lives. The terms of their imprisonments determine that simplicity. The very nature of owning slaves has an economic base. The master of slaves always wants to spend the minimum amount for their upkeep. The nature of slavery guarantees that the Slave is humble. There is little room for ego when you are a Slave.

Finally, I need to mention hope. The Slave has to live in hope. As the saying goes, "Where there is life, there is hope." The reverse is also true. Where there is hope, there is life.

**Archetypal Combinations:**

The archetypal energy of the Slave combines well with the energy of:

Martyr * Servant * Warrior * Peacemaker * Hermit * Rescuer * Beggar * Wounded Child * Companion * Disciple * Coward * Prostitute * Victim

**Effective Use of Slave Energy:**

- Use the energy of endurance and determination to remain strong, mentally and physically.
- Hope should always be the focus of your attention.
- Remember the positive energy of the Slave allows you to be the master of your life. Monitor your attitude for change, and begin the process of changing your life.
- Be wary of your relationships. Make sure they are positive relationships with positive individuals. Be careful of those individuals with strong negative energy that captivates and enslaves you.

# Statesman

The Statesman archetype is home to the individual who can lead with focus, determination, and inspiration. Both men and women may possess the Statesman archetype. These individuals are leaders with charisma. They are often leaders who bring about great change for their people, and their influence may extend beyond the boundaries of their immediate countries or states. The best known Statesmen will generally be Politicians or Warriors. Reformation or significant change occurs through a variety of processes. The changing of laws, the evolution of institutions and political and social reform often occur through the inspiration of the Statesman. Change may be through a political process brought about by the Political Statesman, or it may be through a power process brought about by a Warrior Statesman.

Statesmen have an obsessive focus on change and challenge. Often the most powerful and influential Statesmen begin their quests from a position of deprivation. Martin Luther King, Nelson Mandela, and Mahatma Ghandi battled enormous odds but, through popular support, rose to positions of influence and leadership. Once on their paths, they were able to formulate and enunciate the needs of their people and set out with a determined purpose to achieve those goals. Other Statesmen, such as Winston Churchill, rose to their positions as dictated by external circumstances. In all cases, there is commonality in that fierce determination to focus on the challenges and an obsession to succeed no matter the cost or the odds.

Statesmen have to be orators. They require that ability to identify the challenge, enunciate the change, and focus on the final achievement for their followers. They can put into words what others are feeling. They inspire many to follow the path to a better life or to work through challenging times. This is done through their ability to speak with clarity, conviction, and inspiration. The most important quality of the Statesman is conviction. The most important ability of the Statesman is oration.

Not all individuals with the Statesman archetype rise to the status of world leaders, but they do certainly rise to positions of power. They may be the president of a local sporting or service club, the mayor of a local council, the principal of an educational institution, or even the instigator of a conservation movement. The things they have in common are influence, a steely determination to succeed, and the ability to articulate a common goal.

**Negative Aspects:**

Hidden agenda ~ Confrontational ~ Dictator ~ Avoidance ~ Ulterior motives ~ Self-grandeur ~ Bully ~ Temperamental ~ Power at the expense of others ~ Warmonger ~ Exclusive ~ Fascist ~ Totalitarian

**Positive Aspects:**

Peacemaker ~ Mediator ~ Orator ~ Diplomat ~ Negotiator ~ Good listener ~ Inspiring ~ Bringer of change ~ Patient ~ Determined ~ Resilient ~ Enduring ~ Persistent ~ Hopeful ~ A person of the people ~ Articulate ~ Resonance

**Archetypal Energy:**

The first and foremost quality of the Statesman is charisma. Charisma is the unique energy of an individual that compels attraction. It allows the individual to stand out from the crowd, but it is also a powerful form of identification. It is the crowd saying to one individual that we identify with you. We would like to be as you are. Charisma is also about the trust many put in one person on the understanding that this individual is on their side and has the determination to do what is necessary to assist them in their struggles. Charisma is not a quality that can be packaged. It does not rely on talent or looks. Initially, it does not even rely on a person's actions. Charisma is the energy of attraction. It is after the bond has been formed that an individual's actions are considered. Action then dictates the strength and longevity of the relationship between the people and the Statesman.

The Statesman has empathy. It is not only the crowd identifying with the Statesman, but just as importantly, it is the Statesman identifying with the crowd. Statesmen can feel the anguish and the frustration of those they represent. They can identify with their goals and aspirations. There is a common bond in ideology. The Statesman has the vision as to where others should be. As Martin Luther King so aptly put it, "I have a dream." The skill of the Statesman is to clarify and enunciate that vision to produce a common bond and a common purpose. This skill gives the Statesman the energy of the Orator.

Once the leadership of Statesman is established, he or she calls upon skills as a negotiator. Peaceful change is about compromise, diplomacy, and negotiation. The Statesman is often faced with the task of convincing opponents who hold power to relinquish that power. There may be no better reason than to indicate that it is the correct thing to do. There is never a lot of leeway in that argument. In some situations, it may come down to a battle of willpower. This is when the strength of the Statesman's conviction is sorely tested. It is also when the Statesman's nerve and character are put to the test. However, those with the Statesmen archetype have the endurance factor. They have determination. They have resilience.

Statesmen also have organizational skills. There is always a need to organize manpower and resources to be utilized to their full effect. Resources are often limited, so wise decisions have to be made. If there is an abundance of resources, the role of Statesmen is to put their faith in others. They have to be good judges of character if the whole process is to take root and gain momentum. The Statesman is to be many things to many people. Perhaps that is why there are so few.

**Archetypal Combinations:**

The archetypal energy of the Statesman combines well with the energy of:

Peacemaker * Advocate * Warrior * Politician * Diplomat * King * Queen * Servant * Judge * Hero/Heroine * Gambler * Martyr * Rebel * Rescuer

**Effective Use of Statesman Energy:**
- Use your wisdom, knowledge, and empathy to determine your passion.
- Ensure the challenges that you take on are just and noble causes.
- Be wary of extremism and self-glorification.
- Use your oratory skills to entertain and to inspire.
- Trust in others, for "many hands make light work."

# Storyteller

Obviously, the Storyteller tells stories. This is done in a variety of ways. Stories have their base in the oral tradition. Stories of explanation and custom were handed down within families or within a tribal setting. Storytellers told stories of nature, the wonders of earth and sky, animals, the lives and deeds of past generations, and dangers and pitfalls. Many indigenous stories of creation follow this tradition. As human exploration and adventure increased, the breadth of stories widened. Travellers and wandering minstrels told tales of battles and heroes. They told of strange beasts and mysterious events. They spoke of foreign states with different and unusual customs. They spoke of riches of gold and silver and precious gems. Storytelling became a rich and diverse custom. This was a way of maintaining tradition and culture. It was also a way for parents to warn their children of dangers and difficulties. European fairy and folk tales provide examples of this tradition. Stories like *Little Red Riding Hood* and *The Three Little Pigs* are cautionary tales designed to scare and warn. There were also stories of hope and inspiration that offered relief from the drudgery of everyday living. Fairy tales like *Cinderella*, *Snow White,* and *Sleeping Beauty* sell the dream of a better place and the rewards offered to the pure of heart.

The invention and widespread use of the printing press changed the direction of storytelling. Better schooling also meant that more people became literate. The Storyteller could reach greater audiences through books and magazines. The wealthy and the burgeoning middle class could afford to purchase books. Stories of everyday life were popular, as readers identified with like characters. Cities grew and developed at a rapid rate. There were the associated problems of poverty and crime. This contributed to the publication of detective stories and tales of intrigue. The storyteller was also given the freedom to explore other genres. Stories of fantasy and magic appeared. Psychological thrillers such as *Dr Jekyll and Mr Hyde* found popularity. The world of storytelling had opened its arms to all kinds of topics.

Throughout all of this were the playwrights. They achieved popularity in Greek and Roman civilizations. They reached a peak during the Renaissance and at the beginning of the industrial revolution. In the English speaking world, William Shakespeare reigned supreme. Storytellers such as Shakespeare used stage and theatre as their vehicle. In the twentieth century, the storyteller was blessed with the medium of film and television. Stage and film differed vastly from the oral and written tradition in that they presented the visuals of character and story. The imagination of the reader is not as challenged with stage and film as it is by the oral and written. However, other factors come into play. Colour, costume, movement, action, sound, music, cinematography, and special effects are tools that are available to this storyteller.

There needs to be some discussion on the relationship between Actors and Storytellers. They are two distinctive archetypes. Some people possess both Actor and Storyteller archetypes. Others possess just one of the two. While telling a story, Storytellers may often act, but this does not mean they are ready to jump onto a stage or into a film or perform in front of a television camera. Watching J. K. Rowling launch her Harry Potter novels gave the clear indication that she was much more comfortable in front of her keyboard than in front of the camera.

**Negative Aspects:**

Plagiarist ~ When the storyteller becomes the story ~ Struggle ~ Self-deception ~ Self-centred ~ Failure to be recognized ~ Deceit ~ Self-absorbed ~ Irrelevant ~ Simplistic ~ Delusion ~ Unprincipled ~ Undisciplined

**Positive Aspects:**

Creativity ~ Entertaining ~ Upholds the tradition and passes on the message ~ Self-exploration ~ Keeper of culture ~ Holds up a mirror to life ~ Educates ~ Imagination ~ Broaden the horizon ~ Identification ~ Creative

**Archetypal Energy:**

Creativity, imagination, and entertainment are the cornerstones of the Storyteller energy. Authenticity is also important, especially when the storyteller is the keeper of a cultural tradition. There still are roles for traditional and historic storytellers, but their roles have diminished in importance. The Scribe is the archetype that is more relevant in the cultural and historic tradition. Now that we have become a modern and urban society, mass communication and the need to earn a living plays a larger role in the life of the Storyteller. This demands that the Storyteller be more inventive than factual.

Popular culture demands entertainment. Storytellers have obliged in droves. The bottom line has driven the process. If the publisher, theatre manager, television executive, or Production Company is not convinced of the profitable viability of a product, that product has a tough time seeing the light of day. Storytellers are required to be entertaining. The other consideration is the appearance and disappearance of fads. We have just gone through a fad involving vampire stories. Television is still airing reality shows, and they are pushing the boundaries more than ever before. Successful storytellers tune into the energy of the popular fad and make their mark for a short period of time.

Nevertheless, many Storytellers insist on the creative process as the more important aspect of their craft. Creativity is the energy of true Storytellers: the ability to weave a simple or intricate story, to set the scene, to develop each and every character with identifiable personality traits, and to establish relationships.

Creativity is the process, and language is the tool. Language is so relevant to the Storyteller. It is the flow of words that delivers a good yarn. It is the tone of the words that elicits an emotional response from the reader. The Storyteller has to tune into the energy of language. The artistic Storyteller understands language and understands the genre of storytelling. Language differs with the medium. Novels have a different language from stage. Stage has a different language from television. Television has a different language from film. Even within each genre, the language is different. The language of the children's novel is distinctly different to the language of the adult novel. Detective stories use a different language from what is found in romantic novels. Language is the key that brings the creative process to life.

**Archetypal Combinations:**

The archetypal energy of the Storyteller combines well with the energy of:

Actor * Scribe * Artist * Detective * Wanderer * Networker * Adventurer * Judge * Addict * Alchemist

**Effective Use of Storyteller Energy:**

- Tune in to your creative energy.
- Discipline yourself to your craft with regularity and perseverance.
- Use your intuition and conduct your research.
- Remember to stay within the boundaries of the genre, and always keep in mind your reader and audience.
- Develop your own style, and resist the temptation to copy others.

# Teacher

Genuine and effective teachers are born. They are not made. The person with the Teacher archetype is to be found coaching, educating, and passing on knowledge and information. Teaching is not a nine o'clock to three o'clock job. Teaching is a vocation, and true Teachers are always on active duty. They cannot help themselves. Be it their own children, their children's friends, the students at the local sports club, or their team mates, the teacher is there instructing and encouraging.

Teachers are found in all walks of life. There are preschools, primary schools, secondary schools, universities and tertiary institutions, and community-based education, as well as language schools, sports clubs, performing and creative art schools, craft groups, and spiritual groups, to name a few. Teachers who hold regular employment at a recognized school, college, or institution are professional teachers. Many of the other teaching positions, such as local junior cricket coaches or yoga instructors are often amateur. Nevertheless, they are all teachers, and they all have vital roles to play in passing on knowledge and skills.

It is easy to recognize the Teacher archetype. The more difficult task is to recognize if the individual with the Teacher archetype is using positive or negative energy. This is the focus when assessing the Teacher archetype.

**Negative Aspects:**

Power ~ Control ~ Manipulation ~ Do as I say, not as I do ~ Authoritarian ~ Hypocrite ~ Critic ~ Concerned with recognition ~ Talking down to ~ Sarcastic ~ Belittle ~ Harsh ~ Scam

**Positive Aspects:**

Example ~ Model ~ Mentor ~ Guide ~ Inspires others ~ Empowers ~ Patient ~ Facilitates ~ Imparts knowledge ~ Tolerant ~ Humble ~ Good communication ~ Involved ~ Understanding ~ Role model

**Archetypal Energy:**

A dedicated, effective, and inspiring Teacher is humble. Humility is the prime ingredient in the energy of a great Teacher. There is no equality with the positions of student and teacher. It is so easy for Teachers to misuse their positions of status and power. Great Teachers, however, treat their students with respect and dignity. As a Teacher, you require humility to honour that code. Humble teachers recognize and understand that good teachers are always learning from their students. That is dignity and respect at its very best. Talking down to students, making fun of them, manipulating them, and controlling them with fear and power are things that humble Teachers never do. These mechanisms belong to the negative Teacher who is unable to understand the energy of humility.

Great Teachers are observant and intuitive. They observe their students tactfully yet studiously. They gain an awareness of where their students are coming from, where they are at, and where they can take them. At the time of my teacher training, understanding individual differences was high on the agenda of all trainee teachers. We crafted our skills on the understanding that each of our students had various strengths and weaknesses, and these had to be considered in our programs. All of this required observation and dedication to the task. The intuitive Teachers were well-equipped to deal with individual differences. They knew instantly how a student was learning and functioning and what the best approach was for that individual.

My observation of education and schools today causes me some concern. There is today, and has been for a while, a push for a single curriculum, an ordered and rigid learning program, and a testing regime designed for statistical consumption. Schools have become places of hyperactivity with a totally overloaded curriculum. The result is that bureaucrats and principals are enforcing rigid structures and programs aimed at the average student. This allows the many aspects of an overloaded curriculum to be nominally taught. What it doesn't allow for is the time or opportunity for the individual Teacher or student to explore a passion or diverge on a tangent.

Of course, Teachers must be knowledgeable. They have to know and understand their subject matter. They have to be capable of passing on information that is relevant to their students. Preparation and adaptability is the precursor to an effective teaching session. Above all this, never forget humility. Many primary-age students know a lot more about computers and computer programs than I will ever know, yet I was the Teacher, and they were the students. Peer teaching works wonders, especially around computers and modern technology.

The most revered energetic quality of Teachers is the ability to communicate. When there is quality communication, there is quality teaching. When there is poor communication, there is poor teaching, as well as misunderstandings, strained relationships, and underachieving students. Great teachers understand their students, convey their instructions, and impart information with relevance and clarity. Teachers with good communication skills are quickly recognized, promoted, or snapped up by businesses.

Great Teachers possess other qualities. Patience is definitely one of them. Teaching in any situation is a test of one's patience. Teachers are always dealing with individuals who learn at different rates. An exercise or process that one student understands with a single sentence may need months and a whole variety of approaches for other students. A topic that you taught your students last month may have been forgotten with total abandonment. Try teaching area and perimeter to the student with the Damsel archetype, and you may understand exactly what I am talking about.

Along with patience comes tolerance. We all know of the students who have personalities and archetypal traits that push boundaries. The student with the Rebel archetype always wants to push the buttons of those in authority. Teachers are in perfect positions to receive that kind of treatment. As Teachers, we may never know what is going on inside the heads and hearts of our students. There may be all kinds of turmoil that tests both patience and tolerance. There must be understanding and acceptance before any teacher-student relationship can reach its full potential.

Finally, the great Teacher inspires. Inspiration is like charisma—both enigmatic qualities that are difficult to define yet stir the emotions and raise the standards to levels far beyond expectation. Great Teachers inspire because they are excellent mentors, and they model to students qualities that are meaningful and worthy of adopting. Great Teachers inspire because they are fun to be around. They understand their students and genuinely desire to assist them. They communicate openly and succinctly with their students. They respect and dignify their students at a personal level. They inspire because they possess all of those energetic qualities that allow and expect the potential of their students to become reality.

**Archetypal Combinations:**

The archetypal energy of the Teacher combines well with the energy of:

Mentor * Servant * Advocate * Carer * Shaman * Nun * Monk * Martyr * Judge * Companion * Guide * Wise Woman * Craftsperson * Scholar * King * Queen

**Effective Use of Teacher Energy:**

- Remember that respect and dignity are the keys to successful teacher-student relationships.
- Allow your students to be individuals. Understand the positions from where they come from, and challenge them to expand their horizons and improve their knowledge and skills.
- Knowledge and preparation are starting points to good teaching.
- We never stop learning, and any one individual can teach us many things.
- Be patient. Be tolerant. Never stoop to a student's level of emotion and antagonism.
- Every aspect of your behaviour is observed by your students. You may be an inspiration or a hindrance to any of your students.

# Thief

The Thief is the archetype of the person who continually steals things. Most likely and obviously the Thief steals physical goods and materials. Money, jewellery, computers, and electrical equipment are favourite targets, as they are accessible and easy to transfer into wealth. Art works are for the more specialized thief, and the motor car is the other popular item, but this is often stolen for joyriding and demolition. The Thief is always wanting to reinvent methods. These days, identity theft is on the rise. This may be to secure money, but sometimes identity theft is used for migration fraud and covert or terrorist operations. There is also the emotional and psychological Thief. This Thief pathologically moves from relationship to relationship, from one person to another, leaving a trail of emotional or psychological trauma.

It is not an easy process to readily admit that an individual has a Thief archetype. Part of the energy of a Thief is to remain anonymous. The operations of the Thief are meant to be clandestine. There is limited opportunity to practice your craft if you are caught and placed in prison. Another aspect of Thief energy is denial. The person who has a Thief archetype has good reason to keep that information a closely guarded secret.

We know the obvious Thief. This is the person addicted to a life of crime who accepts spending time behind bars. However, others with the Thief archetype rarely face justice. They are political leaders and their cronies and the top echelon of financiers, bankers, and money marketers. From time to time, a few are brought to justice, but these are rare occurrences. These Thieves are protected by the laws they make or the systems they or their friends oversee. Despite all their legal and political rationale and denial, they still have a Thief archetype.

Some individuals with the Thief archetype are never identified. Modern technology has given them many advantages. These Thieves do not need to run the risk of hiding stolen CDs down their pants or up their shirts. They can download all the music or film material from the Internet they desire. They can do this without fear or trepidation. Stealing articles from the workplace is almost a well-accepted tradition. Stealing from big businesses is often excused by the logic that they can afford it. Stealing from public places is also excused through misconstrued logic. It says something about the Thief archetype when councils need to bolt down benches and seats in parks and shopping centres. It is astounding how many plants go missing after the council workers plant out public garden beds. Consider all the vandalism and tagging that is rife in our cities, suburbs, and towns. It is amazing that individuals can "borrow" items from their neighbours, family, or friends without asking and with dubious intention. This is all the activity of the Thief. Secrecy and denial does not hide the fact that this is the Thief in operation.

**Negative Aspects:**

Disrespect ~ Abuse ~ Denial ~ Need for approval ~ Secretive ~ Rapist ~ Energy sucking ~ Parasite ~ Lack of consideration ~ Immoral ~ Unethical ~ Criminal ~ Damaging ~ Vandal ~ Pirate ~ Bully ~ Inconsiderate ~ Harmful

**Positive Aspects:**

Honour power ~ Self-discipline ~ Ethical ~ Moral ~ Self-support ~ Honour ~ Independence ~ Respectful ~ Clear conscience

**Archetypal Energy:**

The most obvious energy of the Thief is that of secrecy. There is no point in being a Thief if you cannot keep secrets. Secrecy is the inbuilt mechanism on which the Thief energy thrives. Beware of the individual with secrets. Most of us have secrets. There are occasions when we have done things we are not proud of. We are all human. We can all make mistakes. However, Thieves have veils of secrecy that surround them.

The other obvious energy of Thieves is denial or excusing their behaviours. Many Thieves deny their actions. The initial reaction is that "It wasn't me." Another form of denial is that "There are no hard and fast rules." "It is within the law" is always a favourite of the politician or business executive exposed for unethical, immoral, or corrupt practices.

After denial come the excuses. If the Thief has been exposed, then denial does not work, but excusing the behaviour may. How about the rationale of "I deserve it"? Then there is the excuse that "Everybody else does it." The Thief can use the

"They won't miss it" routine or the "They won't notice" dance. There are myriad excuses the Thief can use. It all depends on the circumstances and the audience who catches the Thief.

The Thief may carry out deeds using the energy of envy and jealousy. The self-esteem of the Thief has very little balance. If the Thief has a low self-esteem, then this may act as a justification for robbery. The reasoning goes like this: If the Thief does not feel good about himself or herself, then why should anyone else feel good? Alternatively, if the Thief steals something, then this becomes an ego-boosting achievement. The thieving and acquisition of the article can increase the individual's self-esteem. The extreme is the Thief with the alter ego. This is usually the dictator or politician who plunders his own country or citizens. It is the banker or financier who sells the ordinary citizen a product that is likely to default at the expense of the customer but rewards the banker or financier. It is the heads of crime syndicates who use others to do the dirty work to protect their identity.

Petty thieves, vandals, graffiti taggers, individuals who pirate the intellectual work of others and infringe copyright and so-called joy riders all exhibit energy of selfishness. There is no consideration of others. It is all about meeting their needs at the expense of someone else. The behaviour is selfish, and if the behaviour is continuous, then those individuals have the Thief archetype. Often these individuals change from one activity to another. This is to justify behaviour and deny they are thieves. For example, "When I was a teenager, I used to steal cars and go joyriding. It was just a bit of fun, but I do not do it anymore." Yet, as an adult, this may be the same person who steals items from his or her work place. The behaviour changes, but the Thief archetype still uses the same negative energy.

As with all archetypes, the Thief archetype has positive energy. Negative Thieves do reform. They begin by being responsible for their actions and accepting the consequences. They stop denying their mistakes and admit their misdemeanours to friends and family. They put an end to the lying and secrecy. Reformed thieves start to find their ethics and examine their moral behaviours. They learn to honour themselves and others. They start to treat both themselves and other people with respect and dignity. It takes self-discipline, attitude, and a desire for contentment and appreciation for what life has provided. The positive energy of the Thief is capable of all those things. If we never strive to achieve these qualities, then we never change our behaviours.

**Archetypal Combinations:**

The archetypal energy of the Thief combines well with the energy of:

Victim * Prostitute * Saboteur * Judge

**Effective Use of Thief Energy:**

- Consider your behaviour with objectivity and truthfulness. Are you in denial, or do you excuse yourself?
- How considerate are you of others? "Do unto others as you would have them do unto you" is a useful maxim. "Do to others before they do it to you" is an excuse, and a poor one at that.
- Constantly review your ethics and your morals.
- Consider your relationships. Do you respect and dignify your partner within that relationship, or do you use and abuse them?

# Trickster

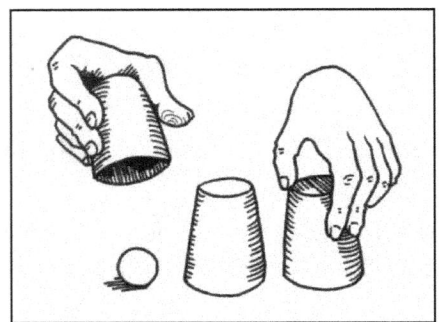

The Trickster is the person who continuously plays tricks on others. The tricks could be frivolous or serious; depending upon the mood of the Trickster and the relationship the Trickster has with the victim. If the Trickster has a vague relationship with the victim, the trick is more likely to be frivolous. If the Trickster has a close relationship with or holds a position of power over the victim, then the trick is likely to be more complicated.

Tricksters play tricks on others for several reasons. The first reason is for their amusement. The Trickster believes that all tricks they play are funny and amusing. They get a laugh out of any situation they have set up.

Tricksters also play tricks to show their cleverness. The more complicated the tricks, the smarter the Tricksters. That is generally why Tricksters play tricks on their friends or, if they are employers, tricks on their employees. Most of us have heard of tricks, most of them quite inane, that senior tradesmen play on young and inexperienced apprentices. The main reason for these pranks is to reinforce the junior position of apprentices. The tricks imply that the employers or senior tradesmen are smart, and the positions of the newcomers are inferior ones. It is the same rationale that condones initiation ceremonies in the armed forces, at expensive public schools, at boarding schools, and at fraternities within colleges.

One of the aims of Tricksters is to make sure there are audiences to witness their cleverness. Initiation ceremonies are group affairs. Making fun of apprentices usually has a whole workshop involved. There is no point for Tricksters to set up gags if there is no audience. The victims of the pranks probably do not see the funny side, but Tricksters have a need to share the mirth and the congratulations of their cleverness. This is one of the reasons that some Tricksters become stand-up comedians. They love an audience to witness their quick-wittedness.

As mentioned previously, there are differences between the Fool, the Clown, the Joker, the Court Jester, and the Trickster. The Trickster is the most egocentric of this quartet. Ego plays an important part in the behaviour of the Trickster. Tricksters are found in all walks of life. The important thing to remember is not to take the Trickster too seriously. The Trickster should not be encouraged to push his or her behaviour to the limit.

**Negative Aspects:**

Deceptive ~ Mimic ~ Low self-esteem ~ Driven by ego ~ Foolish ~ Prankster ~ Sarcastic ~ Put downs ~ Make fun of others ~ Peer pressure ~ Silly ~ Devious ~ Inane

**Positive Aspects:**

Insight ~ Light-hearted ~ Amusing ~ Funny ~ Clever ~ Witty ~ Quick-witted

**Archetypal Energy:**

The archetypal energy of Tricksters is concerned with amusement. Tricksters are intent on satisfying their sense of fun. Tricks are played for their personal amusement. This may be to satisfy their sense of humour, to boost their egos, or to establish and maintain positions of power.

To entertain is another form of energy pertaining to the Trickster. Tricksters have the need to entertain their audiences. They require the acclamation of their peer groups or their audiences. Tricksters can be entertaining, although being on the wrong side of a bad joke is no laughing matter. Most Tricksters' pranks are harmless enough, although there are occasional situations that go bad. The key for Tricksters is to be aware of the social settings and the sensitivity of their intended victims.

Victims familiar with the Trickster's pranks are likely to be less offended than others who are unfamiliar with the prankster. Friends and acquaintances are usually aware of the Trickster. There was an advertisement on television a couple of years ago where mates placed glue on all kinds of objects. Being stuck to your seat or having your mobile glued to a boat would be amusing and entertaining for those guys in that social setting. However, in other social settings, taking a person's mobile would be illegal and cause a deal of angst and disharmony.

One of the benefits of Tricksters is that they are able to ease the tension or take the seriousness out of a tense situation. If there is enough insight, the Trickster can play the role of Peacemaker. This is done through humour, not through negotiation or threats. The Trickster has the ability to show to the protagonists an absurdity or the unnecessary seriousness of a situation. The Trickster also has the ability to "take the Mickey" out of a person who is acting with exaggerated pomposity or stuffiness. In other words, the Trickster has the ability to create that feeling of equality within people. They show, through humour and absurdity, that we are all human and that to communicate effectively, we need to reach a level playing field.

**Archetypal Combinations:**

The archetypal energy of the Trickster combines well with the energy of:

Court Jester * Clown * Joker * Fool * Storyteller * Actor * Mentor * Adventurer * Magician * Rebel * Advocate * Alchemist * God * Goddess

**Effective Use of Trickster Energy:**

- Consider the victim of your tricks. Will the victim appreciate the joke and the humour, or will there be embarrassment and resentment?
- What are your motives?
- Is your trickery used for positive purposes, to create a sense of fun and camaraderie? Is it used for negative purposes, to maintain your power and control, or to enhance your self-esteem at the expense of others?
- Consider your relationship with your audience. Are you succumbing to "peer pressure" or are you consolidating the bonds of friendship?

# Vampire

In recent years vampire stories have come back into fashion. Bram Stoker's *Dracula* is the foundation for modern vampires. In Stoker's novel, Dracula was shown as a character with charm and mystery who disguised his bloodthirsty and sadistic intent. Since then vampires have been portrayed with a sense of romance and intrigue. The sexual aspect of the vampire is often enhanced, and the motives of the vampire have been softened. The intrigue surrounding the vampire has deepened, and in popular culture, the vampire has certainly become a more complex character. This is in line with the archetypal complexity of the Vampire.

Individuals with a negative Vampire archetype literally suck the life force from others. They are very needy individuals, and put in today's terminology, they would be considered high maintenance. They have personalities that draw upon the energy of those around them emotionally, psychologically, and physically. There are various reasons why individuals with the Vampire archetype can be so negative. It is often poor self-esteem. They do not feel content within and are looking for inner fulfilment from sources external to themselves. Negative Vampires feel that the world owes them a free ride. They see their lives as an injustice. Some Vampires feel this should see them looked after, with little contribution on their behalf. They focus on what other people get away with to justify their behaviour. Others committing worse atrocities or stealing vast wealth gives justification for Vampires to behave badly or receive goods, services, or payments obligation free.

Vampires attach themselves to vulnerable or caring individuals. People who are not strong enough to say no are easily drawn into the energy of Vampires. Vampires are the masters of emotional blackmail. These individuals use positive Vampire energy to call upon future favours to satisfy and justify their negative traits. To that end, Vampires assist their hosts. They are pleasant company, do good deeds, and request nothing in return. They share conversations and are extremely social. However, this is all Vampire behaviour, to lull their victims into a false sense of security and a position of dependence. When this has been achieved, Vampires strike. This may be subtle. The victims are likely to experience tiredness, a lack of energy, or irrational concerns. Vampires drain the life force, call in favours, seek emotional and psychological support, and maybe even use their victims' money and possessions. If the strikes are sudden and violent, the victims are left shattered. Vampires are capable of vindictive actions. If their hosts have lost their usefulness, they are discarded and other victims sought.

**Negative Aspects:**

Parasite ~ Energy sucking ~ Vindictive ~ Disrespect ~ In need of approval ~ Taking advantage of ~ Rapist ~ Whine ~ Clinging ~ Sexual predator ~ Abusive ~ Dependent

**Positive Aspects:**

Giving ~ Social ~ Charming ~ Good company ~ Helpful ~ Considerate ~ Honourable ~ Independent ~ Self-support ~ Energetic

**Archetypal Energy:**

The archetypal energy of the Vampire can be charming, honourable, and supportive. What needs to be questioned is the motive. If Vampires have good intentions, their behaviour is independent of any expected reward or support. The period of independence has to be prolonged and consistent. If positive intention underlies the behaviours of individuals with the Vampire archetype, they are utilizing positive Vampire energy. If the motive of Vampires is to gain favour or take advantage of others, then they are employing negative energy. It is easy for Vampires to switch from positive to negative energy. The temptation is difficult to resist. Self-control is a continual challenge to them. The urge to suck energy from others is strong and ongoing, and personal vigilance needs to be constant.

The Vampire has a constant battle for independence instead of co-dependency. The communication skills and social nature of the Vampire can be alluring. This creates dependence on both sides of a relationship. The victim may find comfort from the friendship and the desire to be needed. The Vampire may find comfort from the energy of the victim. The Vampire has to be aware that there is give and take on both sides. This situation maintains a balanced relationship.

The other energetic challenge for the Vampire is to avoid playing the jilted victim. Yes, the world is not a fair place! Some people lead a charmed life, while others are constantly faced with challenges. The key is to appreciate and enjoy the good moments and to work through the challenges. Vampires are blessed with positive personal attributes and can remain focused on their better qualities. It is not important if others have more or less fortune and favour. What matters is an appreciation of what they have. If Vampires can stand tall in their own power, they make a positive contribution to their welfare and the welfare of others.

**Archetypal Combinations:**

The archetypal energy of the Vampire combines well with the energy of:

Victim * Prostitute * Warrior * Detective * Martyr * Companion * Rescuer

**Effective Use of Vampire Energy:**

- Remember that independence is worth fighting for. Stand in your own power, and do not rely on the energy of others.
- Be aware of your motives. Are the relationships you form for the mutual benefit of both parties, or have you something more devious and calculated in mind?
- Use your charm and friendly nature for the benefit of others.
- Do not be envious of others. Focus on your good fortune.

# Victim

Our Victim archetype is the archetype of self-esteem. Our self-esteem is firstly an attitude, quickly followed by an emotion. Our self-esteem determines how we feel about ourselves in each and every situation. It is the measure of our confidence and our risk-taking. One day we may feel on top of the world. Our confidence is sky high, and there is nothing that we cannot achieve. The next day we may be more subdued, a little sceptical, and cautious. Our self-esteem experiences such highs and lows. If we are with friends, our self-esteem is probably in a comfortable place. We are relaxed and happy. However, at a formal gathering with strangers, our self-esteem may plummet, leading to shyness, a lack of confidence, nervousness, and a strong urge to remain within the boundaries of discretion.

Our Victim archetype works hand in hand with our other archetypes. For example, when the Damsel is in love, her self-esteem is high, but when the Damsel endures the suffering of a relationship breakdown, her self-esteem plummets. Our Victim archetype has an especially strong tie with our Prostitute archetype. When our self-esteem is high, we value ourselves more and demand a higher price for our worth and our services. When our self-esteem is low, the value we place upon ourselves is lower. The relationship between our Victim and Prostitute archetypes also influences our Saboteur archetype. When we feel good and value ourselves, we act with more intuition and make positive decisions. When we feel down and devalue our worth, we sabotage our decision making.

Our Victim archetype also has a special relationship with our Child archetype. How we feel about ourselves; how we cope in certain situations; how we react to various events; and how we interact with family, friends, and community is first learnt as children. These social and emotional lessons influence everything we do and become. The more time we spend with positive Child archetypal energy, the more balanced our self-esteem becomes. If, as children, we are subject to negative experiences and dwell with negative Child archetypal energy, it is more likely that we grow up feeling victimized and struggling with low self-esteem.

The Victim is a key archetype. If we use the positive energy of the Victim to raise our self-esteem, we then have a greater chance of fully utilizing the positive energy of our other individual archetypes. It is not an easy task to maintain a healthy self-esteem. It is rare for any one individual to be on a constant high. However, if we understand how our Victim archetype works and monitor our self-esteem, we then have a more rational approach to our decision making, attitudes, and behaviours. We learn to make decisions at the appropriate times. We accept and enjoy each moment of our lives with greater clarify.

As I work with clients on their archetypes, I receive a clear picture of their self-esteem. You might consider this akin to a graph. Some self-esteem graphs are like a mountain range with lots of highs and lows. These individuals feel great for a short time and then plummet to a state almost like depression, before quickly recovering to begin the upward climb to the peaks of happiness again. Damsels and Adventurers seem to have this pattern of self-esteem. Damsels, in and out of love, emotionally high or in doubt, totally dependent or fiercely independent, exhibit this pattern. The adrenalin rush of the Adventurer conjures a similar pattern.

Other self-esteem charts look more like roller coasters with big, rolling highs and long, swooping lows. Actors, Artists, and Rescuers seem to follow this pattern. When the Actor is in work, when the Artist is deeply involved in a project, and when the Rescuer is involved in saving something precious, they participate in this long and flowing, high self-esteem pattern. As their projects and assignments come to a conclusion, their self-esteem goes through the deep valley in search of the next ride to lofty heights.

Other patterns are not as extreme as these. Some graphs are simple rolling hills. Others appear as waves with small highs and small troughs. Some seem to do a loop so the individual can return and re-examine that feeling before moving on to the next challenge. My personal pattern is a continuous bubbly line. There are no big highs or lows, just a continuous line that bubbles up and down. I am always content within myself. I feel a lot of inward joy and rarely show lavish external emotional highs. My dear wife suggests that I am boring. I maintain that I am calm and relaxed and perfectly content with knowing who I am. This doesn't mean that I am happy to stagnate. On the contrary, I am continually striving to improve and achieve.

No matter how your personal self-esteem works, the key to a balanced self-esteem is knowledge and understanding. This gives you the benefit of taking advantage of your emotional highs and an awareness of your emotional lows. Be prepared to monitor your self-esteem. If you have taken an emotional or psychological hit, be prepared to wait before making major decisions. Recognize how you are feeling and work towards raising your self-esteem. Give yourself praise, encouragement, and a pep talk. Focus on the good times and the decisions that have rewarded you. Consider your attitude, and change it if necessary. Ask yourself, is this going to be important in twelve months? If the answer is no, then let it go, and move on. If the answer is yes, then change your attitude, change your behaviour, make a practical decision, and adjust your circumstances to accommodate the situation. Listen to your intuition, follow your gut, and be confident in your instincts.

**Negative Aspects:**

Blames others ~ Learn helplessness ~ Weak ~ Vulnerable ~ Fearful ~ Self-pity ~ Unable to make decisions ~ Prey ~ Bullied ~ Ignored ~ Dependent ~ Succumbs to peer pressure ~ Hopelessness ~ Attributes fault and blame ~ Poor me

**Positive Aspects:**

Stands up for self ~ Assertiveness ~ Protected ~ Victorious ~ Self-assured ~ Choose your attitude ~ Take responsibility for self ~ Confident ~ Content ~ Strong ~ In control ~ Self-disciplined ~ Independent ~ Positive

**Archetypal Energy:**

All thoughts, words, and actions are influenced by our attitudes and how we feel about ourselves. Our self-esteem is all-encompassing, which makes the Victim archetype key to understanding ourselves.

The first and guiding principle of Victim archetypal energy is knowledge and understanding. When we know who we are and understand ourselves, we can be content within ourselves. If we are not content with who we are, we then have the ability and opportunity to change. Knowledge is the first step in the process. Is our self-esteem at a high or at a low? When do we feel confident? What makes us feel confident? What are the causes of the fluctuation in our self-esteem? Knowledge and understanding determine our attitudes and level of contentment. Contentment, or lack of it, is the catalyst for change. We have the ability to change. The key question is; do we have the willpower to change? We have total control over our attitudes, opinions, thoughts, words, and actions. Change our attitudes and we change our levels of contentment.

There are no relevant excuses to justify harmful attitudes. How often do we hear such excuses? "I think that because that's the way I was brought up." Guess what? That is an excuse and not a good one. Here is another. "My friends are all drinking and smoking, so I have to; otherwise, I won't fit in." That kind of talk is also an excuse. Peer pressure is powerful, but we are individuals. If it is not right for you, do not do it. Have the courage to walk away. If your friends do not accept who you are, then they are not true friends. Consider finding other friends who do accept you and your values. Too many friendships are based on bribery. The message sounds something like this: "If you change, then we won't like you anymore." Friendship is based on acceptance as well as shared values. We have the power. Find your own strength, and stay content and happy with the choices you make.

The archetypal energy of Victims revolves around self-belief. When individuals have that self-belief, they express confidence. They trust in their own abilities and the abilities of others. They are assertive and display leadership. They tackle challenges with gusto and celebrate their victories. They take responsibility for their decisions, attitudes, and behaviours. They are also humble enough to admit fault and rectify wrongs they may have caused. The key is always self-belief. When your Victim archetype is cared for, all of your other personal archetypes perform at maximum strength.

**Archetypal Combinations:**

The archetypal energy of the Victim combines well with the energy of:

* All major Archetypes
* There is a special relationship with Prostitute, Saboteur and Child

**Effective Use of Victim Energy:**

- Always monitor your self-esteem. Keep in mind how you feel about yourself and your level of confidence.
- Make key decisions when your self-esteem is high.
- Never make decisions in desperation or when your self-esteem is low.
- You are in control of yourself. Forget "the blame game" and dismiss all excuses.
- Work on those factors that improve your personal development and foster your ambitions.

# Visionary

Visionaries see things beyond the physical world or beyond the limitations of eyesight. Some Visionaries have clear pictures of other dimensions. Our physical world exists on a thin spectrum of light. If we had the ability to move sideways beyond our thin spectrum of light and into other spectrums, we would encounter other dimensions.

Visionaries have the ability to visualize these dimensions. Visionaries do not enter these other dimensions, but they are a channel in which the images of these dimensions are processed. Those individuals with the Mystic archetype can travel into other dimensions, but not the Visionary. Of course, it is possible that an individual has both of those archetypes and has the abilities of both travel and sight.

Some Visionaries have the ability to see entities that may never, or perhaps rarely, take on a physical presence. Our surroundings are vibrating at a speed that we are so accustomed to we do not even recognize their presence. Other entities vibrate at different speeds. So, if we change our vibrating speed, or if other entities change their vibration, then there is a meeting place. Individuals who have the Visionary archetype do not need to change their own personal vibration to observe these entities. It is just a matter of tuning in and refocusing. Visionaries do not spend all their time tuning into their visions. However, when they desire, they have a natural ability to see more than those of us who do not possess the Visionary archetype.

Consider, for a moment, the thoughts of children who have the Visionary archetype. When we are young there are many scary things in the world. Most are in our imaginations. For Visionary children, most of their fears are very real. When we are young, we are encouraged to use our imaginations. Yet, as we get older, we are told to stop making things up. Consider the children who regularly see other dimensions or entities. They may be deemed pleasant by our standards. They may be places of beauty or be entities of human fantasy. They may even be accepted parts of our belief systems, such as fairies, angels, and unicorns. Yet they may also be darker entities with a scary energy. Some might call them nightmares. It is understandable, then, that children with the Visionary archetype are reluctant to tune in to their abilities if these types of visions are common. There are many worlds and entities that are unknown, difficult to explain, and terrifying.

It is also understandable that Visionaries are reluctant to admit to their abilities. The child who actually sees fairies is rewarded with platitudes and labels like imaginative and dreamer. The child who sees ghosts, apart from being very scared, is labelled as strange or weird. As these children grown into teenagers and adults, their ability as Visionaries may be just as taxing. The Visionary is a specific archetype and certainly not common. Humans are dependent on their five senses, and most of us are dependent on our physical sight. It is never easy to explain the things you are capable of seeing, while the majority of people cannot see those things.

To the human mind, the concept of time is logical and necessary. Time is lineal and organizes events in a framework that we understand. However, our concept and embodiment of time is not universal. Worlds that operate on a different vibrating level do not fit into our time zones or our understanding of time. Events that happen in the future do not fit into a neat and recognizable time sequence.

Place yourself in the position of a subsistence-farming family several hundred years ago. Imagine you are a young boy, and your life is working the land. You depend on the seasons and the crops for your livelihood. Your day begins at sunrise and finishes at sunset. Your knowledge is limited to your lifestyle and the few kilometres that you inhabit. What if this boy has a Visionary archetype? What if he can tune into visions of the 1940s? Cities, aeroplanes, ships, bombs, destruction, battle fields, and prison camps fill his visions. Imagine how strange and terrifying these visions would be. Imagine how ludicrous it would be to attempt to place these events in a time frame when all he's known is a simple farming life. The most famous Visionary, Nostradamus, is often dismissed as a credible Visionary due to his lack of a solid time frame and his method of reporting. Consider the fairness of this criticism. Visionaries are not fortune tellers. They can make educated guesses if their visions contain something familiar to the world they know, but truly that is all they are, guesses.

**Negative Aspects:**

Self-seeking ~ Cynic ~ Doom and gloom ~ Fear of rejection ~ Conditional ~ I told you so ~ Pessimist ~ Rigid ~ Limited ~ Fearful ~ Liar ~ Bragger

**Positive Aspects:**

Predictions ~ Bring the message, then let go ~ Self-conviction ~ Confronting ~ Catalyst of change ~ Validated ~ Unattached ~ Courageous ~ Truthful

**Archetypal Energy:**

The archetypal energy of the Visionary relies on courage. Courage is the necessary ingredient for the Visionary's survival and peace of mind. Visionaries require courage to understand who they are and to understand they are different from the majority of their families, friends, and peers. There are very few true Visionaries. They require courage to tune into their visions, many of which are confusing at best and terrifying at worse. They require courage to put their ability into perspective and use them in a productive manner.

Visionaries can be extremely helpful and beneficial in guiding others. When they put aside their visions of things outside of our understanding and focus on visions that are specific and meaningful to themselves, they give purpose and meaning to their gifts. I have one friend who can see people's spirit guides. She is also an artist, and I have the most fascinating drawing collection of spirit guides that she drew for the members of my family. I have another friend who is a medium. She is able to communicate with people who have passed, as though they are standing right in front of her. These are two examples where Visionaries have the ability to understand the purpose of the images they see and to translate the message. Visionaries, working with positive energy, fulfil their potential when they commit to assisting others.

The Visionary also has to be discerning. There are several aspects to consider. The first is the use of the visionary process. The Visionary is likely to invite misunderstanding, fear, terror, paranoia, and even personal invasion if they continually delve into other realms with total abandonment and recklessness. Visionaries have to be aware of their ability to absorb entities and maintain personal equilibrium.

The second aspect is deciding who is privy to their abilities. Visionaries have to surround themselves with supportive family and friends. There is plenty of cynicism in the world, and Visionaries always attract their fair share. They need friends who seek to balance that cynicism with belief and support. The third aspect Visionaries may consider is how to best use their abilities. Is this unique ability to be used at all? Does the Visionary succumb to the doubts and criticisms of the cynics? If Visionaries have the courage to proclaim their abilities, are these abilities to be used to assist others or for self-seeking motives?

The last aspect is for Visionaries to remain independent of their visions. Independence, in this respect, means the Visionary must relay the purity of the message and not tamper with the substance of the message to fit in with personal beliefs or prejudices. These four aspects of discernment either make or break the Visionary.

**Archetypal Combinations:**

The archetypal energy of the Visionary combines well with the energy of:

Prophet * Healer * Servant * Shaman * Rescuer * Divine Child * God * Goddess * Mystic * Monk * Nun * Priest * Priestess * Seeker * Guide * Angel

**Effective Use of Visionary Energy:**

- Use your abilities to give advice, to assist, guide, and heal others.
- Be wary of self-seeking and aggrandizement.
- Be conscious of the limits of your ability and the balance that is required to maintain an independent life.
- Always be discerning in the entertainment of your visions and in the people who surround you.

# Wanderer

The Wanderer meanders through life from one place to another, one job to another, and one event to another. The phrase "go with the flow" applies wholeheartedly to the Wanderer. The Wanderer is a different archetype from the Adventurer and the Seeker. The Adventurer looks for adventure. The Wanderer accepts adventures as they come along. The Seeker asks the questions and takes the appropriate steps to find the answers. If the Wanderer is confronted by a question, it is usually framed in vague terminology, such as; I wonder what it would be like camping on the beach? The Wanderer often moves to a new situation without any thought or consideration of the process. On the other hand, the Seeker weighs up all the options with lists and questions.

In Australian terminology, "the swagman" is a perfect example of an individual with the Wanderer archetype. In Europe there are the gypsies. In the Middle East there are the nomads. Various indigenous tribes are blessed with the Wanderer archetype. These are the obvious examples of the Wanderer who moves from place to place. They are easy to identify. If there is a living to be made in a particular place, then Wanderers are to be found there. When that local economy begins to decline, they move on. When their interests wane, they move on. If there is something more interesting on the other side of the mountain, Wanderers again move on. Some Wanderers change their situations on gut feelings. Their intuition tells them it is time for a change, so off they go. Other Wanderers move on for no apparent reason. Just pack their bags and go.

As you can tell, Wanderers do not hold down the same job for any length of time. They continually move from one position to another. Wanderers make excellent itinerant workers. The nature of Wanderers dictates they have a range of relationships. They are inclined to move from one partner to another. If a Wanderer is in a solid relationship, the Wanderer's partner has to accept the constant moving and changing. Generally, Wanderers have clusters of friends. They are accomplished at moving from one social group to another. At each new job or location, they make new friends. Wanderers are friendly and socially adept at fitting in. There are exceptions, of course. The Wanderer with the Hermit archetype has few friends. The combined energy of these two archetypes dictates to the individual that roaming by oneself is the natural thing to do.

**Negative Aspects:**

Escape ~ Lost soul ~ Lack of commitment ~ Vagabond ~ Insecure ~ No goals ~ Purposeless ~ Unstable ~ Wayward ~ Unsociable

**Positive Aspects:**

New experiences ~ Free spirit ~ Backpacker ~ Adventurer ~ Secure ~ Fun ~ Stability ~ Seeker ~ At home ~ Comfortable with self ~ Go with the flow ~ Adaptable

**Archetypal Energy:**

The most important aspect the Wanderer's energy is the ability to go with the flow. The Wanderer has an attitude that accepts new situations. New experiences are not seen as a challenge but as a way of life. So many people see change as a threat. It threatens their stability and stimulates their fear of the unknown. The Wanderer's energy rails against conservative boundaries and loves the exploration of the unknown. There are no "little boxes on the hillside" for the Wanderer. This way of life is far too restricting. It is the energy that allows the movement from one place to another, from one situation to another, and from one experience to another. It is not a quest but a genuine way of life.

Freedom is the key concept to the Wanderer. It is the freedom of movement, opportunity, and experience. The Wanderer loves to be free. Boundaries are suffocating to the Wanderer. Expectations are trivial. The most fearful situation to the Wanderer is jail or slavery. All other situations represent freedom. The Wanderer is comfortable moving from one situation to another and is totally at ease once a move has been made.

Friendliness is another energetic aspect of the Wanderer. Wanderers are particularly adept at blending into new social groups. They use their good listening skills to learn and understand the values and morals of their new social groups and local habitats. They have to be seen as non-threatening. This gains them acceptance into all kinds of social situations. Wanderers are interesting people to talk to. They have intriguing experiences. They have news and stories of adventure. They pass on information to other people who are set in their ways, and they often live vicariously through others and the media.

How many times have you heard New Age teachers espousing the "live in the moment" philosophy? That is exactly what the positive energy of Wanderers is all about. It is about enjoying life, even the challenges and the difficulties. It is about appreciating each day they are given. It is about valuing their freedom and taking advantage of all opportunities.

The negative side to the Wanderer is lack of responsibility and commitment. It is a challenge to be in a relationship with a Wanderer. By their very nature, Wanderers find it difficult to commit. This places their partners, children, and employers in positions of instability. Wanderers have to consider their nature and their commitment level to a relationship. If children enter the equation, Wanderers have to consider their responsibilities. Wanderers who continually use the negative archetypal energy are prone to move from one relationship to another. They generally have children with a number of partners. They lead lives that resemble a never-ending circle—repeating the same mistakes, never learning from their experiences, and unable to break off in a tangent to set a new and refreshing course of life experiences.

**Archetypal Combinations:**

The archetypal energy of the Wanderer combines well with the energy of:

Adventurer * Detective * Seeker * Storyteller * Prophet * Shape-Shifter * Actor * Beggar * Artist * Explorer * Philosopher * Networker

**Effective Use of Wanderer Energy:**
- Use the philosophy of "go with the flow" wisely.
- Stay with your intuition and gut feeling to lead you to places, people, events, and situations that enhance your life.
- Beware of the lure of false promises and the bright city lights.
- Learn the value of responsibility and commitment.
- Beware of losing your identity and true essence. The loss of self is a result of negative energy.
- Always ask the question; "am I running away?"

# Warrior

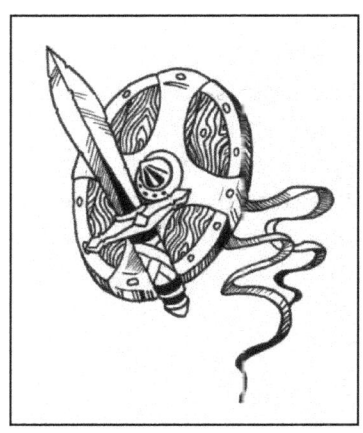

Many people have the Warrior archetype. The Warrior goes into battle for a cause, for the sake of a fight, or for payment. Warriors come in many different forms. There are soldiers who serve their countries or leaders, police officers who enforce civil law, mercenaries who give their services to individuals or causes for payment, and gang members bound by common belief and structure. Their battles are often for territory, identity, or commercial advantage. Others with the Warrior archetype play sport and collectively or individually do battle for pride and the recognition to be the best. Some Warriors fight for social causes, such as personal or civil freedom, legal change, social reform, and environmental conservation.

Most Warriors are identified by a uniform. In medieval times, the warrior knights, as they rode into battle, would carry the flag or symbol of their monarch. Soldiers and police are immediately recognized by their uniforms. Each sporting team has its own colours and totems. The motorcycle gangs have their jackets, emblazoned with club names and symbols. The uniform is used not only to identify the Warrior but also as a powerful psychological tool to instil pride, allegiance, and discipline into a person.

The tools of trade are very important to Warriors. Their successes and sometimes their very existence depend on their equipment. To a warrior knight, his horse, sword, and shield were sacred. For the professional warrior, the role of the horse, sword, and shield has changed dramatically. Now these Warriors use fighter jets, aircraft carriers, battle cruisers, tanks, and armoured vehicles. Weapons are missiles, rocket propelled grenades, and rapid-fire guns.

The modern civil warrior depends on modern transportation. How many young men place pride and importance on their vehicles? The motor bike or car has replaced the horse as the Warrior's form of transportation. These machines are lovingly cared for and maintained with regularity and reverence. The sporting Warrior has seen modern advances too, yet the element of care is unchanged. Cyclists have a duty to look after their bicycles and their uniform equipment.

Olympic glory has been lost through equipment failure. Junior footballers are constantly told to clean their studs and take care of their boots to prepare them for battle.

Physical fitness and mental toughness are characteristics of the Warrior. Most Warrior activities require physical input, and their successes depend on their fitness, strength, and endurance. Despite physicality, often, the determining element of a Warrior's success is mental toughness. In a contest, there may be little between the physical attributes and prowess of the combatants. On many occasions, it is the mental toughness that determines the result. It is the self-belief and psychological endurance that determines victory over defeat, success over failure.

**Negative Aspects:**

Surrender free will ~ Intimidator ~ Corruption ~ Murderer ~ Assassin ~ Callous ~ Vengeful ~ Coward ~ Glorification ~ Bribery ~ Misuse of power ~ Reckless ~ Antagonistic ~ Vindictiveness

**Positive Aspects:**

Saviour ~ Brave ~ Protector ~ Guardian ~ Determined ~ Strength ~ Loyal ~ Guile ~ Physical fitness ~ Mental toughness ~ Principled ~ Heroic ~ Discernment ~ Endurance ~ Resilience

**Archetypal Energy:**

The Warrior energy is about strength, fitness, protection, bravery, loyalty, and mental toughness. The role of Warriors requires them to be healthy and physically fit. If this is not the case, it is possible Warriors may endanger the life and the success of their quests and their tribes. Many Warriors possess natural strength. Most Warriors undertake a physical fitness or weights program to build up strength and endurance levels. Warriors who cannot compete with another's strength compensate for this deficiency with other abilities such as speed, skill, and guile.

Warrior energy is also about protection. First and foremost, there is the protection of self. Many with the Warrior archetype disregard this principle. They show plenty of bravery and are willing to make a sacrifice, sometimes the ultimate sacrifice, in defence of others or a cause. Warriors are the protectors and the guardians of their societies, tribes, and ways of life. Their loyalty is such a strong energetic aspect that they can be blinded to what they're giving up and have no hesitation in doing so.

Loyalty demands that the Warrior be submissive to the tribal or group belief and code of protection. Warriors who become soldiers give away many rights as individuals. They are subject to the will of those in authority and are instructed and trained to obey orders without question. In some cases, this becomes a matter of life and death. Once the decision is made to become a part of the collective, there is often no turning back. The failure of soldiers to obey orders or to retreat in the heat of battle may bring about their own demise. The street gang warrior code has a similar mentality. Once in the gang, members are bound by the code, and breaking the rules or leaving the gang becomes a challenging task.

The archetypal energy of the Warrior is about the tribal power of the collective rather than individual power. The tribe recognizes that solidarity as a whole is a greater strength. As soon as an individual expresses a difference in tribal belief, then the power of the collective weakens. That individual must be expelled or brought into line for the tribal collective to remain strong. Warriors are energetically drawn to this power, as it keeps their world simple and takes away the confusion and frustration of making decisions. The tribal energy and power of the collective is alluring. You often hear things like "We are good; they are bad" and "You are either with us or against us." There is also "United we stand; divided we fall." Nationalism and patriotism survive on the simplicity of tribal energy. The sense of belonging, the fear of being different, and a fear of others are good motivators to join a tribal collective.

All societies have many individuals with the Warrior archetype. As with most countries, Australia is no different. We have nationalistic, flag-waving tribal warrior energy. Our armed forces have been involved in international wars, several of which had no bearing on our security or survival as a nation. Generally, as a nation, we have been free of the warmongering ravages that plague many other countries. Instead, we have tended to funnel the Warrior energy onto sporting fields.

Australia is a sporting nation. This has given our Warriors the opportunity to compete and supplies an outlet for suppressed tribal warrior energy. We support our football teams with passion and pride. We watch the success or failure of our national teams and individual sporting superstars with hope and despair. We do this as Australians in the knowledge that our social structure, our way of life, and our collective persona as a nation is not in any physical danger. In this respect, we are a lucky country. Sport has given us a sense of social peace. To some extent, we have woven ourselves a multicultural society and have thus far managed to marginalize the extremes of the Warrior archetype that feed on division, hatred, fear, and loathing.

The energy of the Warrior is always delicately balanced. There is a fine line between the soldier who kills in the defence of his country and the one who murders innocent civilians to seek revenge on his enemies. This is the fine line between positive protector and negative avenger. The Warrior walks a tight rope, balanced between courage and cowardice, protection and revenge, righteousness and degradation.

All people with the Warrior archetype may find themselves in similar situations. The Warrior who joins the police force may have the dilemma of speaking up to reveal corruption or covering up actions of misbehaviour. The seeker of social justice, the freedom fighter, and the environmental Warrior might have to decide whether or not to act within the bounds of the law or to push the boundaries of what they consider illegal, repressive regimes and regulations.

When does the freedom fighter become a terrorist? How does one react to aggression? Where does the point of compromise begin and end? If winning is everything, where does cheating fit in? If you go into battle for a friend, do you make enemies of others within your social circle? The question of compromise is always present in the forefront of all Warrior action. The key is discernment. The Warrior has to understand his or her individual principles and the objectives of the tribal collective. Discernment gives the Warrior power to compromise and clarifies the difference between moral and immoral action.

**Archetypal Combinations:**

The archetypal energy of the Warrior combines well with the energy of:

Hero * Knight * Athlete * Slave * Adventurer * Peacemaker * Statesman * King * Queen * Politician * Disciple * Explorer * Advocate * Rescuer * Rebel * Wizard * Pilgrim

**Effective Use of Warrior Energy:**

- Be aware that, as a Warrior, you sacrifice some or all of your individual rights to serve the tribal collective system and values.
- Be discerning about your battles and whom you choose to fight.
- Maintain your health, strength, and fitness through a regime of good eating, exercise, and healthy habits.
- Keep in mind that you are a defender and protector.
- Beware the emotional lure of power, revenge, and vindictiveness.

# Wise Woman

The Wise Woman, sometimes known as the Sage or Crone, is the keeper and confidant of knowledge. This knowledge may concern health issues, psychological issues, spirituality, relationships, or a combination of all of these. Historically the Wise Woman played a guiding role in the traditional tribal societies. Her role was especially devoted to the women and children of the tribe. She was the keeper of tribal stories and traditions. She was the advisor with pregnancy, child birth, and child rearing. She was the custodian of knowledge regarding illnesses and remedies. She was the spiritual connection between the tribal members and the Divine. She was the guidance counsellor and the marriage/relationship counsellor. The Wise Woman was a key person in the ongoing stability of tribal tradition and relationships.

As urban development increases and traditional tribal life dissipates, the Wise Woman becomes harder to identify. However, she is still very active in a modern, urbanized society. It is just that the tribe may have become larger and more diverse. The urbanized Wise Woman may be the local midwife, the health-centre nurse, the local herbalist, the alternative therapist, the government or privately employed psychologist, the school guidance counsellor, the school chaplain, or a school's religious education teacher. These positions may draw upon a wide range of clients from a large geographical or social area.

Even in an urbanized society, there are examples of the more traditional tribes with a traditional Wise Woman. This is the women's group that meets on a regular basis. It may be the New Age or spiritual shop or meeting place that holds regular workshops and courses. It may be the playgroup for mothers and their babies. These meetings bring together like-minded people. They form a more tribal community. They have a recognized Wise Woman who has the knowledge and leads the group in discussion and ritual.

Finally, individuals who have the Wise Woman archetype may be stay-at-home mothers or women in a variety of employment situations. These individuals are a wealth of information. Family, friends, and acquaintances recognize the knowledge, empathy, and understanding of the Wise Woman. They seek her advice on any number of matters regarding health, children, relationships, spiritual connections, and the like. These individuals always have a personal library of reference and non-fiction reading material. If the Wise Woman cannot answer a query directly, she seeks the information from other sources. This is no different from the traditional tribal Wise Woman observing nature and seeking answers from her environment.

The archetypal Wise Woman is seen as an older woman. Her life experiences give her the advantage of knowledge and understanding. However, we do not change our archetypes. Our personal archetypes are with us all of our lives. This means there are young people with the Wise Woman archetype. As with a lot of archetypes, their characteristics develop and become more obvious with age. Yet, some young people may be identified early as having the Wise Woman archetype. This is the girl or young woman who is the social group's advisor and confidant. Friends trust her with personal information. They seek her guidance and advice. She leads the various quests and adventures. She is the teacher whom young girls admire and confide in. She may not understand her Wise Woman archetypal energy, but her friends recognize it and are drawn to its knowledge, power, and protection.

**Negative Aspects:**

Nasty ~ Wicked ~ Grumpy ~ Know it all ~ Bitter ~ Busy body ~ Drained ~ Meddling ~ Aloof ~ Gossip ~ Bragger

**Positive Aspects:**

Wise ~ Evolved ~ Knowledge ~ Insightful ~ Elders ~ Mentor ~ Guide ~ Humble ~ Detachment ~ Confidant ~ Advisor ~ Teacher ~ Tradition ~ Trust ~ Practical

**Archetypal Energy:**

The archetypal energy of the Wise Woman is based on her wisdom, knowledge, and the trust placed in her. The Wise Woman is wise and knowledgeable. Some of this wisdom and knowledge is based on her life experiences. Some of it is handed down to her. Some of it is accessed from various external sources. Some of it is intuitive. If there are issues pertaining to women about health, child bearing and rearing, relationships, or spirituality, then the Wise Woman is the person to consult.

Meetings, discussions, and consultations with the Wise Woman and her advice are based on trust. The positive archetypal energy of the Wise Woman allows her to keep individual secrets. Personal matters told to her in confidence are kept private. The negative archetypal energy of the Wise Woman allows for and participates in gossip and rumour. Private information is spread throughout the tribe or community, and the trust is broken.

The Wise Woman is a guide. Only with the trust of friends, clients, or her tribe does she maintain her position as their guide. She is also their teacher. Information must be passed on to others to assist them in their lives. Often the teacher-pupil relationship becomes a closer relationship, and the Wise Woman takes on the role of Mentor. This allows for a one-on-one or small-group teaching relationship. With this type of relationship, the Wise Woman requires humility. The Wise Woman who takes on the status of guru runs the risk of self-glorification. This is the use of negative archetypal energy. Her position becomes one of authority and power, and her humility is lost in the process of personal gain.

The Wise Woman also has to be detached. If she becomes emotionally involved, she runs the risk of her knowledge being corrupted and her judgment being subjective. Detachment is not behaving in a cold, uncaring manner. Detachment is obtaining that fine balance where there is personal support, empathy, and caring while remaining objective and capable of understanding the bigger picture. Detachment allows the Wise Woman to provide personal comfort to her client while maintaining the ability to access her knowledge and wisdom, to think laterally, and to suggest relevant advice.

**Archetypal Combinations:**

The archetypal energy of the Wise Woman combines well with the energy of:

Guide * Shaman * Mentor * Witch * Teacher * Healer * Peacemaker * Rescuer * Priestess * Advocate * Saboteur * Mystic * Judge * Mother * Carer

**Effective Use of Wise Woman Energy:**

- You are the custodian of universal and tribal knowledge and wisdom. Respect your role.
- Use your knowledge and wisdom to assist all those who seek your help.
- Remember to remain humble. Your role is not for self-glorification but to assist others who seek your advice.
- Use your knowledge and wisdom to be objective and to think laterally. Emotional involvement may cloud your judgment.

# Witch

The Witch and the Wizard are the female and male equivalent of the same archetype, but their roles and abilities are somewhat different. The Witch has the dual role of convening with nature and healing. Often the healing is done through the knowledge and use of natural remedies and of reading the signs that nature provides. The healing is the practical use of the theory.

Witches are very much part of the Pagan tradition. They are in tune with nature and her seasons, natural phenomena, plants, and animal life. Pagan rituals and celebrations are built around nature's seasons. In a time when people's livelihoods depended on the seasons, it was important to be in tune with nature. When various religions hijacked Pagan beliefs, rituals and occasions and made promises of eternal salvation, people moved away from nature. With the Industrial Revolution, the rise of science, and the development of cities, people moved further away from their roots. Many industries seem to be in a constant battle with nature, and as a species, we have polluted and degraded our natural environment to the point where our very survival is coming under threat. Nature is rejecting our polluting ways, and as she changes, humanity must face the consequences of its actions.

Those with the Witch archetype are still present in modern society. Many live on the fringe, although some have gained acceptance in mainstream society. The most obvious area for the Witch to have an impact is in herbal medicine. Witches have a broad understanding of plant medicine and know that modern medicine only focuses on a narrow understanding of plant medicine. The practitioner who has a Witch archetype takes into account other factors within the healing process. Modern medicine focuses on symptoms, time, schedules, and profit. The Witch practitioner uses her intuition to make remedies and potions that are suitable and specific to the individual. Modern medicine has a pragmatic, one-size-fits-all approach. The Witch practitioner devotes time and personal service to her client. The general practitioner works to the demands of the clock and a schedule, often with fifteen-minute consultations.

Children with the Witch archetype practice their craft from a young age. They begin making potions and mixtures early. They learn about natural substances and the combinations that work well together. The young Witch is often her own testing guinea pig. These children often struggle at school. They are restricted by the four walls of the classroom and are bemused by the artificial and materialistic wishes of their peers. They are frustrated by a system that teaches the mainstream social values and neglects what is important to the Witch.

It is not just through potions and medicines that the Witch heals. Her expertise lies in emotional and spiritual healing as well. Practitioners with the Witch archetype are aware that treatment is a holistic process, and just treating the symptoms is only scratching the surface. By tuning into nature and the spiritual element of existence, these practitioners offer a deeper healing. This is often done through sacred and ancient ritual. This is a natural healing using the combination of human and natural energy. Ritual is important to the Witch. The Witch practitioner is aware of the rituals that support her connection with nature. She is aware of what is needed for healing both the human spirit and the nature spirit.

Do not be taken in by the popular degradation of the individual with the Witch archetype. The so-called heresy of the Witch was used as an excuse by religions to separate people from popular belief and create an enemy who could be demonized and feared. Throughout history those in power have selected enemies they could portray as threats to a population and thereby keep control over the actions of their communities.

**Negative Aspects:**

Liar ~ Black magic ~ Self-grandeur ~ Narrow minded ~ Power hungry ~ Fakery ~ Deceitful

**Positive Aspects:**

Intuitive ~ Healer ~ Transform ~ Manifest ~ Powerful ~ In touch with nature ~ Ritual ~ Reading the signs ~ Support ~ Herbalist ~ Medicine woman

**Archetypal Energy:**

The archetypal energy of the Witch is defined by her ability as a natural healer. The healing energy of the Witch is multidimensional and multilayered. She calls upon her connection with Spirit and nature to assess, guide, and transform. Many of the Witch's clients and protégés are adults who have a Wounded Child archetype. They have been abused, wounded, or neglected in childhood and require natural, holistic healing that a person with the practicing Witch archetype can provide.

The close relationship between the Witch and nature allows the Witch to read the earth signs for her remedies. Natural plant medicine is the obvious aspect to the healing ability of the Witch, but it is not the only understanding and connection to nature. There is the connection to animals. When we take notice of the animals that enter our lives and understand their messages, we can begin a healing process and a more balanced existence. Every time I receive a visit from my friendly magpie, I am reminded to keep my life in balance. Both the Shaman and the Witch understand the animal connection and what it means to humanity.

Individuals with these archetypes were once key members of a tribal society. The Shaman and the Witch were not only healers but also guides. The tribe depended on their expertise. As humanity has moved away from nature and into a more urbanized environment, we have lost contact with her energy. We have settled on this earth haphazardly. We have wandered aimlessly. We have plundered her ruthlessly. Nature is now beginning to repay us for our arrogance. If you know a person with the Witch archetype, consult her. All of us have the ability to re-establish our connection with nature and Mother Earth. The individual with the Witch archetype can be of great assistance in this regard.

It is not just the plants and animals the Witch understands. The Witch also takes note of the seasons, planets, elements, natural phenomena, landscapes, and the various natural items within a landscape. Some of this knowledge has gained popular acceptance, such as companion planting and planting according to the lunar cycles. As aware and balanced individuals, we can use our intuition and seek the medicines and connections that harmonize body, mind, and spirit. Those individuals with the archetypal energy of the Witch are a relevant source of information and healing for anyone seeking balance and a reconnection with nature.

**Archetypal Combinations:**

The archetypal energy of the Witch combines well with the energy of:

Wizard * Shaman * Healer * Guide * Warrior * Advocate * Mentor * Rebel * Visionary * Prophet * Carer * Nature Child * Wanderer * Explorer * Scientist

**Effective Use of Witch Energy:**

- Always be true to your archetypal Witch energy. Ignore the doubters and those blind with prejudice.
- Use your knowledge and understanding to assist those who seek your help.
- Be aware of the temptation to delve into and use negative or dark energies.
- Practice your skills, and be faithful to relevant ritual.
- Trust your power to manifest and transform.

# Wizard

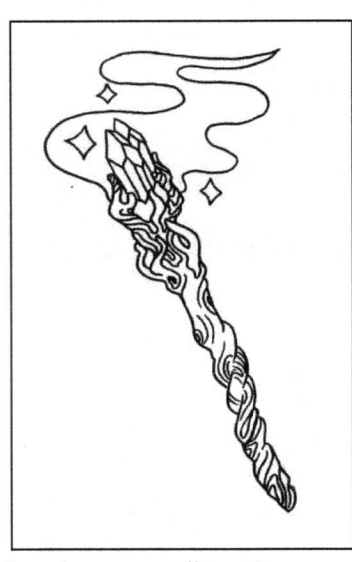

The Wizard is the archetype of that rare person commonly known as a genius. We acquaint the genius with knowledge and understanding, far beyond that of a common person. The Wizard is all of that and much more. There is certainly knowledge and understanding, but the Wizard has a spiritual connection to the divine that enhances his knowledge and understanding to the point where transformation and manifestation abilities become accessible. This gives the appearance that the Wizard is magical, but it is not strictly the case. The Magician deals with tricks and illusions to deceive our views of reality. If the Wizard calls upon all his power, spiritual energy, knowledge, and understanding, he changes reality. He can make the unknown known. He can simplify the complex. He can transform energy. He can manifest situations. He is in the right place at the right time because he has an understanding of how universal laws work.

It is important not to confuse fact with fiction. The Wizards who are portrayed in literature and film are fictional. It is an enhancement of the archetype and the archetypal energy for the purpose of entertainment. Sherlock Holmes and Hercule Poirot are the quintessential Detectives. James Bond is the ultimate Spy. Don Juan is the complete romantic Lover. Hercules is the bravest and strongest Warrior. Dracula is the most dangerous and blood-thirsty Vampire. Harry Potter has taken over the role as the most endearing and resilient Wizard. In real life, Wizards are somewhat rarer than Harry's world suggests. They are also more concerned with a specific and chosen field of expertise. Fictional Wizards are usually inclined to be multi-skilled, as it fires the imagination and makes all things possible.

Albert Einstein, Bertrand Russell, John Stuart Mill, and Leonardo da Vinci are several well-known individuals with the Wizard archetype. They certainly had the ability of a genius. They also possessed other qualities that come with the Wizard archetypal energy. They had a connection to the Divine. They had an understanding of universal laws. They could see a connectedness with many of the aspects that the ordinary person sees as individual components. Wizards are totally restricted by their time on Earth. However, they are only vaguely restricted by their ability to learn, understand, or reason.

Some individuals who possess the Wizard archetype never make the headlines. They are incredibly clever and are capable of remarkable achievements as individuals or as part of a team. They do not, however, seek attention or notoriety. Magicians are different; they are performers who seek an audience. Wizards are not performers and do not need either tricks or witnesses. They enjoy the satisfaction of knowledge, understanding, and achievement. Transformation can be a process that brings about small changes. They do not need to be earth-shattering. The archetypal energy of the Wizard is used in small quantities to achieve small outcomes and contribute to the greater whole.

**Negative Aspects:**

Plagiarist ~ Liar ~ Black magic ~ Self-grandeur ~ Narrow minded ~ Trickery ~ Power hungry ~ Rigid ~ Self-seeking

**Positive Aspects:**

Brilliance ~ Manifest ~ Transform ~ Intuitive ~ Powerful ~ Commanding ~ Adaptable ~ Resilient ~ Flexible ~ Learned ~ Understanding ~ Respect

**Archetypal Energy:**

The archetypal energy of the Wizard is almost fixated on understanding. The Wizard possesses an overwhelming desire to understand how things work. When there is understanding, it naturally follows there can be practical application or fundamental transformation of his project. As there is a connectedness with all things, the Wizard often uses his genius to understand various related topics. For example, there is always a connection between physics and mathematics. You cannot talk philosophy without judging political systems. And if you are dissecting political systems, you have to look into the role of the state, individual freedoms and rights, social and economic impacts, and so on. If you can visualize a flying machine, you need to have an understanding of aerodynamics, available fuels, and useful building materials. The understanding of one component or one situation automatically leads to the exploration of another component or situation.

It is taken for granted that the Wizard is learned. With most Wizards, their intellectual and academic abilities are recognized at a young age. They are usually directed into their various fields of study by family, friends, or economics. As they learn and grow, Wizards adapt and become flexible within their fields and in extending their scope of knowledge and understanding. The ability to adapt and be flexible is learnt quickly. Resilience is another component essential to Wizard energy. The desire to understand and comprehend complex matters does not come easy. Often many factors have to be considered, and the connectedness, in some cases, is like a giant jigsaw puzzle. When the answers to questions are not forthcoming, when experiments fail, or when suppositions prove to be incorrect, the power of determination and resilience is needed to fuel that strong and continuous desire to understand.

Wizard archetypal energy is also intuitive energy. The Wizard not only has an intellectual connection to the paths of knowledge, but he also has a spiritual connection and understanding. For the Wizard to succeed in his quest for knowledge, the power of the intellect is only one of the roads to understanding. If intellect is the only road taken, then progress, in understanding any topic or situation, is limited and narrow. The Wizard uses his intuition to lead him into the specific and into the connectedness of each of the specific.

When the Wizard has an understanding of a particular topic, he then has the ability and power to manifest and transform. There is nothing magic about this process. We all do this. When we know and understand how things work, we are able to make changes to improve our situations. Consider the changes in computer technology, combustion engines, manufacturing processes, building, architecture, and transportation. The intellectual capacity of the Wizard grants him a respect and power that others do not command. It is the scale of knowledge and understanding that separates those with the Wizard archetype from everyone else.

**Archetypal Combinations:**

The archetypal energy of the Wizard combines well with the energy of:

Seeker * Scientist * Artist * Philosopher * Warrior * Scholar * Engineer * Divine Child * Indulged Child * Pioneer * Visionary

**Effective Use of Wizard Energy:**
- Continue the quest for understanding with an open mind and a willingness to explore all possibilities.
- Use your knowledge and understanding for universal harmony, not just for specific advantage.
- Beware of self-grandeur.
- Be aware of the impacts and consequences of your knowledge and research.

# ~ Section 4 ~

# Taking Action

**Action speaks louder than words.**

You have all the words you need, so now is the time to turn those words into actions. Now is the time to develop an **Action Plan**.

Work through the aspects of your life that you wish to change or any improvements that you wish to make. Include everything: possible goals and improbable goals, major life changes, and minor daily or weekly changes. At this stage, all things are in the realm of possibility. Be prepared for this list to change. As you begin an action plan, your priorities are likely to change. What you once considered important may become a minor consideration. What you once considered minor may become a much bigger venture. New people, new factors, and new situations are likely to present themselves, and opportunities and priorities are likely to change in value. An action plan is never static, so be prepared to be adaptable and innovative.

The choice of action plan is up to you. Your plan reflects your archetypal energy. Your archetypes are your friends. When you identify an archetype that is part of you, treat the archetypal energy with awareness and respect. If you identify that you have a Queen archetype, be aware when you take on that persona, and use the Queen archetypal energy. If you have a Mother archetype, be aware when you use that Mother archetypal energy. It may be when you are at home. It may be when you are dealing with your children. However, it may also be when you are working. It may be when you are teaching. It may be when you are dealing with other people's children.

When you have identified your archetypes, be aware of their energy. Are you using positive archetypal energy, or are you using negative archetypal energy? If something is not right; if you want to change your circumstances or behaviour; if you desire to bring certain people, situations, and experiences into your life, check your archetypal energy. Are you constantly using negative archetypal energy? Go to the negative words and phrases. Do they describe your thoughts, your self-talk, your words, or your actions? If so, you are using the negative energy of that archetype. Changing your situation involves changing your use of negative archetypal energy to using positive archetypal energy. Again refer to the positive words and phrases. Adopt those characteristics and qualities so that you begin to use the positive archetypal energy. Change is certain to flow.

Remember that you are unique. Your archetypal combination and the strength of your archetypal energy are like your psychological and spiritual DNA. You are the authority of who you are. You are the authority of your life. You accomplish change with your authority. You do not need authority from anyone else. You decide change at your pace. You decide how to use your archetypes and your archetypal energy. Be aware that if you have and use a Philosopher or Seeker archetype, you are more than likely to make lists; be logical; and use reason, discussion, and argument to decide and engage your action plan. That is fine and perfectly acceptable. If you use your Saboteur archetypal energy, you are more inclined to use your intuition and gut feeling.

### Remember that you are unique!

The other consideration is to be aware that you have and use more than one archetype. Be holistic with your approach. Strive for balance. If you have archetypes with strong archetypal energy such as Damsel, Addict, or Martyr, be aware that they are only a part of who you are. If you allow the energy of only one archetype to dominate your life, then you are excluding so many other facets of your personality and your life's journey. There may be times, in a crisis, when you need to summon all the positive energy of a single archetype. That is all good and well, but this should be for a short and limited time frame. You are much, much more than a one-dimensional character. Be who you truly are.

The model below is there for you to use. Put into practice the entire plan, some of the plan, or none of the plan.

# A Model Action Plan

### Decision

Make the decision to change your situation and behaviour, shift the energy, and turn around patterns. Everything in your life begins with a decision. Isn't it best that your decision be made consciously rather than unconsciously or impulsively, as some decisions are?

### Attitude

Change your attitude. If you do not enjoy a duty or responsibility, cease seeing it as a chore. Look at it as a pleasure. Begin with small tasks, and work up to the larger ones. For example, washing and cleaning the car. Enjoy the experience, and look at the end result. See that your car looks fantastic and that you have done a wonderful job. Are there things around the house that need repair? You can do it if you want to. Consider the process. You have the knowledge, and if you do not, use a book or the Internet to find out how. Have the "yes I can" attitude and self-confidence in your attitude to take action. Is there an annoying person in your life you have to deal with all the time? Visualize love and good wishes to give to them. Visualize sending them a hundred pink balloons filled with joy and happiness. Observe how that person's attitude and your attitude changes and how the relationship improves.

If you find any of the above suggestions do not go far enough, then, make some really tough decisions. If you no longer wish to wash the car, then sell it and buy a bicycle or catch the train. If you have no time for house repairs, then sell the house and buy a property with a property manager, or hire a caretaker. If you have a personality clash with a colleague or the boss at work, then look for another job opportunity. If you have issues with your relatives or part of the family, then cut your ties with them. Your attitude has to endorse positive and affirmative action. When your attitude carries the mindset of a chore, displeasure, frustration, endurance, anger, and the like, then your response and further action derives from negative archetypal patterns. Remember that we are changing from the negative to the positive here.

## One step at a time

Overload causes breakdown, trauma, and ultimately, defeat. If you were constructing a pyramid, you would have to realize the process takes time and methodology. The overall picture and visualization of the final product derives from a well-developed plan of construction. One step leads to another, and you cannot do everything at once. If, along the way, you wish to slightly alter the finished product or need to adopt alternative building methods, then do so. However, the step-by-step process does not change.

It is the same when you work your way from using negative energy to using positive energy. It is a step-by-step process. Improved health and physical fitness is a step-by-step process. There is no overnight miracle. A decision to change your diet to 90 per cent alkaline and start running marathons is doomed to abject failure. You have to begin with gentle exercise like walking or yoga, suitable for your level of fitness. You eliminate the worst of the unhealthy foods like processed or fried food and eat more fruit and vegetables. Step by step, your fitness and energy levels change, and you are capable of more rigorous exercise. Your body loses the craving for sugar and desires more beneficial and sustainable food sources. Quality change is a step-by-step process.

## Determine Priorities

I have found this to be one of the most useful tools that I can suggest.

a) Decide what is important to you. What areas of your life do you wish to change and enhance?

b) Make a list of between three or four subjects. For example, on the list might be partner, family, work, business, house, garden, recreation, saving money, renovating, holiday, new relationship, personal healing, health, fitness, buying a new car, learning a new skill, study, and so on.

c) You have now decided where the majority of your energy is devoted. The three or four subjects on your priority list have your attention. Of course, you must still deal with the basic necessities of life. For example, you may need to cook the evening meal, drive the children to school, or have the car serviced. This is fine, but for every other moment, you focus your energy on the subjects on your priority list.

d) If you need to make a decision, ask only closed questions where the answer is either yes or no. If you have free time, ask yourself if the time is spent on an activity on your priority list. If the answer is **yes**, then you do it. If the answer is **no,** then you do not do it. There are to be no arguments, no justifications, no excuses, and no discussions. This is a brilliant mindset to have. There is no time wasted in decision making and no emotional energy drain. It is easy. Remember, if the answer is **yes**; it fits into my priority list, then I shall do this If the answer is **no**; it does not come within my priorities, so it is not be done.

e) Tell the important people in your life of your priority list, as you are bound to offend both family and friends by keeping secrets and being evasive. When your buddies ring and invite you to the pub or the football, ask yourself if your friends are on your priority list. If the answer is **no**, then the answer to your friends is a simple "No, thanks!" There is no apology, no explanation and no necessary justification.

f) Keep the same priorities for eight to ten months. Give the process time to work and for you to achieve your goals. You may then wish to reassess your priorities. It is best to begin with four subjects on your priority list. This gives you room to manoeuvre around the people and commitments in your life; eliminate the totally useless, impractical, and frivolous activities that you spend time and energy on; and adjust your mindset and willpower to simple **yes** or **no** responses. You may find after eight months, the four subjects on your priority list changes to three, and your life is much simpler.

### Reinforcement

Always give yourself positive reinforcement. Compliment yourself. "Hey! I did that well." "Wow! That was good." "I know I can do this." "I am feeling fantastic."

Accept compliments from others with grace and appreciation. Respond with, "Thanks! I appreciate that." So many people reject a compliment with embarrassment and self-effacement. You must stop saying that you are not worthy. This is your negative Victim and negative Prostitute at work. Remember, always, that you are worth it.

Listen to your self-talk. Is it positive or is it full of self-doubt? Do you continually put yourself down? Are you blaming other people for your situation? Are you jealous of others? Are you wishing and hoping? This is all negative archetypal energy. Turn it around a full 180 degrees. Compliment yourself. Take responsibility for your situation, and seek the good things for improvement. Rejoice in the wealth, good luck, and success of others. Take action, make changes, and achieve with a pragmatic approach to your plan. This is all positive archetypal energy patterning.

If you have a setback, and we all do on occasion, stay positive. Do not take on the emotion of failure. Learn from the experience so it does not happen again, and hold onto the memory of you climbing to success from that failure. Rescuer archetypes, please take note. You cannot keep rescuing lost causes. You cannot change others; only they can change themselves. Setbacks are all part of the natural progression to success. We all plateau between growth spurts. Treat them as catching your breath before the next big surge upwards.

## Assessment

Continue to monitor your progress and reassess your priorities. There is nothing static in this universe. We are all in motion. If your decision is to change, then do so. If you do not like where you are going, then change your path. Remember that this is about you! This is about your life and what you want to do with it. Archetypes have been given to us as tools for understanding ourselves and the people around us. We all have archetypes. We all recognize their energies. Why not use them to our advantage?

## Use your Archetypes

The different archetypes that you have dictate your approach to change. Be aware of how the process works for you and your individual archetypes.

**The intuitive:**

Saboteur, Wise Woman, Alchemist, Wizard, Angel, Mystic, God, Goddess, Guide, Intuitive Healer, and Divine Child are likely to develop plans in their heads and follow their gut feelings.

**The thinkers and planners:**

Philosopher, Seeker, Servant, Engineer, Banker, Detective, Judge, Teacher, Scientist, Artist, Healer, Diplomat, and Scholar are likely to write down their plans with all the options and, the pros and cons and still feel reluctant to begin, just in case they have overlooked something. Remember that nothing is perfect and everything can change so just move on with the process and quit procrastinating.

**The action archetypes:**

Warrior, Athlete, Adventurer, Explorer, Destroyer, Hero, King, Queen, Knight, Addict, Networker, Nature Child, Peter Pan Child, Gambler, Lover, Rescuer, Bully and Entrepreneur are likely to scribble some notes and move quickly into action mode.

**The recalcitrant who lacks the self-confidence:**

Coward, Victim, Princess, Prince, Martyr, Prostitute, Damsel, Disciple, Hermit, Companion, Mother, Scribe, Wounded Child, Celibate, Nun and Priest are likely to be in thinking mode and ponder, can I do this? The answer is, "yes! You can!"

**The contrary archetypes:**

Rebel, Puck, Trickster, Indulged Child, Politician, Clown and Wanderer are likely to disagree just because they can. Remember that this is your life, you have freedom of choice and you may do as you wish!

# Conclusion

**Always remember that your archetypes are your friends.**

**They are who you truly are.**

**Treat them with respect and understanding and you treat yourself with respect and understanding.**

As you gain an understanding of archetypes, you gain an understanding of who you truly are. As you become aware of the archetypal energy and archetypal patterns, you gain an understanding of the relationships you have with all others in your life.

**To change various aspects of your life is up to you.**

Change in your life is dependent on you. It is not dependent on your family, your partner, your friends or your acquaintances. Understanding the energy of your personal archetypes gives you the power to change.

When you look at the negative energy of your personal archetypes and recognize and understand the patterns they create in you, it is an indication that the time has come to change to the positive energy of that archetype and to create patterns that you desire.

**Change is never easy.**

Change requires persistence and patience. Always give yourself credit for those aspects and behaviours that you desire and that you exhibit. Remember that none of us is perfect. When you fall back into traits and behaviours that are negative and that you are trying to eliminate, remember to stay positive. Acknowledge your behaviour, without dwelling on it. Remind yourself of how to change behaviour to the positive and get on with your life.

**Remember that when you change, your circumstances also change.**

Your family is certain to notice the changes. Your friends are certain to notice the changes. Your acquaintances are certain to notice the changes. If they have difficulty accepting the changes in you, remember that those are their challenges, not yours. However, you now have an understanding of their archetypes and their archetypal energy. You have the capacity to understand where their energy comes from. So, if the relationship is important, using positive archetypal energy not only encourages the survival of that relationship but also the growth of that relationship.

**Life is there to be lived.**

**There are good times, and there are challenges.**

**Stay true to yourself.**

**Use the positive energy of your personal archetypes.**

**That is always and only the very best you can do.**

# Index

| | | | |
|---|---|---|---|
| Actor | 18 | Craftsperson | 92 |
| Addict | 21 | Crone - *See Wise Woman* | |
| Adventurer | 24 | Crook - *See Thief* | |
| Advocate | 26 | Damsel | 95 |
| Alchemist | 29 | Destroyer | 98 |
| Angel | 31 | Detective | 102 |
| Architect - *See Engineer* | | Dilettante | 105 |
| Artist | 34 | Diplomat | 108 |
| Athlete | 37 | Disciple | 111 |
| Author - *See Storyteller* | | Diva | 114 |
| Avenger | 40 | Don Juan - *See Lover* | |
| Banker | 43 | Engineer | 117 |
| Beggar | 46 | Entrepreneur | 120 |
| Builder - *See Craftsperson* | | Explorer | 123 |
| Bully | 49 | Facilitator - *See Mentor* | |
| Carer | 53 | Fairy | 126 |
| Celibate | 56 | Father | 129 |
| Child | 59 | Fool | 133 |
| Child – Divine | 61 | Gambler | 136 |
| Child – Peter Pan | 64 | Genius - *See Wizard* | |
| Child – Indulged | 67 | God | 139 |
| Child – Nature | 70 | Goddess | 142 |
| Child – Wounded | 73 | Gossip - *See Networker* | |
| Clown | 77 | Guide | 145 |
| Coach - *See Mentor* | | Healer | 148 |
| Companion | 80 | Hedonist | 151 |
| Computer Nerd | 83 | Hermit | 153 |
| Court Jester | 86 | Hero/Heroine | 156 |
| Coward | 89 | Inventor - *See Scientist* | |

| | | | |
|---|---|---|---|
| Joker | 159 | Rebel | 247 |
| Judge | 162 | Rescuer | 251 |
| King | 165 | Saboteur | 254 |
| Knight | 168 | Sage - *See Wise Woman* | |
| Lover | 171 | Salesperson | 258 |
| Magician | 174 | Scholar | 262 |
| Martyr | 177 | Scientist | 265 |
| Mentor | 180 | Scribe | 269 |
| Midas - *See Banker* | | Seeker | 272 |
| Monk | 183 | Servant | 275 |
| Mother | 186 | Shaman | 279 |
| Musician - *See Artist* | | Shape-Shifter | 283 |
| Mystic | 191 | Sidekick - *See Companion* | |
| Narcissist | 194 | Slave | 285 |
| Networker | 197 | Soldier - *See Warrior* | |
| Nun | 200 | Statesman | 289 |
| Olympian - *See Athlete* | | Storyteller | 292 |
| Peacemaker | 203 | Student - *See Scholar* | |
| Philosopher | 206 | Teacher | 296 |
| Pilgrim | 209 | Thief | 300 |
| Pioneer | 212 | Tramp - *See Wanderer* | |
| Poet - *See Artist* | | Trickster | 304 |
| Politician | 215 | Vampire | 307 |
| Priest | 219 | Victim | 310 |
| Priestess | 222 | Villain - *See Thief* | |
| Prince | 225 | Visionary | 314 |
| Princess | 228 | Wanderer | 318 |
| Prophet | 232 | Warrior | 321 |
| Prostitute | 236 | Wise Woman | 326 |
| Puck | 240 | Witch | 330 |
| Queen | 243 | Wizard | 334 |

# *About the Author*

Brian Dale is an archetype consultant, past life hypnotherapist and workshop facilitator. He is a retired primary school teacher, librarian and storyteller.

Brian's giftedness in archetypes was an amazing discovery. In 2002, he trained as an archetype consultant at the Australian Institute of Caroline Myss. Archetypes are universal personifications, such as, Princess, King, Victim, Warrior, Rescuer and many more. We continually use archetypal energy in our daily lives. Brian realized he could assist people in the discovery and understanding of their true selves, how they operate in the various aspects of their lives and how to bring change for their betterment and the betterment of others.

*Archetypes give us an understanding of who we truly are. They are an incredible tool for self-empowerment. They allow us to change our lives when we move from the negative aspect of an archetype to the positive aspect of that archetype.*

Brian's intuition and insightful observations have assisted many people to fully understand, empower and change themselves and their situation. He has given talks and lectures and facilitated archetype workshops throughout Australia.

Recently, with the passing of his daughter, Tahla, Brian has been inspired to investigate the Afterlife. This has taken him on a new and exciting pathway. He has had several experiences as a medium. He was also encouraged to train as a QHHT practitioner. This is Delores Cannon's past life hypnotherapy technique.

*This is a new and stimulating journey. As a medium and hypnotherapist, I am relishing each and every experience.*

Brian is a published author and his stories for children have been used in standardized tests by both the Victorian and South Australian Education Departments. One of his greatest passions is drama and the performing arts. Brian is owner and teacher of Byron/Ballina Bright Lights Performance School.

Brian and his wife Robyn have been married for over forty years, have three wonderful children, Adam, Jade and Tahla and the most amazing grandchildren, Luca, Lilly and Isla.

## Other Books by the Author

*Tilly and the Magic Potion* (Possumwood, 2013)
*Self-Esteem Matters* (Possumwood, 2015)
*Decoding the Afterlife* (Possumwood 2016)
*The Queen* (Possumwood 2017)
*The Knight* (Possumwood 2017)

## Contact the Author

*Email: briandale1@bigpond.com*
*Web: briandale.com.au*
*possumwoodpublishing.com*

*Notes*

www.ingramcontent.com/pod-product-compliance
Lightning Source LLC
Chambersburg PA
CBHW072003150426
43194CB00008B/983